Working with Weeds

A PRACTICAL GUIDE TO UNDERSTANDING, MANAGING AND USING WEEDS

Kate Wall

With recipes by Sharr Ellson

Illustrations by Kate Wall
Editor and cover design by Heidi Caddies

Kate Wall

Working With Weeds / Kate Wall. —Revised Edition.

First Published 2019

Revised Edition 2024

Copyright © 2024 by Kate Wall.

All rights reserved. No part of this publication may be reproduced, distributed or transmitted in any form or by any means, including photocopying, recording, or other electronic or mechanical methods, without the prior written permission of the publisher, except in the case of brief quotations embodied in critical reviews and certain other noncommercial uses permitted by copyright law. For permission requests, write to the publisher, addressed "Attention: Permissions Coordinator," at gardening@katewall.com.au.

Publisher Kate Wall

Brisbane Australia

www.katewall.com.au

Book Layout ©2017 BookDesignTemplates.com

Working With Weeds / Kate Wall. —Revised Edition.

ISBN 978-0-6487318-4-9

Cover Design: Heidi Caddies

Editor: Heidi Caddies

Recipes: Sharr Ellson

Illustrations: Kate Wall

Contents

Introduction 11
What is a Weed? 14
Why not Herbicides? 19
Environmental Weeds 25
Garden Weeds 33
Getting to Know Weeds 36
    Deep Rooted Weeds 39
    Leguminous Weeds 40
    Shallow-Rooted Weeds 42
    Bulbous Weeds 43
    Sandy Soils 45
    Weeds as pH Indicators 46
    Weeds as Mineral Deficiency Indicators 47
    Weeds of Other Soil Conditions 48
Dealing with Weeds 50
    Soil Improvement 51
    Mulch 53
    Hand Weeding 55
    Composting Weeds 56
    Vinegar 58
    Boiling Water and Steam 59
    Salt 60

- Fire 60
- Solarisation 62
- Weed Matting 63
- Smothering and Cover Cropping 64
- Woody Weeds Removal 66
- Rhizomes and Underground Tubers 67
- Lawn Weeds 69
- Tillage 72
- Livestock 73
- Herbicides 75

Weeding a Neglected Garden 77
- Sally's Garden 82
- Wendy's Garden 84
- Sue's Garden 86
- Ann's Garden 87

Putting Weeds to Use 90
- Edible Weeds 91
- Medicinal Weeds 96
- Fodder Weeds 99
- Compost Weeds 101
- Weeds as Companion Plants 102
- Weeds as Environmental Repair Agents 104
- Weeds as Habitat 105
- Other Weed Ideas: Be Creative! 107

Weed Profiles 116
- Asparagus Weeds 117
- Basket Plant / Purple Succulent Weed 119

Working With Weeds

- Billy Goat Weed 122
- Bindii / Lawn Burrweed 123
- Blackberry Nightshade 125
- Brazilian Cherry, Surinam Cherry, Pitanga 129
- Burr Medic 130
- Canna Lily 132
- Chickweed 134
- Clover 136
- Cobbler's Pegs 138
- Dandelion 140
- Dock 144
- Fleabane 146
- Green Amaranth 148
- Ground Ivy / Creeping Charlie / Alehoof 150
- Henbit 152
- Japanese Knotweed 153
- Jewels of Opar / Pink Baby's Breath 156
- Lamb's Quarters / Fat Hen 158
- Lantana 160
- Madeira Vine 164
- Mallows 167
- Morning Glory 169
- Onion Weed 171
- Paddy's Lucerne, Sida retusa 173
- Pepper Tree 175
- Plantain 177
- Prickly Lettuce 180

- Purslane 182
- Scarlet Pimpernel 184
- Scurvy Weed 186
- Sensitive Plant 189
- Soursob 191
- Sow Thistle 193
- Spear Thistle, Bull Thistle 195
- Spurges 196
- Stinging Nettle 199
- Sword Fern 201
- Vervain 203
- Wild Brassicas 205
- Wild Carrot / Slender Celery 210

Weed Recipes 212

- Weed and Cheese Cobb Loaf Dip 214
- Raw Weed Cheese 214
- Raw Weed Crackers 215
- Stinging Nettle Hummus 216
- Weed Chips 217
- Wild Burger Patty 217
- Wild Weed Pesto 218
- Wild Mustard Mayonnaise 219
- Green Goddess Dressing 219
- Weed Oil 220
- Weed Salt 221
- Chocolate Bark 221
- Iced Dandelion Mocha 222

Soursob Lemonade 222

Sun Kissed Weed Tea 223

Recipe – weed tea, infusions and tinctures for coughs and colds 223

Weed Oxymel 224

Skin Repair Ointment 225

Weed Balm 226

References 229
Index 237

Kate Wall

This book is dedicated to all the plants that have ever grown in a crack in the concrete.

Foreword

An early horticultural mentor of mine once said, "If you can't control your weeds, you better learn to love them."

I wasn't quite sure what he meant at the time, but it made me think; there must be a deeper gardening wisdom to be gained from understanding the role of weeds. Perhaps we could even benefit from them.

Years later, along came a book that made it so much clearer. Kate Wall put the spotlight on weeds and their potential to feed us, improve soil fertility, and provide much-needed habitat for beneficial insects. 'Working with Weeds' was like a revelation, showing us that, with proper management, we can take something that is universally regarded as a problem and use it to our personal benefit and for the benefit of the planet.

Sure, there are weeds that you never want in your garden, and Kate explains how to deal with them, too, without the need to reach for harmful poisons.

This book is far too valuable to be gathering dust on the shelf. It is filled with the practical information we gardeners so desperately need, based on the experience and knowledge Kate Wall has gained from the many beautiful gardens she has created, and the countless hours spent in her own garden, one that bursts with colour and biodiversity. This fully revised second edition has even more of Kate's extraordinary insights to help us work with weeds.
Every gardener should have a copy.

Phil Dudman

Kate Wall

Introduction

Bees enjoy wild heliotrope (*Heliotropium amplexicaule*). This weed is highly attractive to bees and during hot, dry times is often the only plant in flower in parks that have been mown too short.

Weeds tend to be much maligned by gardeners, and indeed too much of our precious gardening time and energy seems to be devoted to pulling them out, spraying them or otherwise trying to rid our gardens of them. Gardeners are such down to earth, happy people in general. We tend to have good mental health, thanks to all that emotional grounding we get from gardening, and yet we can go from Jekyll to Hyde in a matter of seconds when you mention weeds. The word *hate* suddenly gets used a lot.

Imagine a garden without problem plants, a garden without the need for weeding.

It is not hard. We just need to look at weeds a little differently. This doesn't mean we let the weeds take over. It means we get to know them before we judge them. For too long we have looked at weeds as the enemy and tried to eradicate them using chemicals. It's true that weeds are the bane of most gardeners and can wreak havoc in natural environments. The aim of this book is to share the knowledge I've gained over many years learning to manage and eradicate weeds without resorting to chemical weed killers.

I once thought that the only effective way to get rid of weeds was to kill them with herbicides, the active ingredient of most of these being glyphosate. When I first read of impending bans on glyphosate (years later and still waiting for it to happen…), my first thought was *what would we replace it with*? This led me to really delve into the world of weeds. Surely such a critical product could not be withdrawn without giving us an alternative. At first my mind was still on the *kill all weeds* track and I turned to white vinegar. It's certainly a very effective weed killer in many situations, and much cheaper and safer than proprietary poisons. But as my research into weeds progressed and I came to understand and see them as true survivors, my intentions moved away from the need to destroy or conquer them, to ways in which I could use them. I still aim to stop the spread of weeds in my garden, but I've learned to manage them in such a way that they are useful and don't pose a threat to the wider environment.

I've come to appreciate weeds as delicious fresh food and a useful source of medicine. They teach me about the condition of my soil and support wildlife by providing critical habitat. I've even come to admire their beauty. Sure, there are weeds I'd rather live without, but these are a valuable source of compost, if nothing else. Many plants that I once built a career on eliminating, I am now gleefully encouraging in my own garden. My career is so much more joyous and expansive now that it is focused on celebrating life rather than eradicating it.

Knowing more about weeds will help us with ideas to make the task of weed eradication a little easier. We might even use those self-same weeds to our advantage as a food source, soil improver, or an indicator of soil conditions. Many of our common weeds have fascinating folkloric histories. Some of this has been verified by modern science and some is just interesting. This point of curiosity can go a long way to giving us grudging bemusement, if not respect for the role these plants may have played in human history. Dare I say - we may even go so far as to actually enjoy weeds....

What is a Weed?

Patterson's Curse (*Echium plantagineum*) shown here growing with plantain (*Plantago lanceolata*) is so called due to its ability to dominate pastures to the detriment of better forage. It is sometimes called Salvation Jane in South Australia, where it has been the salvation of many flocks of sheep when there is no other feed available during drought.

In essence, *a weed is a plant growing where it isn't wanted*. By this definition, any plant is potentially a weed. A more practical definition might be *a plant that wasn't deliberately introduced into the garden and is having a detrimental effect*. This definition sounds more practical, but it is also open to interpretation. What seems detrimental to one gardener is a joy to another, and we come full circle and return to where we started, with a weed being an unwanted plant.

"What is a weed? A plant whose virtues have never been discovered."

Ralph Waldo Emerson

For many gardeners this is a very black and white issue. A geranium is *good* and cobbler's pegs are *bad*. I hope to show you the many shades of grey (or green) that are weeds, so that hopefully your list of good and bad plants will look a little different by the time you finish reading this book.

Case 1

I'll start with the comparison of geranium and cobbler's pegs. A dainty native geranium (Solander's geranium, *Geranium solanderi*) grows well here. It's very pretty and is native to the region, which makes you think of it as a good plant to have in the garden. It is also extremely vigorous, climbing over and smothering other plants in its path. For me it is a weed that needs to be controlled if I'm to grow anything else in its vicinity. On the other hand, I happily bring home seeds of cobbler's pegs and plant them in my garden. They are good eating so rarely reach the stage of setting seed here before making their way into my dinner.

Case 2

Another case to consider would be the cherry tomato and the sow thistle. You've probably already decided that the cherry tomato is food and therefore *good*, but the sow thistle is a weed and therefore *bad*. I love eating young sow thistles, they are actually very good food. Does that mean they are suddenly less weedy just because they are edible? If allowed to set seed, they can certainly spread prolifically. As can cherry tomatoes, which have a tendency to come up wherever I don't want them and only fruit well if they are not in the vegetable garden. Both can be weeds, but both can also be great food. Sometimes both are welcome, and sometimes both are weeds. I've never planted a cherry tomato and yet every year I weed them out of my garden, hoping some will set decent fruit before I get too annoyed with their sprawling habit and the amount of space they take up in my small garden.

A Subjective Definition

There is still a group of plants that continue to be labelled as weeds, regardless of any efforts to call them plants. Sow thistle and cobbler's pegs are two of these. To some these are edible weeds to be cultivated in the vegetable garden, to others, wild food to be enjoyed. They are still referred to as weeds, even when they are being treated as a useful plant. Some weeds are not so palatable but otherwise useful as agents of soil repair, and some are as ornamental as anything else we might plant. We are often taught that they are unwanted, and war should be waged against them. Sadly, I find that many gardening publications and horticulture classes refer to weeds as a problem in a completely uncompromising way. We are not given the chance to explore their benefits before we are taught to kill them.

To me defining a weed can vary from one garden to the next. I don't tolerate Mickey Mouse bush (*Ochna serrulata*) in my garden, and yet I have a client who really enjoys it. We know it is a highly problematic environmental weed, but it is also one that she can enjoy as it grows and provides green shrubbery, flowers in bright yellow, then develops bright red calyxes. It is easy to prune before the seeds ripen to prevent it from spreading.

In yet another garden, pink oxalis is enjoyed for the abundance of pretty flowers it puts on each year. For another client, we worked on removing clumps of asparagus weed until she tasted the new shoots and decided to keep it in her garden. She realised that the plant had something to offer, and in doing so, went from being much maligned to very much enjoyed (and controlled) almost overnight. I think this quote by Professor William Stearn (1956), taken from John Dwyer's 'Weeding Between the Lines', sums up the subjective nature of weeds perfectly: *"Weeds are not so much a botanical as a human psychological category within the plant kingdom, for a weed is simply a plant which in a particular place at a particular time arouses human dislike."*

Something Green

Weeds are often the only green in a concrete jungle. They have an amazing ability to colonise the most hostile of places. Every time I see a weed growing in a crack in a wall, I am delighted at the power of nature to fight back at humankind's world domination. So often these incredible survivors are harassed with poisons in an effort to eradicate them. Again, this calls for a new perspective. Instead of seeing them as weeds and therefore bad, we should perhaps be grateful for the life they are adding to our harsh urban spaces and appreciate them for being tough enough to survive there. Incredible cost and effort go into trying to eradicate these plants, and if we are lucky even more goes into trying to find ways to green our urban spaces. Would it be so bad to leave some of these survivors alone and allow them to provide us with green life where none other existed?

My challenge to you now is – *what is a weed to you?*

Weeds tend to have a number of key characteristics. They are able to survive and thrive without being cared for. They're able to easily spread through natural dispersal mechanisms and self-propagate easily, usually in large numbers. It is easy to see how dandelion or fleabane fit these characteristics. Less obvious is the jacaranda tree, which has the same characteristics and is a declared weed in warm climate areas. In cold climates daffodils and freesias can act as weeds, as can olives in Mediterranean climates. Interestingly, when people ask for a low maintenance garden, you would be surprised at how often they unwittingly describe weeds – something that is hardy, so they don't have to care for it, flowers well and is abundant. Not many are impressed when I point this similarity out to them.

Perhaps the more appropriate question is *when is a plant a weed*?

All plants can be weeds, and all weeds can be wanted plants. You can be sure that the plant you are battling as a weed, someone, somewhere else in the world, is planting and encouraging to grow. The word *weed* should really relate to a plant in time and place, not to any particular species. When you look at international weed forums, we see the beginning of this. Plants are listed as weeds in one country or region but can exist in other places without that label. I would like to see this broken down further so that a plant's situation, not just region, is being taken into consideration. I know this is very difficult for governments, land managers and farmers to do, but it's not at all hard for gardeners. When it comes to gardens, the situations vary so greatly that I'd like to think no plant should be labelled as a weed and nothing more.

Looking at weeds on an international scale gives a very different perspective. Travelling in Germany years ago, I was extremely impressed with the herbs growing in the median strips and flowering prettily. I later realised that the desirable herbs I struggle to grow in Australia were considered weeds in Germany and left alone to flower. Actually, Europe and the UK have a very different attitude to weeds than we do here in Australia, New Zealand or even Canada and the USA. We have a reasonably modern history of European settlement, during which plants considered valuable to UK migrants were brought to Australia. Unfortunately, many of these plants thrived in the Australian environment, becoming weeds and contributing to major changes to our natural ecosystems. One of these plants was the prickly pear (*Opuntia sp*) which were brought here with the First Fleet, hoping to establish an industry producing the red dye needed for military uniforms from the cochineal insects that feed on prickly pear.

In Berlin I was amazed to see very neat lollipop standards by the entrance to a castle and to realise that these well-behaved pot plants where actually lantana (*Lantana camara*). My German companion was equally amazed to hear my description of the way lantana grows here in Australia, where it can be described as anything but well behaved. Lantana was introduced to Australia as a garden plant around 1841.

Situation and location can make all the difference in whether a plant behaves as a weed or not. In a survey I did of UK gardeners, an ancient native plant, mare's tail (*Equisetum arvense*), rated highly as a disliked garden weed. The gardeners all referred to the ancient origins of the plant, but knowing this didn't change the fact that they found it very difficult to control in the garden – native or not!

There is a wonderful research project in New York called the *Spontaneous Urban Plant Project* (www.sponteanuousurbanplants.org) which encourages people to appreciate and explore the world of weeds in urban settings. I love the title, as it most perfectly describes weeds. They are super hardy and highly resilient plants that come up uninvited, hence the spontaneous part. However, this doesn't mean they can't contribute to the harsh urban environment so many of us live in. By recognising the oft ignored and undervalued ecosystem that is based around these urban weeds, we find life, beauty and even value in plants that were otherwise to be eradicated. In so many cases, removing the weeds from these urban environments removes entire urban ecosystems, replacing them with bare concrete. I think we are better off with the weeds, and I am happy that there are spontaneous urban plants in our cities!

> "In forgoing the forager lifestyle, modern societies have severed their links with nature. Agriculture and civilisation have proved ecologically destructive, and modern urban environments emanate order and artifice.
>
> Fortunately natural processes are still manifest within the city – the thriving weed flora represent a miniature wilderness that can be appreciated like any other. The abundance of edible weeds provides an opportunity for the city dweller to relive, in small part, the hunter-gatherer lifestyle of the past.
>
> The experienced eye of the forager can transform traditional perceptions of the cityscape – weedy vacant allotments and urban wastelands become storehouses of foods and medicine. Where others feel repelled by scenes of urban decay, the forager can find the needs of life."
>
> **Tim Low**, Wild Herbs of Australia and New Zealand

Why not Herbicides?

Brown mustard (*Brassica juncea*) growing with billy goat weed (*Ageratum conyzoides*). Is this a patch of weeds to spray or a wild meadow to enjoy?

We are taught early in the gardening game that the solution to a weed problem lies in a bottle of herbicide available from the hardware store. There is a massive industry out there devoted to destroying weeds. The world herbicide market passed $US30 billion in value in 2023 and is forecast to reach $US40 billion by 2028 according to Mordor Intelligence. The Australian Government estimates that approximately $1.5 billion is spent each year on weed control activities, and a further $2.5 billion is lost in reduced crop yields due to weeds. That is a lot of money. Clearly weeds are causing huge problems, and a huge industry has grown to address these problems. Most of the focus on weeds is directed towards agriculture, as it is here that weeds compete with commercial crops and cost producers in lost income. Herbicides are often classified as *crop protectants* and are heavily relied on for modern food production. Environmental weeds get a much smaller yet still significant slice of the weed budget. I've never used as much herbicide as a professional gardener than I did while volunteering as a bush regenerator in the 1990s. If you read through weed society and horticultural publications, you'll find many ways of using different herbicides to destroy every kind of weed. Given that the purpose of environmental weed control is to protect and improve natural biodiversity, it's surprising that this field is so heavily reliant on chemicals. Could this be a case of relying on a product known to cause harm for the sake of the greater good? Should we try to contain and minimise that harm? Both questions are being hotly debated amongst scientists and those who work in differing areas of land management. It's not hard to find people who are adamant that there is no harm as great as the presence of an environmental weed.

The safety of these chemicals has long been called into question, but in recent times that call is being taken far more seriously. The true toxicity of herbicides appears to have been buried in a multi-billion-dollar industry with a huge public relations budget. Reading through *The Poison Papers* is shocking. This collection of official documents reveals some frightening truths regarding how much was known about the toxicity of herbicides and pesticides, and how much of what was known was deliberately suppressed, even by the regulating authorities. *The Poison Papers* show that there is extensive knowledge about many chemicals still widely used, and that the true toxicity of these chemicals continues to be downplayed for the sake of big profits. The home gardener is a very small player in the global herbicide industry, but that doesn't make us insignificant. Not at all! After all, the volume of weed killers available to us through hardware chains, nurseries and even supermarkets adds up to a lot. Most gardeners will have at least one bottle of herbicide in the garden shed, and many will have been told they need it.

The size of the herbicide industry tells us something very significant about our modern lives – we like a quick fix and are willing to pay money and ignore risks for it. There was a time not so long ago when herbicides weren't widely available.

The History of Herbicides

Herbicides were first developed during the Second World War for use in warfare. They were deployed during the Vietnam War with unforgettable results. Agent Orange, with the active ingredient of 2,4,5-T was used in defoliating forests to expose the enemy. Health problems developed in returned servicemen and birth defects rose sharply in affected areas. It took many years for the full effects to be known, and many more years for the reason to be fully understood. A contaminant of the manufacturing process, dioxin, was responsible, not the 2,4,5-T itself. This highly effective herbicide is now able to be manufactured without the dioxin contaminant, but questions over when and how we should use it remain.

During the 1950s, herbicides became widely available and transformed agricultural practices. They were developed as agents of war, and while they are not used in human warfare any longer, the warfare continues in their use against weeds.

If we look at the language of weed control it is often highly emotive (in a very negative way) and contains many similarities to the language of war, where the enemy must be vanquished at all costs. This language, and the hatred it inspires, is so ingrained that it can be hard for people to see beyond it and look for a solution other than toxic herbicides. The damage done by herbicides (or even some of the other extreme weed control measures like burning or using salt) has often been accepted by gardeners as collateral damage, and wholly justified because when it comes to weeds, we are at war.

Glyphosate

Glyphosate, the most widely used herbicide today, wasn't released until 1974. We have relied upon and completely trusted this chemical for nearly half a century, and it has made weed control easy for us. So much so that when the talk of banning glyphosate first circulated, I, like many others, was shocked and wondered how I'd manage without it. It didn't take long to find copious research into the dangers and ill effects of this herbicide – enough for me to quickly stop using it and wonder why we ever did in the first place.

Since going cold turkey on glyphosate, I've found that I haven't missed it at all. Not once. In fact, since I stopped using any type of herbicide at all (glyphosate is the most widely used but is only one of many herbicides available), I have enjoyed gardening so much more, and have found *less weeds* in the gardens I manage. I now spend very little time weeding and a lot more time on more creative gardening than I did when I was using weed killers. When I stopped relying on herbicides, I started to explore the world of weeds from a different perspective, one where I learned first and then decided how best to act based on the circumstances of the weed. It's not a quick fix but the results are more effective in the long term.

The Cycle of Soil Damage

Logically, if herbicides are so effective at eliminating weeds, shouldn't we begin to see less of them? The reason for the failed logic lies in our quick fix gardening approach, where chemical after chemical is added in response to problems in the garden. Instead, we should be aiming to create a healthy soil and garden ecosystem which is *naturally* free of problems. The constant and repeated application of herbicides is leading to increased resistance in weed species to the point where we now have many weeds that are extremely resistant to herbicides. In conjunction with this, we have soil damage resulting from the use of chemicals, including herbicides, pesticides and non-organic fertilisers, which destroy soil biota and chemically dislodge vital nutrients from the soil particles (see *Earth Repair Gardening* for more on this). The results are poor soil conditions, which in turn favours the growth of those super tough plants that we usually call weeds.

Even if herbicides were found to be completely non-toxic to humans, the increasing volume of weeds that result from their ongoing use should be reason alone for us to question why we continue to use them.

Toxicity to People

Long-term studies are showing just how toxic many of these chemicals are. We are currently seeing huge leaps forward in the public discussion on the impacts of glyphosate on human health, with the World Health Organisation classifying them as a *probable carcinogen*. The difficulty with such a classification is that it is loose in its definition and as such, provides no clarity for either side of the argument. A highly significant 2018 test case in the USA saw school groundskeeper Dewayne Johnson awarded a record $US289.2million (later reduced to $US78m). The jury decided that Mr Johnson developed non-Hodgkin's lymphoma due to regular and constant exposure to Roundup, the active ingredient being glyphosate. A second case was awarded $US81m by a San Francisco court in 2019. At the time of writing a further 11,000 similar cases against the US based manufacturer of glyphosate are lined up before US courts, and cases have also arisen in Australia.

What is so significant in these cases is that Mr Johnston and others like him were using the herbicide in a way that was not outside common usage, and in accordance with the safety directions on the label. It is now apparent is that while glyphosate may not be highly toxic to humans at an acute (single dose) level, the long-term impacts of exposure could tell a very different story.

The true extent of the damage to human health is not entirely clear at this stage. Links between modern lifestyle diseases and glyphosate are the subject of many studies, including the impact of glyphosate to disrupt our gut flora, which then further impacts our overall health.

Glyphosate acts to disrupt the photosynthetic pathways of plants, and therefore should be inactive on animals. A study done at Texas University has demonstrated that glyphosate disrupts the gut flora of bees and is contributing to their decline worldwide through the related reduced immune capacity of the bees. Another study has found that glyphosate impairs the ability of honeybees to navigate and of bumble bees to regulate the temperature of their hives. These are known as sub-lethal effects. In these cases, the chemical exposure doesn't kill the animal directly but leads to death indirectly. Other recent studies have found that high levels of glyphosate exposure can increase the risk of developing non-Hodgkin's lymphoma in humans by 41% and can indeed disrupt the human gut biome. A German study found that low levels of exposure can cause non-alcoholic liver disease. I have no doubt we will see many more similar studies over the coming years as the debate and the research continues.

Where does it end up?
The ability of glyphosate to translocate within the soil is now also becoming apparent. Previously it was thought to be safe, breaking down immediately upon contact with the soil. Traces of glyphosate now contaminate soil samples taken from very remote and undisturbed locations. Damage to soil micro-organisms is also becoming apparent. Soil scientists in Europe have found that earthworm activity was reduced to nothing in a field within three weeks of spraying with glyphosate. Further studies found a dramatic collapse in soil fertility in fields treated regularly over many years with glyphosate. However, this claim could be the result of a complex interplay between various aspects of modern agriculture, with its heavy reliance on chemicals including herbicides, pesticides and fertilisers - none of which support healthy soil biomes.

Traces of Roundup are being found in food, even from organic farms where the chemical isn't used. Glyphosate is so pervasive that it is turning up in water samples, breast milk and children's urine samples. Clearly, it's more persistent within the environment than we have been led to believe.

The key point of this entire discussion of glyphosate is that the true impact of any so-called wonder chemical is usually largely unknown. As with DDT, glyphosate was the chemical to save us from unwanted pests, until we started becoming sick and the unwanted pests started developing resistance. It takes many years for the true long-term impacts of such chemicals to be known. Even now research into the toxicity of glyphosate is largely looking at it as an isolated chemical, instead of looking at the various other constituents of its commercial formulation (glyphosate is the key ingredient in approximately 750 herbicide formulations on the market) including the relative toxicity of those other constituents and how they interact.

What next?

As pressure mounts to ban any one chemical, another will be developed to take its place. Glyphosate is no longer under patent protection, meaning it can now be manufactured by anyone. There are plenty of companies making enormous amounts of it. Chinese production of this chemical is already suspected of outstripping US production.

Are weeds so abhorrent to us that we are willing to take such risks with our health and the environment to eradicate them? Interestingly, the evolution of herbicides hasn't changed our perception of weeds even if it is changing the way we kill them. We still see weeds as an enemy absolute, which not only delays change, but stops us from looking holistically at the weed problem.

A holistic approach may still involve some use of herbicides, but it shouldn't rely solely on the use of these chemicals, and they should be the last resort.

Environmental Weeds

Mexican sunflower (*Tithonia diversifolia*) often forms dense stands on steep creek banks or cutouts, where it holds the soil together, provides dense shelter for wildlife and significantly improves soil fertility.

Although this book is largely directed at garden weeds, it is important to realise that nature doesn't acknowledge property boundaries. What we do in our own gardens by way of weed management, or even by what we allow to grow, has the potential to have an impact beyond our own border. While many of the scenarios presented here describe examples of environmental weeds in Australia, if you change the names, the scenarios are equally applicable all over the world, regardless of climate or geographical boundaries. Environmental weeds, like garden weeds, are a human condition, and occur everywhere that humans do.

Environmental weeds are plants that are not native to an area and yet are performing so well there that they may be contributing to the overall ecology of that area. That contribution is usually a bad thing, as weeds often out-compete and therefore threaten the security of the native vegetation. Many, but not all, environmental weeds are garden escapees. Others have been deliberately introduced as pasture plants, and yet others have arrived accidentally.

As gardeners we have a responsibility to not add to the problem
We can do this by not dumping green waste in the bush, and by being aware of the potential for our garden plants to become weeds. This may be a small issue if our gardens are in the centre of a concrete jungle, but if we have bushland or water courses nearby, we should be more mindful. This does include grass clippings. They don't belong in the bush or on the road reserve. The best place for them is in our own domestic compost systems. There was a time when it was considered ok to throw unwanted plants over the fence into nearby bushland without a second thought. This contributed significantly to the weed problem. These days we're far more aware that dumping unwanted plants in bushland is both illegal and irresponsible. Unfortunately, it's not the only way for plants to escape our gardens.

Flooding and stormwater runoff are significant contributors to the spread of weed seeds. It pays to be aware of the direction of stormwater runoff from your garden – is it likely to enter a drain or watercourse that could act to disperse weeds? Fertilisers, pesticides and even topsoil washing out of our gardens with the stormwater can contribute to weed problems downstream by altering growing conditions.

Even if we don't live near bushland, birds visiting our gardens are one of the major vectors of seed spread. By planting native food plants for the same birds, their droppings will contribute to the spread of natives instead of weeds. This isn't always easy or possible, but something we should consider.

How many weeds are serious?
Nationally, 3000 or so exotic plants account for approximately 15% of Australia's flora. While all of these exotic plants are considered weeds, only a quarter of these are considered serious.

According to the Royal Horticultural Society, there are 1,402 non-native plants established in the wild in the UK, of which 8% (108) are considered to have detrimental impacts. Of these only 43 are covered by legislation. Not all environmental weeds are devastating monsters. Some cause very little disruption to healthy native ecosystems. Some are even beneficial in that they provide habitat and food for wildlife in places where human disturbance has removed the original habitat, and while they may not be as wonderful as the native vegetation once was, those weeds are much better than nothing at all. Of course, there are always exceptions and the Dutchman's Pipe vine (*Aristolochia elegans*) growing in Australia's central east coast region is one of these. It has escaped the garden fence and is rampant in areas of disturbed rainforest. Unfortunately, the vine is closely related to the host plant of the spectacular Richmond birdwing butterfly. The introduced vine is attractive to the butterflies, which are highly specialised feeders, but it is toxic to them. Controlling this weed is critical to the survival of this endangered butterfly.

A similar situation occurs in North America with the invasive garlic mustard (*Alliaria petiolata*) being toxic to the native (and rare) mustard white and West Virginia white butterflies, both of whom are adapted to feed on plants in the brassica family. Sadly, this particular brassica is toxic to them. In its native habitat (Europe, North Africa and Western Asia) the garlic mustard has over 70 natural control agents by way of insects, fungi and others, but in North America, it has none, which has enabled it to dominate so effectively.

Weeds with Environmental Value
The value of weeds outside of the garden fence can be highly controversial. Large areas of lantana are certainly undesirable as a replacement for native bushland, but they are highly desirable for wildlife living on degraded land where the lantana scrub offers shelter and food. The lantana protects the soil from erosion and over time contributes to soil improvement. If we have nothing to replace it with, that lantana is far better left in place. Even if we are planting seedlings of native plants, we need to realise that they're not providing food or habitat at the seedling stage. Controversial? Maybe. It does highlight that the role of weeds and fauna conservation are not mutually exclusive.

Another controversial weed issue arose when a local council poisoned introduced willow trees in Daylesford, Victoria. The traditional approach assumes that because the trees are an introduced weed, they are a problem. Willow trees suck a lot of water out of the ground, which can deplete Australia's delicate and often ephemeral waterways. New research has shown they actually play an important role in slowing flood waters, trapping silt, and even keeping that extra water in the local system instead of allowing it to drain away quickly. The loss of large shade trees overhanging a waterway can cause increased evaporation and exacerbate the impact of the heat and drought on the local ecosystem. Willow trees are increasingly being recognised as important shade trees, with local experts arguing that they shade out another problem weed, the blackberry. With the willows gone, the blackberry can return and with it, increased herbicide use in a riparian zone. In this case, the council was merely carrying out traditional weed control but potentially created issues, most directly with the increase in blackberry but less obviously with water management and shade. In this case the willow may not be the best environmental outcome, but it was limiting a greater problem.

In most urban areas, it is the weeds dominating the degraded creeks and road reserves which provide the greatest amount of habitat for native wildlife, helping it to survive in an urban environment. Without these weeds, a huge number of birds, lizards, snakes, frogs, insects and even small mammals would be lost from urban areas. Weeding and replanting degraded areas with natives must account for the short to medium term habitat loss if it is to have long term success.

When does a plant become a weed?
Amongst the environmental weeds are iconic plants such as Brisbane's jacarandas, and important food plants like olives in South Australia. In North Queensland, coconuts are considered environmental weeds in some council areas and yet are considered natives in neighbouring areas. This highlights the conundrum of when to identify a plant as a weed. Some of our common garden weeds like sida retusa and purslane were here before European arrival, and yet are considered to be weeds rather than native plants. There are many other plants with unknown historical origins over which there is debate as to whether they are native or not. There were no coconut palms growing on North Queensland beaches when Captain Cook sailed past in the Endeavour in 1770. First Nations people collected the seeds as they washed ashore, then ate them. With the European settlers' disruption of their traditions, coconuts remained on the beach and grew.

This problem is greatly magnified in the UK and Europe, where a long and complex history of invasion, trade and travel have very much blurred the lines of what is truly native. If a plant was introduced 3,000 years ago, is it still a weed, or can we by now consider it native? There are some weeds, such as knotweeds (*Fallopia sp*) and giant hogweed (*Heracleum mantegazzianum*), that were introduced over the last couple of centuries and show a clear pattern of invasiveness. Many of the other weeds that gardeners in the UK are dealing with can be described as weeds in some references and wildflowers in others. Even weed legislation in the UK refers to *invasive plants*, not *weeds*, as the term weed is so often used interchangeably with wildflower there.

The discussion of native verses introduced is not always clear, even amongst botanists. The list of plants with doubtful origins is surprisingly long, with some turning to analysis of pollen samples from ancient soils and genetic analysis to try and determine if a plant is native or introduced. Is this going too far? Perhaps a little more acceptance wouldn't go astray.

Recent work by Professor Angela Moles and her students has taken the concept of weed versus native in another fascinating direction. Prof. Moles' work has shown that 70% of the weeds she has looked at in Australia, and 28% of weeds in New Zealand, have shown significant changes to form and are evolving to become separate species from the original parent plants. This carefully controlled work is taking place over an ongoing time frame and is likely to really rock the boat of weed eradication programs. Can a plant still be called a weed if it has become a new species which is now only found in its new homeland?

Potential or actual weed?
The potential and the actual weed value of a plant is another set of parameters giving inconclusive results. It can easily become difficult for the home gardener to really know what is and isn't a weed. For simplicity's sake, we fall back onto the old *unwanted* definition. When it comes to bushland, our garden plants are most certainly unwanted and as gardeners we should be mindful and respectful of that.

Native Australian plants that we have added to our gardens can behave like weeds when planted in regions outside the one they originated from. The cadaghi (*Corymbia torelliana*) is just one of many examples of this. It was widely recommended as a garden tree for Brisbane in the 1980s, until it did so well it became listed as a weed. It is native to Queensland's dry tropics, well north of Brisbane. Morning glory (*Ipomea indica*), which grows and smothers native warm temperate forests is easily identified as a problem weed. But what about kangkong (*Ipomea aquatica*) in the Wet Tropics? It can be very invasive there and problematic, however its origins are pre-colonisation, so is it native, and does that make it okay for it to smother other native vegetation? These examples show just how complex weed identification can be. Amongst formal weed listings, a plant can be classified as an *actual weed* if it is already in an area and misbehaving there, or as a *potential weed*, meaning it is not currently a problem where it is, but it is a weed elsewhere and could become one if left unchecked. It can be somewhat daunting for the gardener to know what is and is not okay to plant. The best place to start is to familiarise yourself with local council weed guidelines and weed identification lists for your area, and then make sure that what you are growing in your garden does not end up escaping the fence.

Climate change also comes into play when thinking about potential weeds. Many experts in the environmental weed management field are concerned that climate change is going to exacerbate the spread and colonisation rates of weeds. Too right it will, and already is. But is this the advance of weeds (especially those that are native but from outside the area, such as the cadaghi), or is it an important part of nature adapting to change?

This man-made change is all happening at rates which far exceed anything evidenced before in the fossil record. While I'm certainly not indifferent to the problems of environmental weeds and climate change, as an ecologist I am also interested in the complex interplay between the plants, soil, climate microbes, animals and more that make an ecosystem function. As one element changes, so too will others, therefore with climate change, changes to vegetation must happen. What does this mean for gardeners? It means we should be mindful of the potential of our garden plants to spread beyond the fence line, and to do what we can to prevent this spread. If a plant can spread easily in our garden, it has the potential to be a weed beyond our border.

Weeds in Pots
Pot plants can be just as much of an environmental risk as plants that are planted into the ground. A large industry is growing up around the trend to grow indoors and in small spaces. Sadly, many of the recommended plants are already problematic environmental weeds. Plants like snake plant (*Sanserveria sp*) make wonderful pot plants, but they also make terrible environmental weeds. This doesn't mean you can't enjoy them as indoor plants, as long as you are careful about where you source them and how they are eventually disposed of. Never buy plants that are declared weeds. If they are a weed, try digging them up from bushland or ask around to see if anyone wants them taken out of their garden. It may be only a very small step towards reducing the weed in the wild, but it also reduces the market for problem plants. Besides, why pay for something that needs to be removed and discarded from elsewhere at a cost?

At the other end of the life span, those unwanted pot plants need to be disposed of with care. Instead of tipping the half dead plant out in the garden, or worse, bushland, where it may grow, it needs to be put into the bin, or appropriately composted.

The Law
It is against the law in most parts of Australia, North America, the UK and Europe to buy, sell or even transport declared weeds. In Australia and the USA, weed legislation is state based and changes from one state to the next. In some states certain plants are prohibited from being brought into that state as they have been identified as having the *potential* to become a weed there. I recommend buying locally – not only to avoid this problem but also to decrease travel miles for our garden. Logically, if we buy plants locally, we have a better chance of buying a plant suited to our local climate.

Weeds Play a Valuable Role in the Environment
Weeds play a role in the broader environment, as well as in the home garden. If we pay attention, they will tell us something – something about the soil, about the climate and about the way we have degraded a landscape that is now in need of repair. If we were to leave a field alone, the first thing to happen would be for weeds to grow. If we were to leave those weeds alone and let them be what would happen? At first it may seem that the weeds are taking over.

However, those weeds will attract insects, the insects will attract birds and even small mammals, all bringing with them seeds from elsewhere. Eventually trees start to grow. In five to ten years, we may still have a weedy paddock but there will be a few tree saplings starting to appear. In 20 years, there will be something of a return to forest. Sure, the weeds will still be there, but so will the native trees. While this mightn't be an ideal situation because it takes too long and doesn't result in a *pure* native reforestation, it is still a healing of the land and of the ecosystem that eventually results in a new equilibrium. If we look a little differently, weeds are succession plants and are playing a critical role in healing damaged land. Instead of seeing a weedy plot as an eyesore, we should recognise it as a *Cinderella Ecosystem*, a term coined by Fred Pearce in his insightful book, 'The New Wild'.

I guess the point I am making is that weeds are not pure evil. They are part and parcel of human existence on this planet, both modern and ancient, and will always be so. I am no purist. I prefer to gauge whether a weed is harmful or not by its contribution to the biodiversity of the area it is growing in. Is that weed increasing the biodiversity? Yes, then it is good. No, then it should probably be controlled. Weeds are usually increasing the biodiversity of heavily degraded spaces but reducing the biodiversity where they are smothering tracts of native bushland. Ergo, not all weeds are bad, but nor are they all good. And that applies in the garden as much it does anywhere else.

Do No Harm

All that being said, *do no harm*. For the weeds that are already around you, exploit, use and enjoy them. There are many different weeds in different locations which have similar uses. Use the ones that are local to you and do not try to introduce others – appreciating weeds is not an excuse to be irresponsible about the very real problem of environmental weeds.

Can environmental weeds have an economic value?

This is a loaded question and one that has been asked and investigated in various ways. Weeds are a source of biomass. Where weeds are present in large amounts, this can represent many tonnes of potentially valuable biomass. There have been numerous investigations into using weed biomass as an ethanol source for biofuels. A project in the USA is looking into the value of a certain prolific weed, the giant reed, *Arundo donax* for use in making paper. The problem lies in the continued supply. As an environmental problem, the intention is to at best eradicate, or at least significantly reduce the numbers of the weed to allow the biodiversity of the region to improve. The Akubra hat industry in Australia is a classic case in point. Their hats are made with rabbit fur. With rabbits being the pest that they are here, this seemed like a perfect way of putting them to use. As efforts to keep rabbits under control have worked, the supply of rabbit pelts to the hat industry has dropped so significantly that this iconic Aussie product is now made with imported rabbit fur. Obviously eradicating the raw material does not make business sense.

A more viable way of looking at the commercial value of weeds would be their ability to perform well in marginal or highly degraded areas. Land considered marginal is usually too arid or too swampy to be of value for agriculture. Weeds have been considered as a way of developing a commercial crop on land that otherwise has no significant food production value, although this begs the question of the natural value of this land. Just because land is considered *marginal* in terms of agricultural values (as opposed to degraded due to human activities, in which case growing weed crops could be a perfect solution) does not mean the land has no intrinsic natural values and perhaps should not be considered for commercial cropping at all. One of the values which make weeds an appealing option for commercial exploitation is their ability to grow quickly and produce large amounts of biomass without the intensive inputs of modern agriculture.

A 2024 study by the University of South Australia has found that the weed prickly paddy melon (*Cucumis myriocarpus*) may have commercial value. Enzymes in the seeds have been found to have effective cementation properties with commercial applications in bio cement production and controlling soil erosion. This weed is both an environmental and agricultural pest. As a weed of summer fallow fields, it may be that farmers can turn it into a second crop to be grown while the fields are resting. In this setting it makes commercial sense. Given that it is an environmental weed of roadsides, degraded areas and on Native Title lands, there may be potential land use conflicts in cultivating this plant instead of eradicating it. As this project is in the early stages, time will tell how the commercialisation of this weed will play out. It may be that the value of a bio cementing agent is high enough to turn this nuisance plant into an accidental hero.

Garden Weeds

Soursob, (*Oxalis debilis*) flowering and adding colour to a pot of chrysanthemums which are not currently flowering. Are the competing or enhancing each other?

While there is a relationship between garden and environmental weeds, the weeds that concern us as gardeners aren't usually the same as the weeds of concern in wild areas. As mentioned, weeds are a human condition and thrive in situations that we have created. This dates back 12,000 years to the very earliest agriculture. From the time humans decided that it was beneficial to have more of the plants we wanted, we have tried to get rid of the ones we don't want to make space for those we do. Through the millennia not much has changed. We are still battling weeds.

What has changed is that we now have gardens, not just crops to weed, and weeding a garden is completely different to weeding a cornfield. We are not going to touch on agricultural weeds here as that is another story, and as with environmental weeds, those that are problematic to farmers are not the same ones that bother us in our gardens.

I've been working with weeds and constantly researching them for many years. Early on I noticed a bit of a disconnect in my workshops when the weeds that *I* found the most interesting and useful were not those that my participants wanted to hear about. The weeds that exist in people's gardens may well be interesting and edible, but they won't necessarily be a bother to gardeners just because they are there. So instead of following the literature about weeds, I decided to ask gardeners. Weeds such as plantain, fat hen, chickweed, purslane and thistles might be the most widespread weeds in the world, but they didn't rate very highly as bothersome.

Hands down, around the world, what bothers us most are weeds that are hard to get rid of because of underground roots, bulbs or tubers, and those that are prickly to touch. Interestingly, lawn weeds bothered us a lot (especially the prickly ones), but lawn grass in the garden beds also rated highly amongst the *worst weeds* gardeners are dealing with - worldwide!

I had initially written this book based on my own experiences and interactions, combined with extensive research. I have now reshaped this to better reflect what over 1,500 gardeners told me was the weed that bothered them the most. There was nothing scientific about my survey, just a question put to gardeners around the world via social media. 1,500 gardeners responded, eager to offload what was bugging them. Most fascinating to me was that the weeds usually featured in gardening shows and publications weren't the same as those we actually deal with.

The least liked weeds in Australia were:
1. onion weeds and oxalis sp.
2. nutgrass
3. cobbler's pegs

4. bindii
5. Wandering trad and couch in equal amounts
6. blackberry

In the UK the least liked weeds were:
1. bindweed (hated by a whopping 28% of respondents!)
2. ground elder
3. mare's tail
4. brambles (including blackberry)
5. couch
6. dandelion, buttercups, nettle, ivy and oxalis

I didn't get sufficient responses from elsewhere to create similar lists for other countries, however, I found I could work out which country a person was from by the weed they hated most.

There was one other group of weeds that featured highly on all continents, and that is anything growing in your neighbour's yard. Amazing how many responses went along the lines of "I don't really mind weeds, but I have a big problem with such and such coming over the fence from next door," or "I don't have weeds, but I have to work so hard to stop my neighbour's weeds from coming over the fence. I wish they would control their weeds".

If we are honest with ourselves, we've probably had a weed spread from our garden without noticing at some stage. We probably didn't realise because it was actually our favourite tree hanging over the fence, our beloved passionfruit vine creeping too far or seedlings from our lovely flowers. How could the neighbours not like them? Let me guess what you are thinking – yes but *my* neighbours have nasty weeds like cobbler's pegs, morning glory and bamboo. Yes, these weeds can be a problem for you, but my point is – what is a weed to you is not necessarily a weed to your neighbours. Conversely what is a great plant to you may be a weed to them. *Weed* is such a subjective word!

Perhaps we could all be more considerate gardening neighbours by simply being more aware of what is escaping our gardens.

Kate Wall

Getting to Know Weeds

This mix of weeds would indicate a soil which is over cultivated, prone to erosion and which dries out easily.

Traditionally, our first response to weeds is to reach for the bottle of weed killer. This is so deeply ingrained in us that for many people, spraying poison onto weeds is done without a second thought. While spraying herbicides may give us quick results, ultimately, we are doing more harm than good, and the weeds just keep coming back. If we look first at why the weeds are there at all, we have the opportunity to deal with them in a way which gives long term weed reduction. Chances are we will find no need to use herbicides at all. Even if you are not an organic gardener, a less toxic approach to weed management has a lot to offer in terms of a greatly improved and more satisfying garden.

Here I will provide useful and fun information about garden weeds, with the aim of making this a handy gardener's companion. I prefer to use an integrated weed management approach. This simply means different approaches for different situations, as opposed to reaching for the poison every time a weed appears. Just as we know to prune perennials at the end of their season, trim hedges when they look shaggy, and prune flowering shrubs as flowers fade, by extending our gardening knowledge to what works for different weeds, we integrate these tasks into our gardening activities, rather than simply *weeding*.

Managing weeds starts with an understanding of why they are there in the first place. It is easier to control weeds once we know why we have some species growing and not others. In this way we learn so much about what is going on in our patch. With just a little knowledge, I have seen gardeners make simple adjustments to their gardening practices which have been transformative.

Why do we have weeds?
There is an important lesson we can learn from weeds, wherever we may find them. Weeds are colonisers. This means they've found themselves an empty space and have grown there. Once they have established themselves in that empty space, many weeds do have an amazing ability to extend that space by out-competing, smothering or even poisoning nearby plants (known as allelopathy). This is not usually a desired trait, and yet the tick trefoil (*Desmodium intortum*) is used as a ground cover in maize and sorghum fields in the Americas as its allopathic properties are useful for suppressing the growth of other weeds. This same habit makes this a very undesirable weed in our lawns as it can very quickly dominate a lawn in poor condition. Natural areas with weeds are often highly disturbed environments with plenty of empty spaces for weeds to take hold in. Roadsides, drains, beach fronts and walking tracks are classic places to find them.

Gardens that are full of weeds are likely to have had many empty spaces for the weeds to happily fill. When we pull them out, we leave an empty space which is perfect for the next generation of weeds. Welcome to the endless cycle of weeding a garden!

The simplest solution is to not leave an empty space in the first place. Grow a plant there instead, or at the very least, cover it with heavy mulch. Otherwise, consider leaving the weeds there until you are ready to replace them with something else, after all, they will simply replace themselves with more weeds.

A densely planted garden rarely has weeds. As gardeners, what better excuse do we need to put more plants in our gardens! This simple truth is probably the single biggest tool in our integrated weed management plan. Every time you despair at the sight of weeds in your garden, instead of buying weed killer, buy a new plant (or propagate a new one). For every weed you pull out, put in a new plant. This immediately turns weeding into a joy as it steers us away from fighting weeds towards more creative gardening. Many people enjoy the look of a full garden where there is very little ground space to see, and yet are quite shy about creating such a garden. The cost of having to buy so many plants to fill a space can be off-putting. By learning to propagate our own plants and choosing types that spread to fill a space (without spreading too far and becoming a weed), we are far less likely to have weeds, and far more likely to enjoy our gardens. Cottage gardening is a classic case in point. We all love the glorious pictures of English gardens overflowing with flowers, but when it comes time to create those gardens for ourselves, I often see large beds holding a smattering of plants with large gaps between them, and gardeners asking me when their gardens will look like the ones in the picture. They won't. They'll need constant weeding for little reward. Fill those gaps with more plants and you will get the look in no time and have almost no weeding to do.

In addition to being colonisers, weeds are survivors. They are generally far less fussy about their growing conditions than are our garden plants or crops. One of the reasons for their huge success is that they can exploit growing conditions which other plants cannot. This particularly relates to poor soil conditions and is the reason they are so successful in disturbed and damaged environments.

Why do we have certain weeds but not others?
While weeds are great at exploiting poor soil conditions, even poor soil conditions can vary extensively. Weeds can be extremely useful indicator plants. Particular types of weeds thrive in certain conditions, so by looking at the weeds in our garden, we can work out the condition of our soil and improve it so that fussier plants will survive in their place.

"Look deep into nature and then you will understand everything better."

Albert Einstein

If we look at some of the general characteristics of weeds, we will see certain soil conditions that are easily amended in the garden. One of these soil conditions is low nutrient availability. Many weeds have the ability to extract certain nutrients that are otherwise unavailable to other plants in that soil.

Euphorbias (spurges) for example are good accumulators of boron. Testing of plant materials grown in the same patch of soil will show higher levels of boron in the tissue of the euphorbias than of the other plants there. The process of these euphorbia weeds growing and dying is making boron available in the soil to other plants. Many other weeds do the same with various minerals and soil nutrients, which is a very useful trait. We call these types of weeds dynamic accumulators. This knowledge can be exploited in a variety of ways. Understanding that the soil is low in plant available boron for example, tells us that the plants doing well there either don't need much boron, or as in the case of the euphorbias, are able to extract greater amounts of boron than are other plants. If we wish to use this space to grow plants which need a little extra boron, such as fruiting plants, we will need to add it to the soil. This can be done by allowing the Eupborbia weeds to compost in situ, thereby returning the boron they have accumulated in a more plant available form, or by adding rock minerals or trace elements. Choosing to allow the Eupborbia weeds to coexist in the space helps to create a natural cycle of boron being made available as the weeds die back and compost in situ. Alternatively, we can recognise that this soil is low in boron and may simply not be the best spot in the garden to plant the passion fruit vine.

Deep Rooted Weeds

Deep rooted weeds are hard to pull out and for this reason alone go into the hated basket, and yet the deeper the root, the more important that plant is in terms of soil security. Deep rooted weeds are bringing nutrients up from deep in the soil, making those nutrients more available at the surface for other surrounding plants. This has the added benefit that deep rooted plants are often highly nutritious both to us and to animals. They also make excellent compost.

Another advantage of deep rooted plants is the role they play in opening up heavy soils, making it easier for worms and the roots of nearby plants to travel deeper into the soil. They are nature's ploughmen. Wild carrots and paddy's lucerne are examples of these.

The act of drawing minerals and nutrients out of the soil is a two-way process. Plants *give back* and will naturally improve the soil around their own roots. The deeper these roots extend into the ground, the deeper the soil improvement. The zone around a plant's roots is called the rhizosphere and is the most fertile and biologically active part of the soil profile. It is estimated that up to 30% of the carbohydrates produced by photosynthesis are exuded from the plant's roots into the soil, feeding this rhizosphere and the beneficial microorganisms that live here. It then goes without saying that having deeper rooted plants (or weeds) is going to be good for creating a deeper fertile soil.

Having an abundance of deep rooted weeds can indicate that you have a heavy and possibly compacted soil, especially if these deep roots feature a tap root. Adding lots of organic matter together with a good quality rock mineral product will make a huge difference in opening up the soil and giving other plants the chance to succeed there. My preferred rock mineral product has a high silica content, and is also biologically active, meaning it contains a large amount of soil microbes. The silica acts to improve the structure of the soil very effectively and easily. The rock minerals add vital minerals and microbes to the soil for good soil and plant health. This two-fold action makes it a very useful product when dealing with any weed problem. If you are able to find a similarly good quality product your journey to good soil will be fast tracked.

By allowing the deep rooted weeds to remain, you will allow them to continue working for you as agents of soil improvement. I cut the tops off any weeds that are too hard to pull out. This keeps them from dominating but allows their important work to continue. The tops are always put to use as food, fodder or compost, as they are mineral rich.

Common garden weeds with a deep tap root include:
- paddy's lucerne / sida retusa (*Sida rhombifolia*)
- wild carrots (*Cyclospermum leptophyllum*)
- amaranths / pigweed (*Amaranthus sp.*)
- sensitive weed (*Mimosa pudica*)
- mallows, including false mallow (*Malva sp.*)
- vetch (*Vicia sp.*)
- trefoils (*Desmodium sp.*)
- dandelion (*Taraxacum offininale*)
- flat weed / cat's ear / false dandelion (*Hypochaeris radicata*)
- bindweed (*Convolvulus arvensis*)
- thistles (*Cirsium sp.*)
- dock (*Rumex sp.*)
- garlic mustard (*Alliaria petiolata*)

Leguminous Weeds

Legumes are plants in the pea family (Fabaceae) and include cassias, peas, beans, and anything with pea like flowers – which does include many weeds. The key characteristic of leguminous weeds is their ability to draw their own supply of nitrogen directly from the atmosphere through the nitrogen fixing bacteria associated with their roots. If you dig them up, you will see little white nodules on the roots. This ability to fix nitrogen gives legumes a competitive advantage in soils which are lacking in nitrogen. Where legumes dominate, you'll be able to break this dominance by fertilising with a low nitrogen fertiliser. Avoid high nitrogen fertilisers in all situations, even lawns. Nitrogen is a highly soluble nutrient. What plants cannot take up immediately is easily lost in runoff to cause pollution in water ways. It is far more effective to use low doses of nitrogen more often. The presence of nitrogen in the soil gives other plants the opportunity to compete and even out compete the leguminous weeds.

Remember that the green waste of leguminous plants is high in nitrogen so makes great fodder, mulch or compost. One of the all-time best soil improving plants is a legume – lucerne. Leguminous weeds are excellent for soil improvement; as compost, mulch, a green manure or just by letting them grow. By slashing and letting them compost in situ, you will not only improve the amount of organic matter in the soil, but also the nitrogen content, making the area more attractive to other plants.

Legumes are well known for their nitrogen fixing abilities and often this is all that is considered when we think of feeding plants, but there is so much more to the story. The exudates from leguminous roots are also providing a constant trickle of plant available phosphorous to the soil through their association with beneficial fungi. The role of leguminous plants in overall soil fertility includes this ability to increase the beneficial fungi in the soil, a process which is only active in living plants. By composting leguminous weeds, you are adding organic matter, nitrogen and other minerals to the soil, but by composting the tops and allowing the root systems to keep working, you have an ongoing soil improvement machine at work for you.

Nitrogen is the key building block of protein, and indeed many of these leguminous plants are good sources of protein. This high protein content can make leguminous weeds such as clover or tree lucerne useful fodder plants. Letting grazing animals into an area can be an effective way of dealing with these weeds.

Legumes include many of our food plants such as peas, beans and lentils. However, these plants also have a tendency to use some of that abundant nitrogen to make cyanide compounds which are highly toxic. So, while this group has provided us with some of our most valuable food sources, it can also be one of the most highly toxic plant groups. *When wild foraging, never eat wild legumes, including peas and beans, unless you know for certain that they are an edible species.* Generally, cyanide compounds give their presence away with strong smells and bitter flavours designed to deter us from eating them – *never ignore a nasty odour or taste, it is often a very important warning to not eat that plant!*

Leguminous weeds which are common in gardens include:
- clover (*Trifolium sp*)
- burr clover (*Medicago sp*)
- creeping indigo (*Indigofera spicata*)
- Easter cassia (*Senna pendula var. glabrata*)
- trefoils (*Desmodium and Lotus sp*)
- vetch (*Vicia sp*)
- tree lucerne (*Leucaena leucocephala*)
- glycine (*Neonotonia wightii*)
- caltrop (*Tribulus terrestris*)

Shallow rooted Weeds

As the soil improves, the weed make-up will change. Shallow rooted weeds tend to be easy to pull out and are indicative of soils with reasonable nutrient values and a friable open soil structure. A mix of deep-rooted and shallow-rooted weeds can indicate a reasonably good surface soil layer but can also mean that the soil is still compacted and in need of further improvement beneath this layer. It could well be a sign that the natural progression towards soil improvement is underway.

Sometimes shallow rooted weeds are an indication of the way we are managing our garden – regular shallow watering combined with regular weeding of small weeds can lead to a proliferation of shallow rooted weeds. This is because all the soil action and life are in the surface layer, and it is only plants with very shallow roots that are able to cope in these conditions. If you have shallow rooted weeds, but a lack of deeper rooted plants or weeds and the soil is hard to dig, you will do well to modify your gardening practices to allow for deeper soil improvement. This is as simple as having a break from weeding to let the plants get roots a little deeper into the soil.

Many shallow-rooted weeds can make excellent ground covers and act to prevent surface erosion. These weeds are also very good at providing a living mulch which doesn't compete with neighbouring plants for water and nutrients. They don't compete with our plants because their roots are in a different soil zone. Generally, we want our garden plants to have roots deeper in the soil than do these shallow rooted weeds. Shallow-rooted weeds like chickweed, lesser swine cress, clover or wandering trad, can be very useful around fruit trees. The flowers help bring in beneficial insects and the leaf cover helps keep the soil cool and moist. Fleshy leafed weeds such as Callisia and wandering trad have been found to have the added benefit of returning extra moisture to the soil and therefore can be very valuable around citrus and other fruit trees.

Water deeper and less often to ensure moisture reaches deeper into the soil profile and allow the surface layer to dry out between drinks. This will help to discourage shallow-rooted weeds, while at the same time helping create a stronger and more drought resistant garden.

When combating shallow-rooted weeds, you need to be aware of two main groups of this kind of weed. The first group are those such as chickweed, nettle, henbit and cobbler's pegs, which propagate via large volumes of seed. In eradicating these weeds, management of seed set will be an important part of their eradication.

The second group of shallow-rooted weeds are those with fleshy surface rhizomes, so are easy to pull out but tend to take away the entire layer of humus with them. Eradicating these is much harder as every tiny piece that is left behind will grow. This can also include weeds like Callisia, buttercups and creeping Charlie. Smothering can be effective with these weeds.

Common garden weeds which are shallow rooted include:
- chickweed (*Stellaria media*)
- henbit (*Lamium amplexicaule*)
- creeping Charlie (*Glechoma hederacea*)
- Callisias (*Callisia sp.*)
- dead nettle (*Lamium purpureum*)
- buttercups (*Ranunculus sp.*)
- catchweed / cleavers (*Galium aparine*)
- common ragweed (*Ambrosia artemisiifolia*)
- gallant soldiers / potato weed (*Galinsoga parviflora*)
- thickhead / nodding top (*Crassocephalum crepidioides*)

Bulbous Weeds

Bulbous weeds such as nutgrass, soursobs and onion weed tend to like heavy compacted soils which are low in calcium. They are also three of Australia's most disliked weeds! Often all are present in the same garden, much to a gardener's dismay. I've found that by significantly improving the soil structure these weeds are less vigorous and easier to control by digging out or if really needed – poisoned. Soursob seems the least upset by the soil improvement, but as it is also the prettiest of the three, and the tastiest, I am happy to let it fill gaps in my garden. Like other bulbous weeds, it will be easier to dig it out when the soil is not so compacted. It is also a good idea to dig them out during dormancy.

All bulbous weeds have a dormant period which will vary according to the weed and the climate it is growing in. Digging them out before they break their dormancy means they will be less vigorous and won't have as many bulblets to worry about. It can be tricky to know where they are, so look for the first shoots appearing and dig them then.

Free ranging chickens or pigs will happily clean out any bulbs for you if you have the option to put a temporary fence around the contaminated part of your garden. The manure they add will help improve the soil as well. Beware of using pigs – they are incredibly effective at removing every skerrick of life in the garden. I had a client with a teacup pig (which was still growing when it reached 100kg thanks to the unstable genetics of some of these heavily manipulated breeds). We made a cute little pig pen in a section of her garden for this supposedly small pig. When the pig moved out to live on a farm, the pig pen was not only completely bare of anything except established trees, nothing had grown in over a year - not a seed, or a tuber or a runner was left.

Viticulturalists in South Australia have found that by letting *Oxalis pres-carpe* grow underneath the dormant grape vines in winter, the soil is well protected. The flowers in spring help bring in the good bugs before the plants die down for summer, so there is no competition with the vines while they are growing. As the grape vines break dormancy in Spring and become perfect fodder for leaf-chomping, sap-sucking insects, the required army of good bugs are ready and waiting to feast, thanks to this early flowering weed. You may find similarly that the weeds are only there for a short time of year and not so troublesome after all.

Bulbs can be exhausted by constantly removing the tops. This is best done at the time of flowering. The bulb has used all its energy to flower and then seed, so is at its weakest point. This is why we are told to let our much-loved bulbs die naturally rather than cutting the leaves off after flowering. Those leaves are *restocking* the bulb after the effort of flowering. For those that seed prolifically such as onion weed, crocosmias, agapanthus and pink baby's breath, pick and enjoy the flowers but cut the plants down completely before seeds can be set. This will not only begin the process of exhausting the bulb but will also prevent any spread via seeding. Nutgrass is more common in warmer climates. It is quite detested because it not only has a tuber (or *nut)*, but those tubers are also all connected by rhizomes which can be very deep. It can survive extended dormancy, including many years under concrete. If the concrete eventually cracks, the nutgrass won't be shy in coming up through the crevices. Improving and softening the soil is critical in dealing with this weed. When the soil is friable you can gently fork it over, lifting the connected tubers en masse. If the soil is not soft and friable, this activity is pointless as you will leave more tubers behind than you remove. While it's unlikely that you'll remove all the tubers this way, it can set the weed back enough to allow you to garden successfully over the top of the little that remains. Nutgrass needs sun, so by covering the area with dense plants taller than 25cm you will weaken it and you won't see it below your plants. Obviously, this only works in smaller patches and not in vegetable gardens, pasture or lawns. In lawns, very regular mowing will help to weaken the nutgrass. Highly toxic and expensive chemicals can be used, but they do have a long exclusion time if you wish to grow edibles, and they need to be repeated several times to be truly effective. These herbicides are specific for bulbous plants, so if you have nutgrass growing amongst your spring bulbs, you are likely to kill your bulbs before the nutgrass. Don't bother with the cheaper herbicides which say they work on nutgrass, they don't. At this point I know many of you will be disappointed – there is no magic bullet for nutgrass. I use a combination of all of the above to combat it. So far, I have succeeded only in reducing its dominance to a tolerable level. This is a serious weed that requires a serious approach. It is also not the most useful of weeds. If you are serious about making perfume, lucky you as nutgrass is used in the perfume industry. It is edible but tastes like camphor. Apparently, the variety more commonly found in tropical areas is good eating. I've never tried it. The variety common everywhere else is most definitely *not* good eating.

Common garden weeds which have bulbs or can be treated as bulbous weeds include:
- Nutgrass (*Cyperus rotundus*)
- numerous Allium species (onion weed, wild garlic etc) (*Allium sp*)
- soursobs (*Oxalis sp*)
- Pink baby's breath / Jewels of Opar (*Talinum paniculatum*)
- freesias (*Freesia alba x leichtlinii hybrid*)
- crocosmias (*Montbretia sp*)
- watsonias (*Watsonia sp*)
- agapanthus (*Agapanthus africanus*)
- onion grass (*Romulea rosea*)

Sandy Soils

At the other end of the scale is red natal grass (*Melinis repens*) which likes free draining sandy soils. I have fond memories of this pretty grass weed from growing up in sandy soils and picking bunches of it to put in a vase (my mother was not as impressed as I was). I am sure it would look lovely as an ornamental grass in my cottage garden, but it has no chance with my heavy clay soils. Many of the weeds which grow in sandy soils have very fibrous root systems, and this includes a variety of grasses. These dense fibrous roots are extremely valuable for erosion prevention as they hold the loose soil together.

Bracken is a weed which will successfully exploit moist sandy soils where it creates a deep root system able to accumulate phosphorous, making it available in the soil as the plant dies.

A mix of weeds that indicate sandy soils will tell you that a garden in that area will need significant soil work first, or you need to select plants for those conditions. These are weeds that are usually very tolerant of drying out and handle the low nutrient levels found in sandy soils. Sandy soils are not always dry, but they do have exceptionally good drainage. Some of the weeds that thrive in sandy soils will still like moist conditions but hate having wet feet.

Common garden weeds which like sandy soils include:
- purslane (*Portulaca oleracea*)
- capeweed (*Arctotheca calendula*)
- vervain (*Verbena bonariensis*)
- fennel (*Foeniculum vulgare*)
- mullein (*Verbascum thapsus* and *V. virgatum*)
- aloes (*Aloe arborescens*)
- wild marigold (*Tagetes minuta*)
- various cactus weeds including prickly pear (*Optunia sp*)

Weeds as pH Indicators

Most plants, weeds included, prefer a fairly neutral pH of 6.5 - 7 for ideal growth. However, there are some that are able to tolerate and even exploit pH outside this optimum range. By knowing which side of the scale they prefer, we can make adjustments to the soil pH to remove the competitive advantage of those weeds in favour of the plants we want.

Elderberry, chickweed, wild carrots and spurges prefer slightly alkaline soils.

Sheep sorrel, chicory, dandelions, plantain, bindii and clover all favour slightly acid soils. Adjusting the pH with garden lime will help to give the competitive advantage to the garden or lawn rather than these weeds. In the case of plantain and sheep sorrel, allow them to decompose in situ and they will act to slowly raise the pH of the soil naturally. They do this by being accumulators of calcium and phosphorus, both nutrients which are limited in the low fertility soils these weeds are commonly found in. Patterson's curse, a common weed in rural areas, has been shown to be extremely effective in raising the soil pH when cut and used as a mulch.

Buttercups like acidic soils that are also poorly drained. If you find buttercup, dock or sorrel increasing in your garden, check your soil. Chances are you have poor drainage, and this is causing your soil to become increasingly acidic. In fact, if any weed is increasing in dominance in your garden, find out what sort of conditions it likes and alter your soil accordingly.

Weeds as Mineral Deficiency Indicators

Mineral deficiencies are a very common soil problem. As gardeners we think to use fertilisers to supply the main plant nutrients of nitrogen, phosphorous and potassium but we don't often think about the other minerals plants need for growth. Often when weeds are thriving where other plants aren't, it is because of mineral deficiencies. The weeds that are thriving tend to be highly efficient extractors of minerals which are in low supply in the soil, giving them the ability to do well in deficient soils. There are some generalisations which can be made. Soils low in phosphorous but high in potassium will favour broad leaved weeds such as dandelions and plantains. Soils low in calcium will favour grass weeds.

Each weed will have certain mineral excesses and deficiencies that it can exploit. It is possible to map exactly what nutrients your soil is deficient in by knowing the preferences of all the weeds growing in that area. Very few of us are likely to go to such lengths, so it is good to know that we can make improvements to our soil without needing to know exactly what the mineral deficiencies are - it is enough to know that our garden is missing beneficial minerals and organic matter. A trace element mixture from a garden centre will help but will not be sufficient alone to correct most deficiencies. Instead find yourself a good quality rock mineral product to deal with mineral deficiencies in a comprehensive and simple way.

Interestingly, many of the most common garden weeds like soils low in calcium and phosphorous but high in potassium. Our increasing use of potash to stimulate flowering (which it does not do - potassium is used by plants for disease resistance, phosphorous is required to set flower buds) only adds to this imbalance. Over watering and heavy rain will cause calcium to be leached out of the soil. Adding a commercial fertiliser is not the answer here as it too will be high in potassium and low in calcium. In Australia, if you live in an area where banksias, grevilleas or other members of the Proteaceae family are common amongst the native vegetation, your soil will be low in available phosphorous. Applying a high phosphorous fertiliser to this soil will kill your natives. A balanced microbial rock mineral product will be a far safer way to get a mineral and nutrient balance back into your soil without causing harm through excessive levels of anything, keeping in mind that the microbes are the true agents of soil fertility, regardless of what you put on your soil. Good quality rock minerals are hard to find, you may need to do an internet search rather than rely on your local garden chain store for these.

Weeds found in over grazed paddocks tend to indicate that those soils have been depleted of minerals and fertility. These weeds are often considered rather unpalatable if they are edible, or they are quite toxic, causing a problem to livestock. Patterson's curse, fireweed, St John's wort and wild heliotrope all fall into this category and can all indicate deficiencies in calcium and copper.

Where weeds have the ability to indicate that minerals are in short supply in the soil, those weeds are usually able to access those minerals from the soil when other plants cannot. By allowing those weeds to compost where they grow, they are making those minerals available to other plants growing nearby and correcting mineral deficiencies in the soil. We call this action bioaccumulation. It is a trait of weeds we can exploit simply by composting those same weeds in situ, in the compost heap or as weed tea. Some weeds able to exploit certain mineral deficiencies and make those minerals available to nearby plants include:

broom	magnesium, sulphur
chicory	iron, calcium, copper
cleavers	iodine, calcium, copper, silica, sodium
comfrey	iron, chlorine, potassium, sodium
dandelion	calcium, copper, iron, magnesium, potassium, silica
dock	iron
duckweed	copper, boron, zinc, phosphorus
fennel	copper, potassium, sodium, sulphur
nettle	iron, potassium, sodium, sulphur
plantain	calcium, sulphur, potassium
ragwort	copper
shepherd's purse	calcium, sodium, sulphur
sorrel	calcium, phosphorus
spurges	boron
thistles	nitrogen, copper, silica
willow	calcium

(extracted, with changes from Newsleaf, Journal of Biodynamic Agriculture Australia, No. 60, p.6.)

Weeds can also be an indicator of high levels of certain minerals in the soil. Creeping wood sorrel can be an indicator of high copper soils and chicory can favour soils with moderately high aluminium levels.

Weeds of Other Soil Conditions

Some weeds, such as sow thistle, chickweed, mallows, fat hen and chicory prefer rich fertile soils. Having an abundance of these weeds is a great sign that your soil is doing well. Many of these weeds are also easy to pull out and great to eat, making a garden full of them more of a vegetable garden than a weed patch. They will all grow larger and lusher as the soil improves and moisture is readily available. Purslane also likes fertile soils but prefers dry conditions.

Yarrow and mustard (wild brassica) weeds tend to thrive in overly dry soils. Other weeds which like dry soils include false dandelion, mullein, amaranths, speedwell, purslane and thistles. If these weeds dominate your garden look at the water holding capacity of your soil. Improvements to organic matter and humus in the soil will help with water retention in the soil and work to break their dominance.

Conversely dock, canna, arum lilies and purple loosestrife can be an indicator of periodically waterlogged soils. Other weeds which favour poorly drained moist soils include buttercups, chickweed, hairy bittercress, horsetail, knotweeds, bindweed, Joe-Pye weed, moss, and quack grass. When these weeds dominate, look at how you can improve drainage in your garden.

Billy goat weed and common ragweed can both be indicators of over grazed paddocks. English daisy in a lawn can be an indicator of dry, worn out, low fertility soils, as can plantain. Wild carrots, dandelion, mugwort, vetch and yarrow all also thrive in low fertility soils. When any of these weeds seem to dominate, soil care is needed.

Regardless of the soil condition, there will be a weed that is well suited to those conditions. If weeds you find troublesome aren't mentioned here, do a little research. If you identify the weed and find out what conditions it likes, you'll be a long way towards understanding the soil conditions you are gardening with. Most local governments have resources for weed identification, such as a poster or online tools. You can also take your weed to a local nursery or garden club or send a picture of it to your local herbarium for identification. If you're unable to identify your weeds for certain, look at their characteristics. What time of year do they grow? Are they deep or shallow-rooted? Do they grow in one part of your garden but not another? If so, what is different between the two sections of the garden? There are so many weeds in the world that no book will ever cover every one of them. My quick survey of gardeners resulted in a list of over 150 different weeds that we don't like. If you assume that weeds have something to teach you and you are able to observe their characteristics, the information here will still help you to read them and learn something about the conditions in your garden.

You can even learn about your soil from the number of different weeds found growing in your garden. The greater the diversity of weeds you have, the more likely that you have fairly good soil which is not too dry or wet, has a neutral pH and average fertility. This is a good indicator that a diverse range of garden plants will also grow in your garden. The more extreme your soil conditions, the greater the dominance of weeds that favour those conditions will be. At the other end of the scale, if you have bare soil and very few weeds, you have real trouble with your soil!

Kate Wall

Dealing with Weeds

A garden full of snake plant, basket plant and Singapore daisy will be a challenge to deal with, but these weeds can all be effectively eradicated without needing herbicides.

In spite of the many great attributes of weeds, there will come a time when you want to replace them with other plants. In this case, think of the weeds as volunteer plants that you are not responsible for. This is also true of other plants you have but no longer wish to keep. Regardless of the reason or the plant, there are many ways of dealing with unwanted plants in a way that doesn't damage soil, the environment or our health. I suggest only using herbicides as a very last resort.

Whatever methods you employ to deal with weeds, soil improvement should always be considered as an important ongoing process of good gardening. Our aim is to achieve a garden environment with less weeds, and this will never be done by pulling or even poisoning the same weeds over and over. Something needs to be done differently if a different outcome is to be achieved, and soil improvement is a great place to start.

Soil Improvement

Soil improvement is a vital part of good weed management. Remember I said that weeds were survivors? They are usually able to withstand poor soil conditions far better than our garden plants or lawn and are working for us by improving that poor soil. If we were to let the weeds have their way for a few years and then try planting, we'd find that plants would do better than they would have without them. I've seen it very poetically written as "weeds are nature's Band Aids healing a damaged landscape". Waiting years for weeds to improve the soil before starting a garden is not really practical so we need to speed up this process.

How many times have we weeded the garden before we fertilised because we stubbornly refused to share the fertiliser with weeds? We should really fertilise *before* we weed, as most weeds don't really like it. They have the competitive advantage in poor soils, and as we improve our soil, the weeds lose that advantage as our plants gain it. As the soil improves the weeds naturally become less dominant. Sure, great soil can grow great weeds, but it will also grow great plants and make the weeds easier to pull out. Generally, the weeds that grow in good soils are not the same as those in the bad soil. Many of the weeds that thrive in good soils, also happen to be the best weeds for eating which immediately makes them more desirable.

When fertilising, we might worry that the weeds are going to thrive on the fertiliser, and that in doing so these weeds will rob our gardens of those same valuable nutrients. If we have deep-rooted weeds, they are feeding in a different soil zone to the shallower roots of our vegetables and garden plants, reducing any chance of root competition. Those deeper-rooted weeds are providing much needed support to our garden plants by making deeper nutrients more available to them. Recent studies have shown that plants do indeed *share* nutrients with each other through a complex interaction of the soil fungi surrounding plant roots. Often after fertilising we can get a flush of fast-growing annual weeds and again, we think they are robbing *fertiliser* from our plants. What they are actually doing is storing the excess fertiliser to use later. Such flushes of growth are often caused by over fertilising. In the absence of this flush of weed growth, that same fertiliser will be washed away and wasted, or worse, cause algae blooms when it finds its way into waterways. By allowing the annual weeds to grow, they are trapping and storing this fertiliser, to be released back into the soil as they die. A reminder that we should compost weeds.

Fertiliser *is not* a soil improver. It is designed to feed plants and nothing else. A soil improver improves the structure, microbial life, water holding ability, porosity and the plant available nutrient levels within the soil. As these aspects of the soil are all improved, the need for fertilisers is greatly reduced. Overuse of fertilisers can cause nitrogen burn to plants and leads to nitrogen pollution in our waterways and atmosphere, as well as a build-up of salts in the soil. Excess salts in turn cause other soil problems, such as locking up many of the minor plant nutrients, making them unavailable to plants. Combined, it creates the perfect environment for weeds to flourish.

My preference is to avoid fertilisers altogether and instead feed my soil once a year with a mixture of aged horse manure or homemade compost, together with my favourite microbial rock minerals. This mix allows for excellent improvement in all soil types as well as ensuring that a full range of minerals are brought back into balance in plant available forms. Many gardeners dislike using horse manure as a source of organic matter largely due to the tendency of weed seeds to pass through the horse's digestive system and grow. This is one of the reasons I like it so much. The horse manure breaks down rapidly to improve the soil and the weeds that grow are not only easy to pull out, they are most often wonderful edible weeds such as nettle, mallows, sow thistles and chickweed - plants the horse has eaten.

In his book 'Weeds, The Guardians of the Soil', soil scientist Joseph A. Cocannouer describes the plight of a commercial orchard in California. He talks to an orchardist who had been using an expensive commercial fertiliser for years without any other soil care practices. After a few very successful years the trees began sickening. The orchardist was advised to remove all the trees and start again on a new site. Instead of pulling out his trees, he walked away and left the orchard abandoned for a year before returning. A year later the weeds were thriving and in the absence of fertilisers, the trees had not only recovered, but were looking healthier than ever. The orchard was saved and from then on the orchardist used only weeds and legumes as fertiliser for his trees. A key to his success was the action of deep-rooted weeds to help break open subsoils and build stronger, deeper soils.

Any plan to reduce weeds can include putting the weeds that are already there to good use. Cut the weeds (or even mow or slash if you have large areas) and leave the tops to compost in situ. In this way the minerals they have drawn out of the deficient soil is returned to be available to other plants. By leaving the roots in place, they can keep working for you. Repeatedly cutting the tops off weeds will deplete the root system and eventually cause the plant to die. It also prevents them from seeding so the weed cycle can be broken, gradually eradicating the weeds while improving the soil.

Mulch

Mulch will help to suppress most weeds. It does this by stopping the sunlight from reaching the soil. Most seeds will only germinate if they are at or near the surface of the soil where there is light and warmth. Mulch buries seeds deeper, reducing the chance of them being able to successfully germinate. There are some exceptions of course. Large seeds are happy to be that bit deeper, as are the seeds of deciduous plants such as the Chinese elm (*Celtis sinensis*), which drop a thick layer of leaf litter over the top of its own seeds, so they have adapted to germinate exceptionally well under mulch.

Seeds under mulch may remain dormant but still viable for many years. They won't grow until that mulch is disturbed and they find themselves at the surface again. In most cases mulch won't kill the weed plants, nor will it kill the seeds, it simply stops them germinating. By mulching a garden after weeding, we reduce the likelihood of the seeds left behind germinating and have less weeding to do next time - until the mulch breaks down and those dormant seeds find themselves once more at the surface that is. By topping up the mulch regularly so that it continues to work effectively as a barrier to seed germination, we are also constantly topping up the organic matter in our soil and improving it – so in a roundabout way we can still thank the weeds for improving our soil!

It is recommended that mulch be applied *after* weeds are pulled out. Thick mulch over the top of the weed plants can work if you follow the smothering technique described below, or if you are covering tiny seedlings. A realistic mulch layer for a garden bed with plants in it is no more than about 3-5cm, which is not enough to kill off anything but the tiniest plants growing below it. Mulch much thicker than this will work to smother weeds but will also make the garden bed unsuitable for other plants.

If you have concerns about the seed load in your soil, an even better method is to weed the bed, then water it well. Don't mulch it until you see a carpet of tiny green weeds sprouting. Mulch will kill these tiny seedlings by smothering, and you will have eliminated some of the seed from the soil seed bank.

A well mulched garden will have far fewer weeds. Mulch has many other benefits to a good garden, including conserving water and protecting the soil, making it a perfect example of how good garden care can contribute to less weeding work and a better garden.

Seeds

There is a saying, allow weeds to seed in one year and have them for the next seven years. Seeds can be hard to get rid of and can make the fight against unwanted weeds seem endless. They are a key survival strategy of weeds, many of which live reasonably short lives but compensate for this by creating hundreds or even thousands of seeds per plant. In creating a garden which is not ideal for weeds, we need to be aware of this survival mechanism and arm ourselves against it.

Removing weeds before they set seed and mulching the soil to prevent seeds from germinating are two of the most important strategies in overcoming weed seeds. With a little time and vigilance, it is entirely possible to break the seed load in the soil and stop further weeds from coming up. I have successfully ridded large gardens of cobbler's pegs (*Bidens pilosa*) by ripping them all out and laying them down as mulch – seeds and all, after all there was an overabundance of seed in the soil already. As new plants grew, they were pulled out and lain down as mulch, this time without adding any more seed to the soil seed bank. If using this method, make sure that every time you pull out the weeds, you also water the bed. Pulling the weeds gives enough soil disturbance to bring more seeds to the surface to grow, and by watering we hasten the growth so that we can pull out the next generation. For this method to work well you need to be patient and vigilant – once they get away from you and start to set seed again, you'll be back to the beginning! On the upside, all those seeds can be turned into wonderful green manure. The garden where I used this method was large and overflowing with cobbler's pegs as high as my chest to start with. Within a year I had only the very odd plant still coming up. Now years later, the property has been sold, the garden demolished and left bare, and still no cobbler's pegs have come up. We broke the seed load in the soil very successfully, without using any poisons and without removing any seeding plants from the site. By composting all those wonderful cobbler's pegs plants, we also managed to create some wonderful soil.

Gardeners often panic about the idea of leaving weeds which are seeding on the ground. In truth if your weed has gone to seed, you will already have a seed load in the soil, and those seeds still on the plant are only adding a small amount to this load. It doesn't matter if you have five seeds or 500 seeds in the soil, you'll still need to come back and address the new weeds germinating there before they can grow and set more seed. As soon as you move weeds with seeds on to anywhere else to compost or dispose of them, you risk spreading the seed.

Far better to leave the weed to compost in situ so that you know exactly where the seeds are to deal with. The compost value of those weeds left to break down on the soil surface is enough to warrant a few more seeds in the existing seed bank. Plan to be consistent in pulling out the seedlings for a little while and the long-term results will be well worth the short-term effort.

I strongly recommend that you avoid using pre-emergent herbicides. These are poisons which prevent seeds in the soil from germinating. The key word being poison – we simply do not need more poison added to our soils. Instead create a garden or lawn environment where seeds do not germinate easily. Bare patches of soil are the perfect place for germination, so avoid empty spaces by filling them with mulch or plants.

As mentioned previously, burying seeds under mulch is another valuable strategy. Some weed seeds such as dandelion and false dandelion are only viable for a couple of years, so mulching is effective in beating them. The seeds of other weeds such as amaranths and fat hen can be viable for 30 years or more. Beware that once the mulch breaks down or you dig over the bed, those seeds may still be there ready to sprout.

Hand Weeding

Hand weeding is the most ecofriendly way of weeding. Use your pulled weeds for compost, either in situ, in the chook pen or the compost heap. If you have a lot of weeds to pull out, work on it as methodically as you can, even if is bit by bit. This means choose a starting point and work from there so that you can see your progress and acknowledge your achievement. By working randomly, the weeds can seem to bounce back into the gaps before you've had a chance to put anything else in the gaps.

Allowing weeds to compost in situ means leaving the weeds laying on the ground where you pulled them. This is always my preference as it not only saves me the effort of cleaning up after myself, but it also means that whatever nutrients those weeds have taken from that section of soil are returned directly to where they are most needed. It may seem unsightly, but I then tuck them under a nearby bush or cover them with mulch if I want a neater result. Otherwise, I look happily at the very temporary mess knowing that I am doing the soil a big favour.

Once you have mostly got control of the weeds, there will often still be spot weeding to do. Pull each weed as you see it – perhaps while you are doing other jobs or just admiring your garden on the way to work. Pull out one weed and lay it back down and keep going. This means that when the weekend comes you don't have a big weeding job because it has been progressively done already.

If you have a lot of deep-rooted weeds or ones that are hard to pull out easily, break the tops off and put your efforts into soil improvement instead. I have a few like this and instead of worrying about getting the roots out, I leave the roots to keep working on improving the soil for me. By regularly breaking off the tops, I just get more compost and more benefit from these weeds being there.

Hand weeding can be an arduous task if you have a lot of weeds, and most gardeners will have their favourite tool to help with the job. I have seen some pretty impressive collections of hoes, making me wonder at the amount of time some gardeners have spent on weeding.

With persistence and effort, hand weeding can beat any weed, although many readers are probably swearing at me after reading that statement. It is true but it isn't fun. That's why I have included numerous other weed management strategies here as well. Hand weeding often needs to be done in conjunction with other methods to be realistic. Weeds that sprout from tiny pieces of broken root or stem are unlikely to be beaten with hand weeding alone.

Amongst the weeds that gardeners told me they really disliked are those that hurt to touch. Nettles came out pretty high on the list. The idea of sticking your bare hand into a patch of nettles may not be tempting but they are easily dealt with using a long-handled hoe. Most gardeners tend to find they have nettle by accident. It only takes one small plant to get this weed onto the most hated list. I prefer to work with bare hands, but if there is any risk of nettles, I make sure I wear gloves. Prickly weeds in general are difficult to hand weed. Protective clothing is a good idea, as are whipper snippers (weed whackers) and long handled tools.

Another group of weeds that we particularly hate to hand weed are those with sticky seeds. I personally don't mind cobbler's pegs but the sticky seeds of silver leafed desmodium drive me batty. I usually spend much longer trying to remove seeds from head to toe than I do actually weeding. Cleavers is another weed much disliked for its sticky seeds, but there are many more. These are the sort of weeds we prefer to deal with without getting too close, so we need to look at other weed control options. These weeds may be better dealt with using boiling water or steam which will also kill those annoying seeds.

Composting Weeds

There is a lot of advice telling us not to add weeds with seeds to the compost. Unless you are hot composting your backyard compost set up will not harm seeds. The compost heap can be a great way to grow some extra veg as pumpkins, tomatoes, paw-paw, capsicum and avocadoes (to name a few of our kitchen scraps) love to germinate in it.

Seeds are less likely to germinate if the compost is buried under mulch after being spread (which is better anyway). Keep an eye on it and pull any weed seedlings out while they are still small and before they can set more seed. If you are hot composting seeds will be killed. To achieve a hot compost the pile needs to reach at least 60° Celsius and will usually be a pile of at least one cubic meter.

I have already mentioned that my preference for dealing with weeds is to compost them in situ. This still applies when those weeds have seeds on them. When the weeds have gone to seed, the soil below them is going to have a stock of seeds in it anyway, so whether you add the ones on the plant or not, you still need to deal with the seed load in the soil. Laying the plant down on the spot, seeds and all, will not change this fact and allows you to keep the seeds in one area and deal with the one seed bank instead of spreading them around. Then keep an eye on it and weed before the weeds are big enough to seed again.

Remember that the weeds have grown and taken something out of the soil. In a healthy balanced system, we need to replace these nutrients. The best (and cheapest) way to do this is to compost and return those same weeds to the soil. Any weeds with deep roots are especially valuable in the compost as they have drawn nutrients up from deep in the soil and so are mineral and nutrient rich. Leguminous weeds are excellent for adding extra nitrogen to compost.

Weeds with seeds can also be composted under water by making weed tea, which is a great alternative for weeds that are likely to take root in the compost. This includes running grasses or succulent weeds, weeds with tubers such as madeira vine, bulbs like oxalis or onion weed, or fleshy ground covers like tradescantias or Callisias. All of these weeds can be made into weed tea very easily. Put them into a large garbage bin or similar, fill it with water and put the lid on. After a couple of weeks, it will smell truly foul as the weeds rot in the water. Adding a bit of nitrogen in the form of chicken manure or a nitrogen-based fertiliser will speed up the decomposing process (in the compost heap as well as in the weed tea). A week or two later the smell should start to reduce, and this is your signal that the compost is ready to use. Scoop off the liquid and dilute it to the colour of weak tea before splashing it around the garden as a foliar feed. The sludgy weeds at the bottom can be added to the compost if they are looking rather indistinguishable, but if you can still easily recognise which plant is which, add more water and make another batch.

If you want to use the weed tea before it has lost its smell, apply it straight to the soil rather than as a foliar feed. This is particularly fabulous when preparing new garden beds. As the weeds rot in the water and the mixture starts to smell, a form of fermentation is occurring. Weed tea is more than just mushed up weeds diluted in water. It is alive with beneficial microbes which are very valuable for plant and soil health.

Vinegar

For weeds in gravel pathways and similar situations, spray with neat white vinegar. This is very cheap and safe. By using a spray directly onto the leaves, you will not be acidifying the soil. Spray during hot weather for faster frying – the vinegar works because it is an acid that effectively burns the leaf. For weeds with waxy leaves dilute the vinegar 50/50 with water and add a little detergent to help it *stick* to the leaves.

If you have an abundance of weeds and are using vinegar often to manage them in large areas of the garden, then there is a chance the soil will acidify. This is fine if you plan to grow strawberries or gardenias, but otherwise ensure you add plenty of organic matter to the soil before planting the garden as this will buffer any pH issues that may result from using so much vinegar. Fortunately, it breaks down quickly to carbon dioxide and water in the soil so any acidifying will be temporary. For this reason, vinegar is not considered useful to achieve long term pH alterations to alkaline soils.

Weeds with deep tap roots will be harder to kill with vinegar and will need a few goes. The vinegar works by burning off the leaves. This is enough to kill many plants but in the case of tubers, bulbs or deep tap roots, it isn't as effective. These types of plants are best dealt with through soil improvement and then a helping hand from vinegar. Vinegar is not systemic and will not be drawn into the tissue of the plant. As a bonus it is safe to let the chooks or livestock forage on weeds that have been sprayed with it.

There is a new generation of organic weedkillers on the market which are based on pelargonic and other plant acids. They work in exactly the same way that cheap vinegar does but cost a lot more. I have worked with both and have not found them to be any more effective than vinegar. They are gaining popularity however, as people like to buy products that tell them what to do in the name of the product. I am sure if the company making the cheap vinegar put different labels on the bottles – weedkiller, surface spray, window cleaner and so on, they would sell a lot more bottles of exactly the same stuff! Don't laugh, if you take the time to read the detailed information on the back of fertiliser packets you would realise that this is already happening – change the label but not the contents and you will sell twice as much.

There are many internet sites recommending a homemade salt and vinegar spray to deal with weeds. I very strongly discourage this. The vinegar is effective without the added salt, which damages the soil and therefore is not recommended as part of long term weed eradication.

Boiling Water and Steam

You can use a kettle of boiling water to easily deal with weeds in the paving. Make sure you don't splash yourself, otherwise this is pretty much completely without side effects. If you are using boiling water to destroy bulbous weeds, dig a hole around the bulb first to get the water straight to it. This can be tedious, but it effectively cooks the bulb and will work on things like oxalis and onion weed; weeds that have many bulblets attached to the main bulb and spread when you try and dig them out. Boiling water used too often will also kill microbes in the soil, so use it in small areas at a time and give the microbes time to recover before repeating.

Some very progressive councils are using steam instead of herbicides for weeding footpaths and public places. This is *great* news and I hope that it gains momentum. The steam works just like the boiling water or the vinegar in that it burns off the foliage. In most cases this is all that the weedkillers are doing anyway. The steam tends to burn things off quickly, so it is obvious that an area has been sprayed and there is no risk of a passerby munching on a tasty weed without realising it had just been sprayed. What doesn't die but grows back will have no toxic residue and will be safe to eat which is great for foragers – human or otherwise. One of the disadvantages of weedkillers is that they're not instant. It can take several days for the effects to be seen. In that time, they remain as invisible poison to foragers and can be toxic to pets that walk over the sprayed weeds then lick their feet. I have known cats to be terribly ill from walking over a neighbour's grass after a weed and feed treatment was used.

The main cost with steam is the set up. Once you have the equipment, just add water. This represents long term cost savings, which is not always easy to see when looking at short term outlay. I really hope this situation changes, as steam is probably the most realistic large-scale alternative to herbicides for use in public places. The other great advantage that steam has over herbicides is that plants will never develop resistance to it.

In the home garden, you can give your steam mop a second job by using it to weed the paving. Steam weeding is particularly effective for seedlings and for shallow rooted plants or ground covers. It is also great for succulent weeds. For all of these, burning off the tops will kill the plant. Some of the hardier ground covers that have dense leaf growth protecting their stems or runners may need a second go as the leaves will reshoot.

Steam is useful on any soft leafed plant that doesn't have an underground storage organ. It's particularly good for shallow rooted ground cover weeds that root at nodes, making them difficult to hand weed without leaving a little behind to regrow. This includes weeds like buttercups, creeping Charlie, Callisias, tradescantias and commelinas. Steam weeding can also be useful for succulent weeds such as mother-of-millions (*Bryophyllum delagoense*). After pulling out the main plants and disposing of them (solarisation or weed tea are ideal for this), you can use steam or boiling water to stop the many fragments left behind from growing back.

Salt

Someone once told me that as a child she used to follow her father around, and as he dug up a nutgrass weed, she would put a spoonful of salt down the hole. I assume this would work for onion weed, soursob and other bulbous weeds as well. Of course, this is not something to be repeated often as it causes salinity problems and is probably best done a week or so prior to heavy rain to help flush excess salt from the soil. Salt isn't an option for weeds growing in close proximity to garden plants as it travels in the soil and affects nearby plants.

Many people recommend adding salt to vinegar sprays, but this isn't necessary and is damaging to the soil. As we have already mentioned, the vinegar alone is an effective weedkiller and causes no damage to the soil, until you add salt to it. Wherever you use salt as a weedkiller, be aware that it will burn plant roots, kill soil microbes and reduce soil fertility by changing the form of soil minerals so that they are no longer able to be absorbed by plants. This makes the soil better for weeds and is counterproductive for weed eradication. Even when adding salt to the cracks in paving, think about where the water runs off as salt is highly soluble. I have seen many people on social media suggest that the damage done to the soil by adding salt is all worth it to get rid of hated weeds. I have even seen someone proudly showing off their garden bed white with salt. Sadly, this garden may never grow another plant in the gardener's lifetime! Do we really hate weeds so much that we think such drastic measures are worthwhile? it seems many do.

Fire

Burning weeds can be a very effective way of getting rid of them, although it comes with certain risks. I had a neighbour two doors down who decided to weed the garden by simply setting it alight. He did this during drought and with vines channelling flames into treetops. Our neighbourhood is entirely timber houses so you can see why this was not a good idea! If you plan to burn off weeds make sure you're able to control the fire, which includes checking that nothing can catch alight and spread the flames out of your easy reach.
Burning can damage the soil structure, burn soil organic matter and kill soil microbes, so it's not usually recommended, plus there is the obvious risk of setting the garden alight to deal with weeds.

Burning is effective for woody or fibrous weeds such as gorse, velvet leaf, sida retusa, mallows, lantana, Mickey Mouse bush, privet and leucaena, or grass weeds (which are also very fibrous and flammable plant material). Be aware that where you have large stands of any of these weeds, you may have more success to cut the weeds (especially the ones with trunks) and lay them over the base of the plant before burning. This tends to keep the fire from getting out of control and concentrates it around the base of the plant where the fire can kill the growing buds in the woody stems.

Fire can be useful in clearing thickets of blackberries, though the blackberries will probably grow back from underground roots that are unaffected. Once the difficult prickly tops of the plant are gone, controlling the blackberry as it reshoots is far more manageable. Goats will eat the shoots, or you can mow or hoe them. If you stop the shoots from maturing, they cannot feed the roots and the plant will become exhausted and die.

Any use of fire *must* be controlled and *must* comply with local fire regulations, especially fire bans. This includes the use of flame weeders, which used carelessly in dry weather near sugarcane mulch for example is a huge risk. A flame weeder is usually a handheld gas fuelled flame. It burns the top off the weed and is useful on small plants contained in small areas. It's not as useful on deep-rooted or bulbous weeds as the tops will burn but the weed can reshoot (as in the case of the blackberry). When using one, you don't need to catch the plant alight, just blast it with the blue flame until it steams. At this point the plant cells are destroyed, and the job is done. This works well for succulent weeds such as Tradescantia, Commelina, Callisa, and Kalanchoe, which effectively cook due to the high water content in their leaves. Commelina can have deep roots, so if you don't get the crown it will reshoot after flame weeding.

A flame torch can work well for weeding paths, paved areas or weeds in gravel. In this case the flame is great not just for killing the weeds but will also destroy the weed seeds. Not all seeds are killed by fire. Holly leaved senecio (*Senecio glastifolius*), and black wattle (*Acacia mearnsii*) have both shown improved gemination afterwards.

The flame weeders available in garden centres are often too small to be very effective and can end up being an expensive solution to the weed problem. Larger models can be tricky to use but very effective. Remember to be safe when using flame weeders and keep a hose handy. The flame can shoot out to as far as 15cm, so you also need to be careful with nearby plants, organic mulch, garden lights or anything else that may be damaged by the heat. For this reason, using fire is usually a last resort and is not recommended for suburban gardens.

Solarisation

Solarisation is the process of using the sun's heat to kill weeds. It works by covering an area of weeds with black plastic and letting the sun heat it up enough to cook everything underneath. This is usually a quick process in Australian summers with temperatures consistently over 30°C. In the temperate northern hemisphere, this can be a much longer process and not always as effective. It works best to slash or mow the area as low as possible first, then water well before laying down the plastic. You can leave the slashed material in situ as it will compost quickly in the heat. If you can get the area hot enough it will kill weed seeds as well. To achieve this amount of heat, it is best done in full sun during the hottest time of year. Black plastic will get hotter than other colours, but it needs to be nonporous. Shade cloth or weed mat will not work for solarisation. The tiny holes will allow the heat to escape and reduce the effectiveness of the cooking process.

Watering the area works to help transfer heat and speed up the cooking process. Along with slashing, it also stimulates the weeds to grow. The lack of sunlight forces the weeds to grow soft and weak, sending out long pale shoots which are easily damaged. These soft shoots will rot easily in the heat under the plastic. Should they still be alive when you lift the plastic, expose them to the hot sun for a day before covering them again. The sudden direct sun will burn and further weaken them. This method relies on the lack of light as much as the retention of heat, so make sure the edges are trenched into the soil or very securely held down. It's important to ensure there are no underground runners extending out from under the covered area and happily soaking up the sun nearby. Use a spade to cut a line around the edge of the area and make sure any underground runners are severed.

As plastic degrades in the sun, heavy duty plastic will be more effective, especially if you are doing large areas of solarisation. Small patches of a suburban garden can be solarised with black plastic garbage bags held down with rocks, but even then, I prefer to use a heavy grade of plastic that can be reused and won't contribute to the single use plastic problem.

The timing will be based on how hot the area gets. In some areas two weeks will be plenty, but I usually recommend four. Keep the plastic on for longer if the weather is mild. The area shouldn't have any sign of living plant matter, including sun-seeking white shoots when you lift the plastic. If it does, repeat the process. Once it is complete, you will have a totally clean area ready for planting.

Solaristion can be done on a small scale by placing difficult weeds into a black plastic bin liner, tying off the end and leaving it in the sun for a couple of weeks. This works very well for succulent weeds which are naturally full of moisture and therefore cook well in the plastic bag. The resulting mush can be added to the compost without risk of the weeds resprouting.

Solarisation is a blanket weed treatment and only applies to areas that you want to completely cleanse of plant material. It won't work in shady areas or in garden beds between plants. It is a wonderfully effective way of cleaning large areas in readiness for creating new garden beds. It doesn't work on bulbous or dormant plants. Bulbs that are close to the surface might be killed but deeper bulbs such as nutgrass or cats claw creeper will be unaffected. It does work well on Singapore daisy - a common warm climate weed that spreads by rhizome or even root pieces, forming dense mats. To be effective however you must cover the entire infestation and dig a spade line around the edge, otherwise any stray pieces of exposed weed will feed the other sections of weed left in the dark. It is also effective to treat other persistent ground cover weeds with solarisation, but only when they are growing in reasonably warm sunny locations. For ground cover weeds in shady locations, smothering is better.

Weed Matting

Weed mat is so often recommended that most people assume it must be important. I hate it and never use it. Sure, it slows weed growth, but only temporarily. As mulch builds up over it, weed seeds land on top and the roots grow through. Super tough weeds like nutgrass and couch grass just laugh at weed mat and keep on growing! In a year or two, you have as many weeds as you would have had without it. Weeding when the weeds have their roots enmeshed in a mat is not fun. Planting into a garden bed with old weed mat in it is not fun either. Weed mats have a long life, but only a short useful life. Once that useful time is over, there is a long time of cursing the day you laid it.

Weed mats also reduce air flow into the soil – yes healthy soils have an ongoing exchange with the air above them. Soils underneath the weed mat become oxygen depleted, which plants and soil microbes don't like. Thick paper or cardboard can do the same job as weed mat in the short term, but in the long term will decompose and are no longer impacting on the garden in any way. The only place worth thinking of using weed mat would be under gravel paths or driveways – places where it doesn't matter if the soil is sour because there is no intention of ever planting there. But then, thick paper or card works just as well so why bother with the expense of weed mat? And why add plastic to the environment unnecessarily? Over time soil and seeds will accumulate on top of the weed mat and you will once again be dealing with weeds in the gravel.

Although weed mat impedes oxygen exchange with the soil, it is porous enough that it won't effectively solarise weedy areas. Water vapour will escape, and heat will be lost.

Smothering and Cover Cropping

Any form of smothering weakens plants. An example of this is when weedy vines take over treetops, smothering the tree foliage and weakening the tree. We can turn this tactic around and use it on the weeds we don't want, although we will have more control of the process if we apply it to weeds much smaller than trees!

One commonly practised form of smothering is no-dig gardening. By placing thick layers of newspaper, cardboard and organic matter over an area to create a mounded garden bed, you are very effectively smothering the weeds that were growing there beforehand.

Unlike solarisation which relies on heat, smothering relies on completely restricting light. It takes a little longer to work than solarisation, but in the case of situations like no-dig gardens, the covering is designed to be permanent, so it doesn't have to kill the weeds quickly, as long as it kills them eventually.

Cover cropping works by growing plants with a taller and denser leaf cover than the weeds you need to get rid of. As the cover crop grows, it shades out the unwanted weeds below. Plenty of vegetables work like this. Many of the cucurbit family (watermelon, zucchini, pumpkin etc) produce sprawling plants with large leaves, perfect for shading out small weeds below. Hand weed around them in the vegetable garden when they are small, then as they grow, let the weeds be and the cover crop will simply out compete them.

If you are planning to use cover cropping as a way of out competing weeds in vegetable or ornamental gardens, you'll have more success if you grow certain types of plants closely together, for example, beans grown under corn or nasturtiums under camellias. Plant closely together as this allows the cover crop plants to shade out the weeds faster. To have success with cover cropping you need to think along the lines of a densely planted garden. Where sunlight is not reaching the soil, not only will seed be far less likely to germinate, but small weeds there will be quickly deprived of light and die.

Smothering and cover cropping can work very well in combination against difficult ground cover weeds, weeds that might not be beaten by either one of these methods alone. Weeds like wandering trad, Callisia, Singapore daisy, grass weeds and even mother-of-millions are good for this method. Firstly, cut the weed low using a mower or whipper snipper, then smother. Do not water underneath the smother layer this time, as we don't want the plant to have the energy to regrow through the layers. Smother with thick layers of cardboard or newspaper and mulch. This is not a no-dig garden, so we don't need to add layers of compost for planting into the entire area. Instead make some holes through the smother layer for planting into. Within those holes you will need to clear the weeds and add compost for fast and successful growth of the cover crop. Then plant your cover crop. Something that can be temporary and dense is usually the best option. Pumpkins and sweet potatoes are ideal for this job. Their dense growth will cover the area and where the weeds do manage to come through the smother layer, they still need to compete with the cover crop. This isn't a fool proof eradication method, but it does weaken a weed to the point that it's no longer a problem and becomes easy to control through hand removal. During this time, you're also producing a crop and improving the soil for any future, more permanent planting. Win-win!

If you use sweet potato as your cover crop, you may need to think of it as a permanent replacement plant. It can be nearly impossible to find all the sweet potato tubers and this plant can be hard to get rid of. Sweet potato is a good plant for soil improvement however, as the tubers encourage beneficial soil life. It can be whipper snipped down regularly to allow fruit trees to grow together with the sweet potato. As the fruit trees grow, they benefit from the regular mulch provided by the cut leaves of the sweet potato. In time the sweet potato finds it too shady under the fruit trees, thins out and other more shade tolerant ground covers can take hold.

Pumpkin vines are more of a short-term cover crop as they are annuals, and popular for covering over plants such as bindweed which likes to entangle itself in other plants. The spiky stems of pumpkin are disliked by other plants and so they won't try to climb them looking for light.

Smothering in combination with cover cropping is particularly useful for large areas or for sloping areas that are difficult to manage.

Smothering and cover cropping are usually designed to work over many months. Of course, it's fine to create a permanent cover crop. This method is mainly used to transition to a more permanent garden without weeds. The end goal of any weed control method is improved soil and dense planting to reduce further weed problems.

As with solarisation, smothering only works if you cover the entire patch of weeds. If some of the weeds are able to poke out of the edges of the cover, they will continue to feed the rest of the plant underneath. Smothering works in shady situations because it doesn't rely on heat. It can be useful for ground cover weeds such as creeping Charlie, violets, field bindweed, mints, and wandering trad.

Woody Weeds Removal

None of the above weed eradication methods are suitable for weeds large enough to have developed a woody stem. Removing woody weeds can be challenging, especially when they are large trees. Obviously, trees should be removed professionally – if they need to be removed at all. Wherever we live, large trees have an important role to play as habitat, for temperature regulation, in flood mitigation and in soil care. Even if that tree is a noxious weed species, think twice before removing it, especially if there aren't many other trees around.

Small trees or woody shrubs can usually be cut down with a hand saw. Cut them as low to the ground as possible. Many species won't re-sprout if cut low enough - usually just below the soil surface. Other trees, such as liquid amber and crepe myrtle, will sucker and be quite a nuisance. In this case, stump removal does help to end the problem. It can be very difficult to remove the base and roots of woody weeds, in which case poison is an option, as long as the plant has not developed resistance to the herbicide. I once poisoned the same base of a stand of Chinese elms and Mickey Mouse bush so many times it was ridiculous. Now I cut shrubs down, let them grow and break off any regrowth I see with my foot so that it comes away at the very base of the shoot. This way I damage the growing tissue while it is small and reduce the ability of the base of the woody weed to resprout. Eventually it won't be able to resprout at all. This is not the same as cutting off the shoots! When you rub off the shoots, you'll notice they leave a little hole or depression in the trunk where they come off. This means you've removed the growing bud, and that bud cannot regrow. There will be other growing buds so there will be more sprouts, but you can easily deplete them if you keep an eye on it. If you cut off the new shoot with secateurs, you're left with a stump rather than a depression, the growing bud is intact, and it will just keep growing.

By leaving the base and roots of the tree in the soil, the roots can continue to bind the soil and prevent erosion, even in death. As the roots breakdown they of course add organic matter to the soil.

Sometimes woody weeds are useful in sheltering the plants underneath. I like to allow an Easter cassia to grow in my garden in summer. It provides some dappled shade through the heat of summer, flowers gloriously in autumn and then I cut it back as mulch before it can set seed, letting in some extra winter sunshine. Being a legume, the cassia makes nitrogen rich mulch, but is also working on looking after my soil as the base continues to grow.

Trees can make for controversial and emotive weeds. The reason for this is simply the size of the plant. The larger the plant the larger the feature it can be. Trees are rightly being valued more as agents of environmental cooling, as habitat and as critical soil care. They have certainly caused many a dispute amongst neighbours.

Always think twice before acting on removing a tree, regardless of its weed status. I usually recommend that where you have weed trees, plant seedlings of more desirable trees immediately and plan the removal of the weed trees over a period of at least ten years to allow for succession. An absolutely ingenious way of doing this in warm climates is to plant a young strangler fig directly into the weed tree. Strangler figs naturally germinate in the crevices of other trees. As they grow, they gradually take over and kill the parent tree, replacing it with a huge, magnificent native tree. There are approximately twelve species of strangler fig worldwide. These are tropical and subtropical trees and are native to regions with tree weed problems – places such as northern New South Wales with the camphor laurels, or Florida with tea-tree (melaleuca). By planting the strangler fig into the weed tree, we allow a native tree to gradually take over without ever losing tree cover. There will still be seed set from the parent weed tree. To deal with this, keep the area around the tree well mulched and densely planted. In rural areas be careful not to allow overgrazing, which leaves bare patches that are perfect for weed seeds to take hold.

Rhizomes and Underground Tubers

What are rhizomes? They are a form of modified stem which is often mistaken for a root. This modified stem can grow at or near the surface (as is the case for many irises) or can be very deep in the soil as is the case for many that become problem weeds, things like couch grass or snake plant.

Many of the world's most disliked weeds are those with an incredible hidden survival mechanism – underground tubers or rhizomes. You may think from the surface that you've got the weed out and yet it will be back before you blink, worse than before. This is because the means by which the plant survives and reproduces is still in the ground, full of energy and ready to burst back into full growth, even from a small, broken piece of rhizome. Sometimes the very action of weeding is enough to break the rhizome into many smaller pieces, all of which will regrow, which is why it can seem like the more you weed, the more of these weeds there are. Unlike seeds, which emerge as fragile new plants needing to establish themselves, the regrowth from underground storage organs is coming with an established root system. These include Japanese knotweed, bindweed, couch grass, running bamboo, Singapore daisy, madeira vine, the many morning glory species, blackberry, nutgrass, cat's claw creeper, arum lilies and countless others. A great many of them are vines.

Never till weeds that have underground tubers or rhizomes. Controlling these weeds often requires a multipronged approach and hard work, bearing in mind that they all have an advantage in compacted soils. The more compact the soil, the more likely you are to break the rhizome and leave some behind. Soil improvement should therefore be your first line of defence. I like to cut the tops off, then compost heavily. This may seem counter intuitive in that it is feeding the weed, and it *is*, but that's ok. This is an important stage in the battle where we are trying to improve the soil. Feeding the weed does not work against us in this instance. As our composting is improving the soil, particularly the surface layers first, the weed will exploit this improvement. The vigorous new top growth will be softer and easier to deal with than the old growth was. It will be nutrient rich and great for composting (remember to choose a composting method suited to the weed as some above ground parts might regrow). Keep on cutting this new growth back and composting it. All the while you are continually improving the soil. Most importantly, any new underground growth will be concentrated in the upper layers of the soil where the compost is and will be much easier to access to dig out. While it hasn't removed the original deeper tubers or rhizomes, any new ones will be easier to get to. As the soil improves, those deeper tubers or rhizomes will also become less of a challenge.

For some of these weeds, such as Singapore daisy, the smothering action of the compost will really set them back; for others such as bamboo or Japanese knotweed, it will not bother them at all. Over time as the soil softens, the job of removal becomes more likely to be successful. Always use a fork rather than a spade, and gently loosen the soil to shake out the rhizomes in as large a clump as possible. The improved soil will aid regrowth but will also make it easier to find and remove the bits you missed. This is a process which takes time. It might be that while you are waiting for the soil to improve, you are also repeatedly cutting the tops off the weed. This will exhaust the underground storage organs. A plant that cannot photosynthesise will not be able to utilise the goodness of the compost.

If your rhizomatous weed is a low growing ground cover or a weakly twining vine, you can add a cover crop for extra effect. This works for things like bindweed, nutgrass, and Singapore daisy. A cover crop like pumpkin works well because it is fast growing and densely shades anything underneath it. Weakly twining vines such as bindweed don't like the prickly stems of pumpkins and won't climb it.

If your multipronged approach includes using herbicides, I don't recommend spraying the leaves. I've seen numerous experts recommend pulling vines out of trees and shrubs, laying them on the ground and spraying them with herbicide. Initially this results in a lot of dead material but rarely does the poison translocate to the rhizomes and tubers sufficiently to give long term results. Cutting all those same vines at the base will achieve the same result, without the use of herbicides. The top will be dead, giving a reprieve for the plant it is smothering, but underground nothing has changed. Often the new growth is less tangled and easier to see. This is the best time to deal with the tubers. I use the cut-and-dab method at this stage for particularly aggressive and problematic vines that I cannot get to the roots of, things like cat's claw creeper, morning glory and love lies bleeding. Otherwise, this is a good time to dig out the tubers. The new growth highlights where the tubers are so you know where to dig. If your weed is an edible weed, these new shoots will be the best eating for us and for livestock. At this stage the plant is trying to re-establish itself. By harvesting and never allowing the new shoots to develop to the point of photosynthesis, you will eventually exhaust any tubers which are too difficult to dig out. If, however, you allow some shoots to develop green leaves they will be photosynthesising and feeding the underground tuber, which will work against any plans you may have to exhaust it.

Weeds with tubers and /or rhizomes include:
- canna (*Canna sp*)
- knotweed (*Fallopia japonica* and *Fallopia sachalinensis*)
- cat's claw creeper (*Dolichandra unguis-cati*)
- morning glory vines (*Ipomea sp*)
- bindweed (*Calystegia sepium* and *Convolvulus arvensis*)
- bamboo (*Phyllostachys sp, Bambusa sp*)
- madeira vine (*Anredera cordifolia*)
- comfrey (*Symphytum officinale*)
- couch grasses (*Elymus repans* and *Cynodon dactylon*)
- Singapore daisy (*Sphagneticola trilobata*)
- arum lilies (*Zantedeschia aethiopica* and *Arum maculatum*)
- blackberry and brambles (*Rubus sp*)
- nutgrass (*Cyperus rotundus*)

Lawn Weeds

> "In my experience at the Royal Botanic Gardens, Sydney, by improving our horticultural care of turf we eliminated many pernicious weeds without using even organic herbicides. Turf also became more resistant to wear and tear and this significantly reduced the cost of returfing." Jerry Coleby-Williams, 2012

Interestingly most lawn weeds are deep rooted and are usually growing in lawns which have become bare through scalping and compaction. Fix the compaction problems and the weeds lose their competitive advantage.

Other common lawn weeds are legumes, clover being one of the most common. Clover is a wonderful weed. Like all legumes, it fixes nitrogen from the air, giving it a sizeable advantage in nitrogen deficient soils. Mow short enough to remove most of the leaf from the clover (and feed to chooks or add it to the compost, it is good stuff) then feed with a low nitrogen fertiliser to give the grass the advantage over the clover. If the clover is particularly thick in the lawn, lucky you, clover is so much prettier than grass. However, if you would prefer it wasn't there, you'll do best to repeat the above regularly, but feed lightly each time to give the grass a small regular boost. By taking the leaf off the clover, the plant will become depleted fairly quickly. Be aware that as clover is more of a winter than a summer weed, you will need to do this at a time when the grass is not growing much. Best to do it as the weather starts to warm up in spring but before the clover disappears for summer. Fertilise lightly but regularly as nitrogen leaches from the soil easily and the lawn will not be able to suddenly take up large amounts when it is not growing as rapidly. The other reason for the light feeding is to gradually improve the fertility of the lawn. You can achieve this by using bagged compost from the garden centre rather than fertiliser as this will help to improve the soil, not just feed the grass and weeds. Other leguminous lawn weeds such as burr medic, creeping indigo, vetch and silver leafed desmodium can be treated in the same way.

Good lawn care means never mowing too low. A weed filled lawn immediately calls for a change to your lawn care regime. Lift your mowing height, mow more frequently and mow without the catcher. Mowing without the catch will only work if you mow often and do not have a lot of clippings. It will allow the clippings to compost back into the lawn feeding the soil naturally. By using this method, you will gradually turn your weedy patch into a lawn without the need for returfing or chemicals. Be patient, it may take up to a year for a complete transformation into a weed free lawn.

Lawns that are mown too low stress the grass and create openings for weeds to take hold. A thick healthy lawn will require less water or fertiliser and will keep weeds out more effectively than a lawn in poor condition.

Aeration is needed to stop foot traffic and mowing from compacting the soil. Compacted soils will favour deep tap rooted weeds, so it is not surprising that many lawn weeds have tap roots. Aerate the lawn and then top dress with a fine compost instead of fertiliser. This helps to add organic matter to the soil which in turn limits compaction. A good quality rock mineral product which is high in silica will also help to open compaction. Over fertilising and over watering are amongst the most common lawn problems. This results in weak growth that is readily attacked by pests and diseases, in turn creating bare patches for weeds to grow.

Of course, if your lawn is filled with wonderful weeds such as clover, dandelion, plantain and thistles, you may prefer to call it a very successful meadow rather than a failed lawn. It might even be far more valuable to the environment as a meadow than it could ever be as a lawn. The meadow argus butterfly was once very common in Australia but is in decline as people weed out their lawns. Plantains are one of its host plants. Children can have just as much fun in a meadow amongst the bees and flowers as they would on a green monoculture called lawn. Interestingly, while we love our lawns and like the idea of a weedless green carpet, lawn grasses themselves also ranked very highly in every country as some of the most disliked weeds. Chief amongst them was couch, but kikuyu was also mentioned repeatedly. Both are aggressive and vigorous plants with creeping rhizomes which makes them so perfect for lawn but a problem elsewhere. They have a tendency to escape the lawn and venture into garden beds where they are very much not wanted. In a garden bed these grasses are deep rooted, entangle with the roots of plants and are almost impossible to get rid of without huge disturbance to the plants in the garden. Keep in mind that the better your soil, the easier it will be to get these roots out.

The best way to deal with grasses in garden beds is to prevent them from growing in the first place. The single biggest cause of lawn grasses becoming problematic in gardens is lack of attention to lawn edging. If you're not willing or able to regularly trim your lawn edges, containment is going to be critical for you. Wide flat pavers used as edging are great as they allow you plenty of time to see the grass heading over them and into the garden, giving you the opportunity to cut it back. If they are flush with the grass, you should be able to mow over the edge of the paving to keep the grass in check. Narrow edging offers no such buffer. Uneven edges such as rocks are also troublesome as it's not easy to cut the grass in all the nooks and crannies. Think also of depth. Grass rhizomes love to go underneath edging to get into the garden, especially when the garden beds offer better access to water and nutrients. Lawn edging needs to be buried at least five centimetres deep to be effective.

If raised garden beds are to be placed over an area of lawn, you first need to eradicate the lawn. Smothering can be effective if it is deep enough but will not work if the grass rhizomes are still connected to the lawn outside the garden bed. Always cut around the outside of the bed to ensure the rhizomes in the lawn are not feeding the ones you are trying to smother under the garden bed.

This entire discussion about weeds in lawns assumes that you haven't resorted to using herbicides. There are numerous herbicides available which have been developed to kill broad leaves plants (dicots) but not grasses (monocots) and are marketed for spraying weeds in lawns. While there is a place for herbicides in weed management, this is not it. All herbicides will cause some damage to your soil conditions, which is the last thing we want when trying to eradicate weeds in the long term. Removing weeds in lawns, or anywhere else, without addressing the growing conditions, will leave bare patches allowing the weeds to return. Popular weed and feed products do not address this issue. The feed part of the formula will feed the weeds as well as the grass and work against the action of the poison. This product is working against itself, which is the main reason so many gardeners report its low effectiveness. In response to this low effectiveness, many gardeners use it again or use it in greater quantity to try and get a better result. All the while they are doing more and more soil damage and missing the key to successful long term weed management.

> **The Trouble with Nitrogen**
>
> Nitrogen is a key plant nutrient which is needed to grow green leaves. It is also a highly soluble nutrient which tends to leach out of soil rather than wait there for the plant to want it. Nitrogen to plants is like sugar to children. A little is great and even highly important in the right form, just as we need sugars in the form of low GI carbohydrates. Too much is not so good. Plants put on a surge of fast growth which is sweet, soft and attractive to pests, contributing nothing to the long-term health of the plant. The unhealthy plant then needs treatment for pest problems. As it dies it leaves gaps in the garden which are ideal for weeds. This pattern is particularly obvious in a monoculture like a lawn. Typical lawn fertilisers contain approximately 20% nitrogen, and overuse of these fertilisers is one of the key factors in setting up the negative spiral of other lawn problems. A healthier lawn can be achieved using a fertiliser that is no more than 5% nitrogen, in combination with good lawn care and attention to soil care.
>
> Plants will only take up nitrogen when they are actively growing, have plenty of water and are not stressed. What nitrogen the plants do not take up is leached out of the soil to become a problem elsewhere. Even plants like lawn grass, which like lots of nitrogen, do better with small amounts often than they do with occasional large doses. Our aim is long term soil improvement and with that, permanent weed reduction. Short term nitrogen boosts do nothing for this end goal. Ultimately, the best way of keeping a soil rich in nitrogen is to have a good amount of organic matter in the soil to act like a sponge, holding nutrients and microbes, which in turn release the nitrogen slowly and as plants need it.

Tillage

Tilling or rotary hoeing is not something commonly done in backyard gardens anymore, possibly because gardens are shrinking in size and there is less garden space to till. Tilling involves turning the soil and, in the process, weeds are dug, cut up and turned into the soil. Some gardeners still like to dig over garden beds, which is a simplified form of tillage. On a larger scale, most farmers practice tillage to get fields ready for planting. Of course, on this scale it is a mechanical process. Rotary hoes can still be hired for use in the home garden.

I don't recommend using a rotary hoe to weed your garden. Tilling destroys the natural structure of the soil and kills worms. The freshly dug, exposed soil is now highly susceptible to erosion and therefore even more problematic if you have a sloping site. Our aim is to improve the soil as our first defence against weeds, so any method which causes damage to the soil is going to be counterproductive. In the home garden, tillage causes far more soil disturbance than is required in most cases. Hand hoeing is effective in removing large areas of weeds without deep soil disturbance. If you are planning to use a rotary hoe to break up the soil and dig in weeds, keep the blades high to reduce the depth of digging and subsequent damage to soil structure - as much as possible.

Tillage can work against us for certain weeds. It can bring seeds to the surface and cause a flush of weed growth. This flush can be easily dealt with by a second tilling to dig the seedlings back in. More problematic are weeds that easily regrow from pieces. In this case tillage can very effectively spread those weeds. Succulent weeds are particularly good at regrowing from pieces but so are others such as Singapore daisy, knotweed or kikuyu.

I've often had people ask me if they should rotary hoe an old weedy lawn and start again. The answer is almost always no. As discussed above, weedy lawns can usually be revived with good care. A little patch of nutgrass or onion weed in a corner of the lawn will be delighted to be rotary hoed and spread around the entire lawn.

Recent research in the USA and Spain has shown that tillage in fields can actually encourage weeds in a very different way. Ants are a natural predator of seeds and tilling destroys ant nests. With less ants around, less weed seeds are removed from the system. Ant nests with their tunnels and waste chambers play an important role in soil system health. Once again, we see something that is generally considered troublesome turn out to have an important ecological role. God Bless Mother Nature!

Many agriculturalists are now seeing the advantages of reduced tillage and with this comes a change to their dominant weed species. No till methods will favour seeds which are viable when they remain on the soil surface, including fleabane and sow thistle. Mulching is highly effective at burying these seeds in the home garden and has many other benefits for the soil, which reduces any need for tilling.

Livestock

Overgrazing of paddocks can be a huge contributor to the success of weeds, but it is also possible to use livestock to help control weeds. The key to doing this is to match the right animal to the situation. If grass is your problem, for example an unmown lawn that you would rather turn into a garden, sheep can be very effective at seriously handicapping the grass. Sheep will eat grass very low and even pull it out by the roots. They will also eat young ragweed plants and many other weeds as well.

In the average suburban garden, farm animals are not such easy weeding machines. Chickens are quite manageable and very effective at keeping weeds under control. With all their scratching, the chickens are not very selective and what they don't eat often gets dug out. For this reason, few gardeners are keen on allowing chickens to free range in the garden, myself included. Instead use a small mobile chicken home or allow them temporary access to a fenced area. They will eat the more palatable weeds and scratch up everything else. Chickens will eat the seeds and bulbs of many weeds, including oxalis and nutgrass. Leave them in a particular area until there is nothing green left and the topsoil is well scratched over.

Ducks and geese are preferable to chickens for controlling weeds. Both are more selective and quite partial to many common garden weeds like chickweed and sow thistle. In addition, water birds don't scratch so will do much less damage in the garden than chickens. Ducks have the added benefit of eating snails. Both are also fond of lettuce seedlings, so you will still need to protect some areas of the garden or only allow the ducks and geese access to the garden at certain times. Turkeys tend to like a high protein diet with less greens than other poultry so are not usually good for weed control, however I have heard that they have a liking for brassica weeds, which could be useful if you have a lot of wild brassicas.

You can also control weeds with a pig. They are especially good for rooting out bulbs of nutgrass and the like. There isn't much that can withstand the efforts of a bored pig in a confined space. Not so many of us are able to try this out, but if you do happen to know someone who would lend you a pig, they will fix your nutgrass problem. One weed to watch with pigs is Noogoora burr (*Xanthium occidentale*). It can cause poisoning if they eat large amounts of it.

Another farm animal not often encountered in the home garden, but great for controlling weeds, are goats. Goats are well known for eating anything and everything and this includes weeds. Unlike horses, cows and sheep, which are grazers and prefer to eat grass and soft low growing weeds, goats are browsers and prefer to eat non-grassy plants. Goats have been found to be super effective at controlling weeds in difficult terrain. Steep sites are no problem and because they are happy to eat a variety of plants that other animals won't, they are a very ecofriendly way to weed. Goats have been used in parts of Australia to control bushland weeds and will eat plants like Mexican sunflower, billy goat weed, fireweed and even blackberries, which are highly problematic in rural areas. Goats like a varied diet and will nibble at different things, so they are not so happy if you want them to tackle a single weed problem. This tendency to nibble various plants allows them to eat small amounts of usually toxic plants without poisoning themselves. As cattle and goats have different dietary preferences, goats can be a valuable method for landholders to control pasture weeds without poisons. There are companies here in Australia, the USA and other countries that will rent out a small herd of goats for weed control to local councils and businesses.

I have heard that heritage breeds of pigs, sheep and cattle all have broader dietary preferences than modern breeds and therefore are better for weed control. Perhaps diversification of breeds for our farm animals would help manage weeds on small holdings and in paddocks.

A highly beneficial side effect of using animals to eat out problem weeds is manure. The animals leave behind digested weeds in the form of manure, which is wonderful for soil improvement and free.

Herbicides

Sometimes these methods aren't enough, or complete eradication is required. In this case some use of herbicide is needed. Always take care when handling herbicides and remember they are toxic chemicals, so avoid skin contact or breathing in the vapours. Choose your herbicide wisely. There are a number of cheap weed killers on the market that claim to kill nutgrass. They don't. You will be needlessly adding poison to your garden if you use them. Only the seriously expensive stuff works on nutgrass, and even then, it works much better if the soil improvements discussed above are also implemented. Be careful – it will also seriously hurt other bulbs and tubers such as daylilies and does have an exclusion time if you wish to grow edibles. Interestingly, there seems to be some folklore alive and well out there that says covering the patch of nutgrass in the lawn with chopped potatoes will eventually kill it. I have not tried this so offer no recommendations to its success.

I still apply herbicides *very occasionally* using the cut and dab method. This method involves cutting the stem of the weed and immediately placing a drop of undiluted herbicide directly onto the fresh cut. It needs to be immediate as the plant will start to seal the cut and once this happens the herbicide will not be absorbed. To be effective, cut and poison each stem one at a time.

The cut and dab method works for weeds that will regrow if the base is left in the ground, and when digging the roots out is not an option. I've found it to be the only effective control for cat's claw creeper which has multiple underground tubers that are almost impossible to dig out. It's also useful for woody weeds where you may prefer the roots to remain in the ground to prevent erosion, or where the crown of an asparagus weed is under the roots of a tree and cannot be dug up. Be very careful if using this method as it is so very easy to splash the chemicals on yourself and on nearby plants. I like to use an eyedropper for the herbicide and also wear gloves. Happily, I rarely need to do this.

Because this method allows the herbicide to be drawn instantly into the plant's tissues, there is almost no risk (except spillage) of it affecting nearby plants or entering the soil. It also means there is much less risk of our pets and children coming into contact with herbicides on the leaves near where they are playing.

Good weed management requires an integrated approach and sometimes herbicide does play a part, however we should look at chemicals as only a small part of the solution, instead of the only choice. Soil improvement and understanding the role of weeds will help make any program of eradication either more effective, or even redundant.

Weeding a Neglected Garden

The new owners of this old home will need to deal with an extensive weed seed load in the soil.

Facing a garden that has been neglected and is full of weeds can be a daunting task, and one that many gardeners will shy away from. I have found that when gardeners are overwhelmed, they either neglect the garden further which only exacerbates the problem, or they call in the big guns to clear fell and start from scratch, which can be a very expensive solution.

Starting from scratch can represent a clean slate and for some gardeners this is exciting, for others this is just as daunting as being faced with an overgrown jungle. Unfortunately, if an overgrown and weedy garden is cleared using machinery, or even if it is blanket sprayed with herbicide, weed problems can re-emerge with a vengeance. Weeds with underground rhizomes, bulbs, tubers and crowns can regrow quickly. Any seed bank in the soil can now take full advantage of the open clear conditions to sprout. People often lay new lawns, only to find that although they scrapped the soil below and sprayed herbicides, the nut grass grows back thicker than before.

Instead of rushing to have a new garden installed, it is better to take some time to find out what we are dealing with - the rewards can be well worth the extra effort.

What lies hidden?
Gardens that have been neglected and the weeds allowed to grow out of control present us with not just hard work, but an opportunity for discovering what may be underneath. I've found all sorts of fabulous treasures hidden under the weeds of old gardens, like rare old plants, stone walls and pathways, birdbaths, statues and even old concrete pots filled with rare orchids. All of these I have rescued from gardens which were deemed as overgrown and weedy messes. Sadly, I've seen much more lost to bulldozers brought in by overwhelmed or disinterested gardeners. These hidden finds have value to anyone who appreciates them, but for the gardener who works to uncover them and rebuild a garden around them, they have even greater value, and can give history and timelessness to a garden, things that no amount of money can buy.

Weed Clues
Even if you find little in the way of wonderful old plants or other treasures in your neglected garden, taking the time to clear and restore it will give you enormous advantages as the gardener. It gives you a chance to fast track your knowledge of the garden. By observing which weeds are growing where, you can learn so much about your soil and the conditions in different parts of your garden. You can see where you have good soil and where the soil is in need of improvement. The weeds can also give you clues as to how to improve the soil. Does it need improved drainage? Or a more open structure? Or do the weeds indicate a pH problem? You cannot restore a neglected garden without observing what is there and what needs attention. This process of observing both before and after weeding will be your greatest teacher, if you take the time to pay attention.

Where to Begin

The first thing you need to do in an overgrown or overrun garden is to cut back the weeds and overgrowth just enough to find what is underneath. Hand pull what you can easily, the rest just prune for now. Clearing weeds is often needed to find where garden beds are supposed to be and uncover garden paths. Valuable garden plants might well be lurking underneath the overgrowth. If there is nothing to save beneath the excess growth, then you can just go mad with some of the broader scale approaches described above. In most cases you will potentially find more fabulous old plants than you had expected. Clearing around them will help you to see a plan of what must be done first, and how to approach the different sections of the garden.

If you have vines which are tangling shrubs and trees, pull them back. Don't worry about the roots of the vines at this stage because until you know what lies underneath, you won't see the bigger picture. Some trees and shrubs can be so badly damaged by smothering vines that they're not possible to save, but you'll only find out once you remove the vegetation.

The areas of the garden with nothing to save are the easiest to deal with. Whichever method of weed management you choose, keep in mind that these weeds have been here for quite some time, and therefore have had the chance to become well established and to extract plenty of nutrients from the soil. Composting them and using this compost in the new garden will be hugely beneficial in returning those nutrients. Regardless of how you choose to get rid of the weeds, take the time to see what they are and what they might be able to tell you.

Smothering

I prefer to approach garden restoration by smothering weeds where I can. In any neglected garden chances are the soil could do with some support. Smothering combines overcoming weeds and improving the soil through added organic matter, both of which are essential for the success of a new garden.

Many annual and ground cover weeds will be killed by smothering, and it will help to bury seeds and reduce seedling emergence in the same way as mulch will. More persistent weeds will re-emerge through the smother layers. This can be a good thing because it highlights which are the more difficult weeds that need a targeted approach to control. Give your smother layer time - time to work and time to see what it won't work on. Most gardeners would rather know they have missed a bit of couch grass when the bed is in the preparation stage than find it emerging from in between their flowers later.

The sort of weeds likely to reshoot through a smother layer are those with deep tubers, bulbs or corms, and those with rhizomes. This can include things like nutgrass, or knotweed, bamboo, couch grass, Singapore daisy, morning glory, cat's claw creeper and bindweed.

If you have asparagus and have left the crown in the ground, it too will shoot through the layers. Weedy asparagus crowns are best dug out. You only need to get the actual crown, which is the bit where the roots join the stems. Some asparagus weeds have very long roots with nodules on them. These are water nodules and will not regrow. They can be left to rot and return their stored water to the soil.

The extra organic matter and nutrients used in a smother layer will correct a lot of soil problems and make the area more suited to the plants you wish to grow. The weeds which once dominated have now been composted, and their natural role as soil improvers has simply been fast tracked. This process is very similar to the process of creating a no-dig garden, although with less layers. You can use a no-dig approach or simply let all the organic matter act to smother what remains of the weeds and do amazing soil improvement. At this early stage solarisation is also a good option and perhaps the best option if the garden contains succulent weeds.

Bulbous Weeds
More difficult to deal with are bulbous weeds like nut grass, oxalis or onion weed. Heavy duty poisons can be used but they have long exclusion times for growing edibles, which is an indication of how toxic they are. The only other option is digging them out by hand. A tedious process, but one that is much easier in softer soil, so do the soil improvement first! If you have the time and the garden is well fenced, try running some chooks or even a pig in the garden for a few weeks or months, depending on the size of the area. They will do a great job of cleaning the weeds out, and in the case of bulbs, they are happy to eat them as well. If a garden bed rather than lawn is planned for the area of the garden with bulbous weeds, you may consider that the bulbous weeds aren't such a problem. If the garden plants are intended to be taller than the weeds, they will shade and cover the weeds and prevent them from dominating. Those weeds will still be there, but in reduced numbers, and you are unlikely to get more than the odd glimpse of them below your beloved (taller) plants.

Woody Weeds
Woody weeds may need to be dealt with more severely. Digging out the roots is an option for smaller shrubs, but stump grinding or burning might be an option for larger, more difficult woody weeds, or for large areas of them. How you deal with woody stumps will be based on whether or not cutting the top off has killed the plant, or if it is likely to reshoot. Often cutting just below the soil line will be enough to stop many woody weeds from resprouting. Some, such as crepe myrtle, Brunsfelsia, Plumbago or various Clerodendrons have a tendency to

sucker. The more you cut them back, the more they will sucker. These plants will need the entire woody root system removed or poisoned to stop it coming back. Please don't pour petrol or engine oil over stumps to kill them. This is only adding to the death of your soil and ongoing soil contamination issues.

Woody stumps that are dead and therefore will not reshoot may still need removal to allow soil space for new plants. Holes or cuts made into the surface of a tree stump and old milk poured over can help a stump to rot away faster. You can burn out woody stumps by lighting a small fire over the top of the stump and letting it burn down into the stump. This can be difficult on newly cut stumps where the wood is still green. It may also be illegal in your council area or prohibited under fire bans based on weather conditions. If conditions and regulations allow you to burn out a stump, build a fire pit around the stump with bricks first to keep any fire contained and safe.

Clearing the Green Waste
Clearing the bulk of the green waste is usually required to see where the base of woody weeds or vines begin. Often this green waste can be left in a pile for a couple of weeks for the leaves to fall off before you need to worry about dealing with the stems. This results in a nice pile of leaf mulch, and a pile of sticks for the fire. A mulcher to chop the entire amount up is great as long as you don't feed it with plants that regrow from small pieces! This includes Japanese knotweed or Singapore daisy, which should never be mulched. It's worth hiring a mulcher if you have a big project.

Now that you've cleared enough to see the garden properly, you can get a feel for what it once was, what it could become, and more importantly, what you want it to become.

Break it into Sections
Tackling the entire garden in one go will be overwhelming and it is likely the weeds will return faster than you can beat them, so once your plan takes shape, divide the garden into sections. Work on one section at a time so that you can see the progress you are making. Like any big job, small rewards along the way are critical to keep us inspired to keep going.

Weed a section, then plant up that section. Take a little time to care for this section before moving on, keeping on top of any weeds that reappear in that section before they can become problems again. As this section begins to need less maintenance, you are ready to tackle the next section. Each time you go out to work in the garden, start with the section(s) you have already done, just to make sure any little bits of stray weeds still there are not getting a foot hold. This ongoing small weeding work will get less each time and will ensure that the job is done thoroughly enough that the weeds do not return while your attention is focussed elsewhere in the garden. It also means that each time you go into the garden you are starting at a win point, which helps you to feel inspired to tackle the next weed patch with gusto.

Proper Preparation Matters

A neglected garden often has a diversity of weeds and types of weeds, requiring a mix of strategies to get on top of them. Diversity is a good thing – the more diverse your weeds the better your soil probably is. Sometimes the approach is not so much about eradicating all weeds as choosing which weeds are most important to eradicate and creating a sliding scale of how much they bother you. Put your energy into the ones that bother you most, rather than the ones that bother other people. Afterall it is your garden, not theirs. Effort should be directed first into the ones that are the hardest to control. Digging up a new garden to get to a weed that you didn't pay attention to earlier can be heartbreaking. Weed seedlings are easy to pull out without disturbing the garden, while those with underground tubers or rhizomes are hardest to remove. Start with the hardest and you'll see that many of the other weeds have succumbed in the process.

The more effort that is required to remove a weed, the longer it will be until you can establish a new garden where the weed once was. You will be tempted to rush this process. I have and I've regretted it. Take the time to dig out your problem weed, to improve your soil, to wait for your weed to reshoot, then attack it again, and improve your soil some more. For some very persistent weeds this cycle may need to be repeated more than once for complete weed eradication, or even to just control it enough so it no longer dominates. By including soil improvement along the way, when it is finally time for new plants, they will be so much happier and more successful in a shorter space of time. You will be grateful then that you took the time. Taking your time also allows you to find weeds that are dormant throughout winter or in certain weather conditions, such as drought.

Start with the least weedy section. You will have greater success more easily and this will help to keep you inspired to tackle the more challenging sections of the garden. Yes, psychology plays a part in tackling any big job, overgrown gardens included.

Sally's Garden

A client of mine, Sally, had a professionally landscaped garden that had been neglected for a number of years when life got busy. It was time to try and resurrect it so that it could be enjoyed once more.

The front garden had a collection of small untidy trees with struggling plants beneath them. It was a tangle of cobbler's pegs, grass, other annual weeds and spider's webs. The plan we devised was to start from the pathways and work inwards, pulling out annual weeds and grass. In order to see the structure of the garden, the untidy lower branches of the small trees that were tangling into the weeds need to be removed, creating a separation between the tree canopy and the rest of the garden below. With the worst of the weeds pulled out and the shape of the garden now easy to see, we were able to make decisions about which plants to keep, which to move and what to pull out altogether because they didn't suit the garden. At this point serious soil improvement can be done, and the future of the garden can be imagined and created.

In another section of Sally's garden, a narrow strip of natives, mainly grevilleas and bottlebrushes, was filled with couch grass, sow thistles and commelinas. This section was highly inaccessible, so very difficult to maintain. Happily, the natives were all tall enough so that the weeds, while prolific, were not obvious from a distance. In this section we decided that to crawl through and weed it roughly would suffice. The area could then be heavily mulched with woodchip to suppress some of the weeds, although mulch only temporarily slows the couch grass. Given that the ground layer wasn't highly visible, we decided that it wasn't worth battling with the grass. The shrubs were healthy, and the weeds were not impeding their growth. The weedy ground layer here had already created habitat for lizards and insects, which Sally appreciated.

In yet another section of Sally's garden the struggle was with vines. A tall old chain wire fence for a tennis court had become a complete green wall of weeds, hiding the rest of the garden behind and making the entire property look much smaller than it was. The vines had not stayed on the fence but were happily spreading over every piece of ground that was not regularly mown and smothered everything in their path. The height of the fence meant that the vines were out of reach and difficult to control. The only way to really deal with this was to remove the top two thirds of the fence. With the fence reduced to chest height, the weed vines are now easily managed by running a hedge trimmer over them occasionally to keep the fence neat and green. At this height the weed-covered fence is easily managed as a hedge. It no longer hides the section behind it and now hints at the garden beyond. The section behind the hedge was filled with small rainforest trees and a World War II bomb shelter, so was worth exploring! The weed vines not only hid this section of the garden from view, but they had also wandered from the fence and begun to smother this area of the garden as well. The vines were able to be cut and removed from the rest of the garden, with the main roots left to cover the now manageable fence. The fact that these vines are weeds, including cat's claw creeper, does not matter. As they have a dedicated fence to grow on, and can be controlled there, they are no longer a nuisance elsewhere and their value as dense green plants is appreciated. These are vines that are incredibly difficult to eradicate, so a system of strict containment can be effective and less troublesome in the long run.

Wendy's Garden

Wendy's large garden is filled with fabulous old plants. It was a garden she inherited from her parents, and while she loves it, she doesn't have time to keep up with it. When I first saw it, the front garden was filled with annual weeds. Wendy has only been able to garden occasionally which meant weeds were constantly seeding and ensuring their ongoing presence. With a bit of consistent weeding, combined with mulching, this area of the garden was quite easy to restore. Dealing with the weeds by allowing them to compost in-situ with mulch over the top reduced the problem of seeds in the soil, but also effectively improved the soil and helped the garden plants to thrive.

Other sections of the garden were not so easy. They were overgrown with weed trees such as Chinese elms, Easter cassias, Cocos palms and vines such as morning glory, cat's claw creeper and Singapore daisy, not to mention large patches of basket plant and snake plant. Underneath all of this was an old garden. This area required time, patience, and a lot of hard work. Working one section at a time, we cleared and mulched heavily using newspaper and lawn clippings. The plan was to smother the Singapore daisy. A cover crop of dog bane went in. The cover crop needed to be tough, able to cope with very occasional care and hot dry weather. It also needed to be attractive and easier to control than the Singapore daisy, with the option to replace the dog bane with other plants in the future.

The small trees were chopped out just below the ground. The basket plant was able to be smothered but the snake plant (mother-in-law's tongue) needed to be dug out carefully. Digging out large areas of snake plant and making sure that no pieces of root are left behind is a large job. In Wendy's large garden it was tackled bit by bit, working on one section at a time. This allowed us to see any pieces of root left behind which had started to reshoot and was therefore easily dealt with. It also meant an overwhelming task was made manageable.

The cat's claw vine was probably the most difficult weed here. It develops multiple woody underground tubers which can be both deep and large and are almost impossible to get rid of. I have been able to get it under control in other gardens by cutting each stem and dabbing with neat poison, but this is a very tedious task. Initially in Wendy's garden, we kept the tops pulled off to stop it going places until we were ready to tackle it more seriously.

In other sections of the garden, I simply covered the weeds with large amounts of leaf litter and grass clippings. This garden was a long-term project, so by doing this some weeds were smothered. If nothing else, this smothering improved the soil and gave me an advantage when I came to tackle those sections. I only returned to these in winter when the snakes were less active, given that the overgrown back garden was highly snake prone.

Snakes.

Weeds are often beaten into submission through a fear of snakes. In countries like Australia or America where snakes are not uncommon and are potentially deadly, a fear of snakes in the garden is not unhealthy. In truth it does not matter if it be a plant or weed, any dense growth could harbour snakes. Once a garden starts to get out of hand, it is often a fear of snakes that prevents a gardener getting back into it. Fear is no way to garden, so being aware of snakes and being realistic about the risk is worthwhile.

I have never been bitten by a snake, but my ex-husband is lucky to be alive after being bitten by an eastern brown snake in an inner suburban garden, two doors down from Wendy's garden.

Snakes like to keep out of our way, and despite all the myths, you are really only likely to get bitten if the snake is unable to get away from you. This can happen if you surprise it. Snakes have no ears so will not hear you coming (if you are sure your snake has ears, it is a legless lizard). They do have excellent eyesight, and excellent ability to sense vibrations, so the best thing to do is to stomp a lot when approaching an overgrown section. Work in from the edge of the garden. This way a potential snake has time to retreat easily before you stumble upon it.

I prefer to garden without gloves, but if I am reaching my hands into thickets of weeds I do put on gloves, in case there is more than weeds in there. I don't mind getting my hands dirty, but I prefer not to get bitten by snakes, spiders, centipedes, ants or anything else hiding in the weeds.

Slashing overgrown areas first can also be a good way of making sure you can see where you are weeding. Protective clothing is sensible in overgrown gardens, to protect against scratches as well as bites.

Snakes will hibernate over winter, so this is usually a good time to get into overgrown sections of a garden. Be aware that they may be hibernating in a pile of old logs under the weeds, so you still need to be cautious. A hibernating snake will be slow to react, so keep your distance and let it move away. In summer the snakes will probably see or feel you long before you have any idea they are there – if you give them the chance by stomping and working from the edge.

Spring can be one of the most dangerous times, as snakes come out of hibernation and are looking for food and mates. They are very active and more territorial than usual, so take extra care at this time of year. Personally, I like to work in such a way that I have a clear view of my feet if there are likely to be snakes around, regardless of the time of year.

Part of the strategy in Wendy's garden was to establish new plants where weeds were removed. The new plants were not only for visual appeal, but they were also designed to fill gaps to reduce the opportunities for the weeds to come back. This was a staged process. Removing the weeds was only stage one. Soil improvement and planting hardy space fillers was stage two. Eventually the garden will be ready for stage three which means replacing some of the space fillers with more desirable and interesting plants.

As long-term neglect is a major factor in this garden, soil improvement is a key part of the garden restoration, and a very useful tool for helping me battle the weeds here.

Restoring this garden has been hard work but also very rewarding. I found some truly wonderful old plants, including variegated gingers, alocasias, silver philodendrons, caricature plants and rare bromeliads, as well as a rocky creek bed, a rock spiral wrapping around an old stone bird bath and some lovely stone steps, remnants of the garden her father had built over 50 years ago. These lovely details would have been lost completely if a more heavy-handed approach had been taken to restoring the garden.

Sue's Garden

My first impression of Sue's garden was a tangled mess of asparagus fern, Easter cassia and Mickey Mouse bush. Once I got into the garden, I was excited to see old roses, blechnum ferns, clivias, daylilies and cordylines underneath the weeds. This was a small garden with great bones crying out to be a semi-wild cottage garden overflowing with exuberance. The strategy was to remove the overgrowth in order to work out a plan for what was below, then go hard with soil improvement. There were natives full of small birds in the neighbour's garden and a couple of great bottlebrushes in the front, so we decided to add as many bushy natives as we could to the front garden - but first the weeds had to go. We started with the annual weeds and allowed them to compost in situ under mulch. A sudden crop of cherry tomatoes, exploiting the empty space, was allowed to grow and fruit only until we were ready to put something more permanent in their place. Loads of asparagus fern was dug out (after good rain so the ground was soft) but some had the crowns underneath tree roots and had to stay. Now that Sue knows the new shoots are edible and delicious, this bit of asparagus is enjoyed rather than hated, and is not likely to get out of control now that it is being eaten.

Masses of white shrimp plant (*Justicia betonica*) have been removed to clear around the old roses, which responded by bursting into profuse flower. A small patch of the shrimp plant has been allowed to stay after witnessing usually shy carpenter bees enjoying it so much that they ignored onlookers. In allowing this weed to stay in patches, we have created a task for ourselves – we must ensure we cut it back after flowering or it will be everywhere again. One of the roses has a super tough false mallow weed (*Malvastrum coromandelianum*) growing at the base. This has been deliberately left to act as a *mother weed*. Its deep roots are feeding the rose, and it attracts beneficial insects which are helping to keep the rose pest free. Interestingly, this rose was by far the strongest and most prolific flowerer of all the rose bushes. The mother weed has been a huge benefit here.

A prickly Mexican poppy (*Argemone mexicana*) popped up and was left in the garden. This weed can be highly attractive but also invokes childhood memories for Sue, so was enjoyed. With plenty of mulch for soil protection and improvement, its seeds cannot germinate easily, so it could be enjoyed without taking over.

The Easter cassia is still there, providing summer shelter to the new plants below. A hard winter cut back will happen each year until it is no longer needed and then it will be cut off at ground level. The ochna is similarly being regularly pruned to allow it to shelter other plants but not to seed and spread.

In this garden weeds are gradually removed and replaced with more desirable plants. This process is however limited as the weeds demonstrate useful properties. Sue (like me) has a very tolerant attitude to weeds. She keeps native bees, so when the weeds are flowering both Sue and the bees are appreciating them. Sue is also finding that as she learns more about the edibility of various weeds, she is eating more from her garden than ever, despite not growing vegetables. Purslane and chickweed have become two of her favourite edible weeds, and cobbler's pegs are left for the bees and butterflies. Over time this garden still has an abundance of weeds, but they are no longer the first thing you see. Now when I visit Sue, my first impression is always the joyful riot of colour from so many flowers, and the busyness in the garden as I dodge the bees and butterflies.

Ann's Garden

When I started work in Ann's garden, it was a mass of snake plant (*Sanseveria sp*, previously known as mother-in-law's tongue) and guinea grass. It couldn't really be called a garden at all. The first job was to remove the guinea grass (*Megathyrsus maximus*). This could be left in big piles to compost in situ, despite the fact it was seeding, as there was already a seed load in the soil. The second job was to dig out as much of the snake plant as possible. This was a huge task as any piece of root left in the ground would regrow. It also produced large amounts of green waste, which had to be safely disposed of through the council green waste collection service. The council green waste is composted in huge piles, large enough to generate the heat required to kill and compost the tubers. The third job in Ann's garden was to add lots of organic matter. A large deciduous tree in the garden gave a huge amount of leaf drop once a year, and for the rest of the year, the neighbours mowing man left piles of grass clippings under a street tree which needed a better home. Ann's garden was a much better place for these grass clippings – added as compost and not as mulch of course.

This area is now a lovely, lush garden, full of greenery and flowers, which has provided so much pleasure. A couple of years on and the soil is rich and the garden completely full. It still gets the odd weed, but only ever needs weeding around the edges where it gets walked over and there are bare patches. The odd bit of snake plant does still pop up but is not a bother and in small amounts is easy to control.

Now we are at the stage of taking the garden to a new level. Weeds are no longer a problem, and the garden is full. We are gradually replacing plants which no longer appeal with ones we like more. The garden is full of plants that are easily able to be transplanted to elsewhere or given away in favour of something else. The plants that went in to replace weeds did not all have to be the forever plants of that garden. Those initial plants needed to be hardy to cope with less-than-ideal conditions in the garden and be able to fill the garden quickly to prevent the weeds regaining their dominance. The makeup of those plants can now be refined over time and as we fancy. Gardens are not static, and it is ok to change our plants in time as our desires for the garden evolve.

In the early stages we left some green Syngonium in the garden. There was not much of it and it filled a space. Now we no longer need it to fill the space, but it has thrived to become a weed in itself. It is now being gradually weeded out to make room for purple tradescantia and Euphorbia 'Diamond Frost', giving more colour under the shade of the tree. Scurvy weed is also prevalent in the garden, but the blue flowers are cheerful and attractive to butterflies, so Ann doesn't mind it. It is easy to pull out the excess when it gets a bit out of hand, and then my chooks are grateful for a feed, especially as it usually comes with caterpillars, being a butterfly host plant.

Ann's garden also has patches of nutgrass and soursob. The soursob we have learnt to enjoy with its masses of pretty pink flowers in spring. It is not much of a bother really as it dies away over summer. Nutgrass on the other hand is a nuisance. We are not using poison on the nutgrass in the garden beds because it is growing amongst Zephranthes bulbs, and the poison which works on nutgrass works on other bulbs as well. In other sections of the garden we have removed the majority of the nutgrass by digging it out. This worked by using a fork to loosen the soil well before trying to pull it out. By pulling on a clump rather than a single stem, you are more likely to get the bunch of connected roots with nuts attached. An advantage of nutgrass is that all the individual bulbs are connected by a system of roots. By gently forking the soil it is possible to lift the entire clump. Obviously, the soil needs to be loose for this to work. As nutgrass likes to grow in compacted soil, we made an effort to soften the soil by improving it with compost before trying to dig it out. We have decided to let the nutgrass coexist with the mondo grass around the edge of the garden. They grow to the same height, so the nutgrass is actually giving an appearance of a denser stand of mondo grass (if you don't look too closely). This saves a lot of heartache in trying to get rid of a super tough weed, and an occasional hand weed keeps it from spreading.

Putting Weeds to Use

Brown mustard (*Brassica juncea*) is very attractive to pollinators and is useful for attracting them into your garden.

Now here is the fun part - putting weeds to use. When is a weed not a weed? When it is a desired plant! Simply by learning to value some of the plants we know of as weeds, we can take heart in leaving them in the garden because suddenly, the amount of weeding we have to do is wonderfully reduced!

Edible Weeds

> "When I see these plants, I see a lot of wasted nutrition and deliciousness," says Philip Stark, U.C. Berkeley statistics professor and the lead researcher of a new report: 'Open-Source Food: Nutrition, Toxicology, and Availability of Wild Edible Greens in the East Bay.' "I see missed culinary opportunity, and I see missed opportunity to reduce the carbon and water footprint of our diets."

Of all the ways we can turn weeds into a resource, eating them is probably the most rewarding. Edible weeds are a growing movement in western countries and foraging courses can be found in most major cities. I love edible weeds; they are so much easier to grow than vegetables because they do it all by themselves. My vegetables certainly don't do that. Unlike vegetables, weeds haven't been highly bred for greater productivity, nor are they growing in places they don't like – they choose where to grow. This is usually in locations with unimproved soil where they are likely to thrive. The same cannot be said about most of the vegetables we eat. For this reason, many of the edible weeds are far superior to our vegetables when it comes to nutritional value. It has been suggested that eating one large handful of weeds is nutritionally comparative to eating 1kg of organic vegetables. I haven't seen this claim substantiated but amongst the weeds there are certainly some very nutrient dense foods that are worth getting to know and eat. Chickweed, green amaranth and pink baby's breath are among my favourite weed foods, closely followed by cobbler's pegs, sow thistle and purslane. They may well be amongst the world's first superfoods, and often tastier than plant food that has been bred for production.

A study by the University of California, Berkley in 2014-15 looked at the nutritional value of six wild harvested weeds found growing in the San Francisco Bay area during a summer drought. The research team compared the nutritional value of dandelion, chickweed, dock, mallow, nasturtium and oxalis to that of kale. The results were no surprise to the seasoned weed eater.

With the exception of vitamin C, all nutritional values were either similar to that of kale, or well above its nutritional value.

Even more surprising was that the levels of heavy metal contamination were very low, despite the weeds being sourced from roadsides and degraded areas. The team concluded that high quality food was readily and freely available from weeds, even during periods of severe drought.

Foraging Weeds
Foraging for wild food plants (be they weeds or otherwise) is a dietary staple for many people around the world. In Vietnam, wild foraged vegetables account for up to 65% of the diet of people living outside cities. This is probably similar for many other countries as well. Historically these figures would have been much higher, even in Europe. In our overdeveloped world, the art of foraging for wild food is being rediscovered. Foraging workshops are becoming increasingly popular as we look to reconnect to lost knowledge. Whilst I hope that this book, and others, are of great value to you, I strongly urge you to look for local classifications and learn to recognise the weeds in your local environs. Many of our weeds are cosmopolitan, but there are so many others that are more local in distribution. By adding local knowledge to what this, or any other book provides, you will have a much greater selection of wild food plants available to you for foraging.

There are a few precautions to be aware of when wild foraging. Most importantly, be aware that it's not possible to tell if a weed has been sprayed with herbicides just by looking at the plant. Recently sprayed plants can take a few days to show signs of dying. Foraging is best done after good rain, when anything unpleasant is likely to have been washed away and it is unlikely that plants have been sprayed in the preceding 48 hours. Where you see a patch of multi-generational weeds (i.e. both young plants which have not yet flowered and old plants which have set seed), it is unlikely that the area has had any herbicides applied for some time and is most likely a good place for foraging. If you see weak and unhealthy-looking plants, don't eat them.

Although the study mentioned above found very low levels of heavy metals in the weeds that they harvested from roadsides, I would still treat these with caution. Other studies have given a very different result. It is entirely possible that the answer to these different findings can be explained by the work being done by the team at Delprat Garden in NSW. They are working on phytoremediation of a contaminated site adjacent to a disused steel works. Phytoremediation is the use of plants to remove contaminants from soil. This project is looking at how different plants take up heavy metals, where those metals are stored in the plant tissues and the follow-on impacts. If heavy metals are stored in the flowers and pollen, this will have serious implications for pollinators for example. They are finding that certain vegetables can be grown in highly contaminated soils and still be perfectly safe to eat, as the heavy metals are stored in the plant roots. The rest of the plant, including the parts we like to eat, has been found to be completely free of heavy metals. In other vegetables they are finding heavy metals in all parts of the plant. It may well be that the weeds assessed in the California study are storing and isolating heavy metals in their root system and the foraged leaves are safe to eat. Until we know more about which weeds are capable of isolating contaminants in certain parts of the plant, we should assume that weeds grown in contaminated areas will be unsafe to eat. In highly polluted areas be aware of the potential for the weeds to have taken up pollutants. The verge of a busy road is not a good place for foraging even if the weeds look healthy there. There is a high risk that they have absorbed pollutants from the road. Similarly, heavily industrialised areas pose a risk of contamination as well. Contamination from a passing dog lifting its leg is easily and safely dealt with just by washing the greens before eating.

One of the downsides to foraging is finding a great area full of wonderful weeds and coming back to find it has been mown. Ultimately the best place to grow and forage for weeds is your own garden. This doesn't mean you should not be opportunistic and harvest great weeds as you find them. Do be aware of harvesting weeds in public and make sure you are not removing desired plants. Also take care when harvesting weeds that you are not spreading seeds and propagules around. By harvesting weeds our aim is to enjoy them and limit their spread, not to spread them further.

Eating Weeds
I use the term *potherb* frequently when discussing edible weeds. This is an old-fashioned term which means *herb of the pot*, so can be used anywhere you would use something green – such as spinach. These edible greens can also offer huge nutritional benefits to us in green smoothies, as sprouts or as micro greens. There are so many ways to eat weeds, and most revolve around the way you would eat any green leafy vegetable. If we use *spinach substitute* as a guide, we have a good start for eating weeds – young leaves are good in salads or on sandwiches, older leaves are better wilted or cooked. Think of all the ways you may be able to use spinach, or indeed Asian greens, and you can substitute these with seasonal edible weeds.

Some weeds offer more specific flavours. Flickweed, swine cress, peppercress and shepherd's purse, or indeed any of the wild brassicas can be very peppery and can be used to add the zing that we enjoy from rocket or water cress. Peppery flavours like these support the circulatory system and can be incorporated into a diet to support holistic health.

Others, like wild carrot, are usually too small to provide much substance in a meal but offer a good alternative to parsley as a garnish. I had a person attend one of my talks only to discover that the weed in abundance in her garden was wild carrots, which are edible. This inspired her to make a pasta dish of wild carrot leaves wilted in garlic and butter that same evening. It may be a small weed, but when you have plenty of it, you can still get a decent feed.

I personally enjoy the flavour of Emelia (*Emilia sonchifolia*) and like to nibble on this one fresh. If you have an abundance of great edible weeds in season, there are ways of preserving them. Sometimes you need to weed them out to make way for other plants but don't want to waste the harvest. Most can be blanched and frozen. Freeze your blanched weeds in meal sized portions for ease of use later. Soft leaved weeds such as chickweed or creeping wood sorrel do not need to be blanched before freezing. They can be chopped and added to ice cube trays to create portions that are easy to measure. Others can be dried, and the leaves crushed into a green power to add a nutritional boost to food and drinks. They contribute almost no flavour when used this way, which is good for those who aren't keen on eating greens. Drying works well for leaves without succulent properties as the extra moisture in the leaf makes drying more difficult. Weeds such as pink baby's breath, purslane or madeira vine are best frozen rather than dried.

Weeds with medicinal values can be made into flavoured oils or vinegars for salad dressings and drizzling (often in combination with more flavourful herbs), made into tinctures and salves for medicinal use or even soaps and lip balms for daily care. How far you go depends on you. If I don't have time to make all of these wonderful things with weeds, I can still throw large handfuls of them into everything I cook, knowing that I'm giving myself and my family nutritionally dense food.

If you're keen to eat weeds (and why wouldn't you be?) please take the time to identify them correctly. While many of the weeds discussed in this book are familiar to us, they can be confused with similar plants that might not be safe to eat. Don't rely on one picture alone to identify a weed. Plants growing in different conditions or at different stages of their life cycle can look very different. I highly recommend doing an internet search using the scientific name (*not* the common name as common names vary enormously) and look at multiple pictures. In most cases toxic plants are very unpleasant to eat. They will be extremely bitter or have a repugnant smell. These characteristics are a warning not to eat it, afterall, it is in the plant's best interest to stop us before we damage or destroy it. Let your sense of taste and smell guide you. If you are put off by the taste or smell of something, that is your body's way of telling you to not eat it. Follow these instincts! If you are not sure of something, nibble with caution or leave well alone.

Oxalic Acid

A note here about oxalic acid. Many of these wild foods contain high levels of oxalic acid, as does spinach. Large amounts of oxalic acid are not good for you, especially if you have calcium or vitamin D deficiencies. Our bodies process oxalic acid better in the presence of calcium, which might play a part in the fabulous pairing of cheese and spinach in many traditional dishes.

Oxalic acid is thought to be neutralised by cooking, and many of us also prefer our spinach cooked, or if we do eat it raw, we eat young leaves which have a much lower oxalic acid content. Other references suggest that cooking does almost nothing to neutralise it. Blanching (dropping the leaves into boiling water for a minute and then removing and discarding the water) does remove some of the soluble oxalic acid. Let the water cool and use it on plants, it will contain other soluble minerals as well. Insoluble oxalic acid tends to be in crystalline form and passes straight through us without impact, and as such is not a problem. I personally find that cooking does help, even if that means adding chopped leaves into a dish just before turning the heat off. By treating many of these edible greens as you would spinach, eating them becomes easy.

The actual amount of oxalic acid in a plant can be quite variable and has been hard to measure accurately. I haven't provided comparison charts here as various sources provide completely different results – with parsley measuring 1.7% in one study and 0.1% in another. Instead let your body guide you as to what suits you. The oxalic acid content of a species of plant can vary with the age of the plant, time of year, the soil and climate conditions. Oxalic acid content is higher in dry conditions, but then the reduced amount of water available to the plant is likely to make all phytochemicals more concentrated and the leaves less juicy and palatable. With so many variables, the job of quantifying oxalic acid is not so straight forward. There are many websites discussing oxalic acid and its negative effects on the body. Each website has a different list of vegetables and nuts that have high levels, as well as those that don't - and the same vegetables will be listed as high on one website and low on another. No wonder we get confused!

In addition to the oxalic acid content of vegetables varying according to growing conditions, people's ability to metabolise oxalic acid also varies. When I talk about oxalic acid in a workshop, I describe a metallic taste or a tingling in the mouth when you have eaten too much silverbeet or spinach. Some people will be nodding, and others will be looking confused – not everyone experiences these symptoms regardless of how much they eat. This is an indication of your personal tolerance levels – your body is telling you what suits it. Listening to the cues your own body is giving you will be far more reliable and relevant to you than any other source of information. Rarely do we sit down to a bowl of nothing but spinach for a meal, and the same goes for the weeds we are eating. Like any vegetable, we tend to mix and match and add many other ingredients to make a meal. This mix of ingredients - such as cheese and greens, is more likely to give a balance of nutrients, which will help metabolise oxalic acid and other phytochemicals. If you do have trouble with metabolising foods high in oxalic acid, gut health can also be a factor. The Lactobacillus bacteria found in yoghurt is very beneficial in breaking down oxalic acid, making the Green Goddess dressing recipe later in this book a perfect way to eat weeds! Another gut bacteria, *Oxalobacter formigenes,* is able to break down oxalic acid in the gut, but not everyone has these.

I have mentioned that calcium and vitamin D deficiencies can reduce our ability to metabolise oxalic acid. People who are prone to gout or kidney stones, or who have thyroid issues may also need to be careful to limit oxalic acid in their diets.

It is interesting to note that the warnings around oxalic acid often apply more heavily to wild greens, rather than cultivated vegetables. Spinach was hugely popular as a healthy green not so long ago. Now kale is all the rage. While we see so many edible weeds discussed with warnings about oxalic acid, we do not see the same warnings on common vegetables, even though many contain as much or more oxalic acid than the leafy greens we have mentioned here. Parsley can be very high in oxalic acid, as can broccoli, kale and pistachios. Personally, I find I can only eat very small amounts of parsley comfortably. I can eat huge salads of dark green leafy vegetable and weeds without any effect, but not every day. If I cook my weeds, even sightly, I can tolerate large amounts on a daily basis. When you are aware of how your body reacts to oxalic acid you can find the ways to eat and enjoy weeds without triggering reactions in your body.

By far the most sensible approach is to realise that instead of looking for that one *superfood*, the quick fix that can be taken as a little green pill, we need a diverse diet. Modern diets are extraordinarily limited. We tend to eat the same basic ingredients over and over. Our so-called *fresh* food comes from supermarkets, and we don't think about how long they have been in cold storage, what chemicals were used to grow and preserve them, whether the soil they were grown in has any real value or if the plant has been force-fed artificial fertilisers. All these factors impact on the true nutritional value (not to mention the taste) of the food we eat, and on the oxalic acid content of that food.

A diverse range of greens gives us the opportunity to not only ensure we are not potentially overdosing on oxalic acid, but also allows us to gain the benefits of the different nutritional value of many different plants. By far the best way to do this is to eat fresh and seasonal. What could be fresher and more seasonal than eating the weeds as they pop up in our own gardens?

Medicinal Weeds

Many of our common weeds are wonderful medicinal plants. Some require special preparation before safe use, but you might be surprised at how many will be of huge medicinal benefit if we simple go and chew on a leaf or two, make a simple cup of tea or rub them onto our skin. Here are some of the ways I turn to my garden for medicinal support before I turn to the medicine cabinet:

Pain and headaches: sow thistle, prickly lettuce, basket plant
Tummy upsets: sida retusa, mallows, basket plant
Sinus trouble: sida retusa, mallows
Wound healing: plantain
Antimicrobial: cobbler's pegs, nasturtiums
Bites and stings: billy goat weed, chickweed, dock
Warts and Sunspots: radium weed (external use only!)
General pick me up: pink baby's breath, stinging nettle, mallows, madeira vine, chickweed
Asthma, breathing issues: alehoof, basket plant
Brain fog: gotu kola
Kidney and liver support: dandelion, false dandelion, sow thistle
Colds and coughs: plantain, cobbler's pegs, sida retusa, wild brassicas, basket plant
Summer hydration: purslane
Breath freshener: cobbler's pegs
Nose bleeds: shepherd's purse
Kick start the day: wild brassicas
Skin rashes and daily care: plantain, mallows, chickweed, basket plant
UTIs: dandelion, false dandelion, cobbler's pegs, nasturtium, sow thistle
Insomnia: prickly lettuce, vervain
Stress: nettles, sensitive plant, vervain

This list is not exhaustive by any means, it is just a brief starting point. You'll find more information on each of these plant's medicinal uses in the plant profiles contained in this book. I do not have these plants available to me every day as many are highly seasonal in my climate. I use what is available to me when I have need of it.

In addition to weeds with specific uses such as those above, there are many general characteristics of plants that correspond to general medicinal properties. Plants with a high mucilage content, often evident by leaves with a slightly slimy texture or silky sensation in the mouth, are good for reducing inflammation and boosting immune system functioning. Examples are madeira vine, pick baby's breath and all weeds in the mallow family.

Plants with a pungent or peppery flavour act to stimulate circulation and release endorphins. This includes all of the wild brassicas.

Plants in the dandelion/sow thistle group with yellow flowers and milky sap are good diuretics and give liver and kidney support. Do not confuse this group with the euphorbias which also have a milk sap but are highly toxic (though good for burning off warts).

Weeds with a sharp lemony flavour are particularly high in vitamin C, which of course is great for health, including general immune system support and even cancer fighting. This includes the docks, sorrels and oxalis weeds, but all fresh leafy greens will contain vitamin C.

The notion of food as medicine comes into play here. Many of the weeds I've discussed are beneficial as food medicine due to their high nutritional content. By including these plants in a diverse diet, we can boost our health without needing a detailed knowledge of their medicinal properties.

When using any plant as medicine it is important to understand that therapeutic doses are often much higher than the amount you would eat as part of a healthy diet. While a daily dose can help us maintain health and reduce the need for higher and more therapeutic doses, if a stronger dose is needed, you may be able to achieve it simply by eating more of a particular weed when required, or by making a herbal tea. Sometimes a stronger dose again is a good idea, or you may wish to preserve some seasonal weeds for medicinal purposes throughout the year. In this case an alcoholic or cider vinegar tincture made from the weeds can be beneficial.

Always research further if using herbs or weeds medicinally. A quarter of our modern pharmaceuticals are directly derived from plants, highlighting how powerful they can be. It's a safe rule of thumb to stick to weeds that are edible as well as medicinal. There are many non-edible weeds that are effective as medicine. Use these with caution and care as they can be very harmful if used incorrectly. The weed vinca, (*Catharanthus roseus*) is a case in point. It is effective in treating Hodgkin's and leukemia, but it also contains toxic alkaloids which cause serious side effects, including hair loss, nausea and low blood pressure resulting in death. The cancer drugs Vincristine and Vinblastine are derived from this plant. Clearly a powerful medicinal plant but not one that we should self-medicate with.

While so many of our modern medicines are derived from plants, they have come a long way from their original form. Aspirin is derived from willow bark, digitalis used for heart conditions is derived from foxgloves, Silymarin extracted from the seeds of milk thistle (*Silybum marianum*) is used for the treatment of liver diseases and Artemisinin from the traditional Chinese plant *Artemisia annua* is used to combat multidrug resistant malaria. What modern pharmaceuticals have done is isolate certain phytochemicals from plants which can then be synthetically manufactured for use as modern drugs. While this is highly effective, it does tend to negate the many other phytochemicals within the plant. Some of the reason why many herbal medicines are not able to be easily synthesised into drugs is due to the complex and little understood interplay of the many different phytochemicals within a plant. Put simply, much of the medicinal benefit of plants is based on the many different plant chemicals within that plant working together rather than in isolation.

The field of plant medicine is enormous, with much of it still based on hundreds, even thousands of years of practice. The science of plant medicine will continue and is a fascinating study, one that offers us huge benefits and I look forward to what it continues to offer. However, I also highly value the age-old wisdom of herbs and wild plants. This includes the ones to leave alone as much as it does the ones to use abundantly.

> Ragweed can be a significant allergen for hay fever and asthma sufferers. Ironically, it can also provide the remedy. Try making a tincture of the leaves of ragweed in vodka for an effective hay fever cure. Common ragweed has deeply divided ferny looking leaves and can look similar to the highly poisonous hemlock which is in the Apiaceae family (ragweed is in the Compositaceae or daisy family). You can identify hemlock by the noxious smell released from the leaves which warns you to keep away.

Fodder Weeds

Even if you're not excited about eating weeds, you might find that your animals are. So many of the weeds we've been discussing as useful are also sought out by animals as great food plants.

If you are wondering if a weed is edible, offer it to your pet guinea pig or rabbit. They have a very similar digestive system to ours and what they are happy to eat is usually also safe for us. Chickens are also a good guide. I've never come across a chicken that has poisoned itself. They will pick out what is good to eat and leave the rest. This doesn't necessarily mean we will like the same foods, just that we can eat them. Chooks love eating maggots too, which while a potentially great protein source, I am not about to add to my diet. Most animals will choose to eat what is good for them if they have the choice – choice being the key here. When food worth eating is in short supply, food not worth eating gets eaten in far greater amounts. If animals are poisoned by eating weeds, it is usually because they are placed in weed infested paddocks where their grazing choices are very limited. This isn't a problem for suburban gardeners, who may only be feeding the guinea pigs and the chooks, if anything. However, there are many semi-rural gardeners and permaculturalists with enough space for animals and plenty of weeds. Happily, those animals can be incredibly useful in managing those weeds, even in suburban gardens.

Weeds that we don't consider worthy of eating ourselves can often be a valuable source of food for animals. Burr medic and other medic weeds are related to alfalfa (lucerne) and considered to be very good fodder weeds. Thistles, stinging nettles, amaranth, ragweed (*Ambrosia artemisifolia*) and bindweed (*Convolvulus arvensis*) have all been found to be great stock feed, producing good quality meat and milk supplies. Ragweed is a controlled and restricted invasive species in Queensland, often found in overgrazed paddocks. It is deep rooted, and as with so many other weeds, plays a role in soil repair. All these weeds can be controlled by letting stock graze on them before they seed, then leaving the paddock fallow for the soil to recover. Allowing stock to graze again before weeds can seed involves regularly moving them. The effort is worth it if it means weeds are controlled, the stock is well fed, and the soil is in recovery.

Like burr medic, clover is a weed hated by lawn lovers and loved by permaculturalists. It makes an excellent soil repair agent and a good protein rich stock feed. The expression *rolling in clover*, meaning to have plenty of money, comes from how happy cows are in a field of clover. Yet another legume is an important fodder plant and an invasive weed - *Leucaena leucocephala*, or tree lucerne, is a fast-growing small tree capable of producing large amounts of high protein fodder quickly. It has been touted as a miracle tree for its high yield, especially in subtropical and semi-arid environments. It has also been known as the conflict tree due to its ability to spread prolifically. It is valued throughout much of India and Asia as a wood (fuel) and pulp source in addition to fodder. In places where other fuel and fodder sources are readily available (including southern Europe, the USA and Australia) it is considered little more than a noxious weed. Even in these countries, many farmers are keeping small patches of Leucaena on their land for emergency drought feed. A research project I recently came across in Queensland is working on developing a non-weedy variety of Leucaena. A project like this recognises both the economic value of the plant to farmers and the environmental impacts of this weed. I don't know if this project has also recognised the importance of this plant to bees. Most non-weedy varieties of plants are developed as sterile hybrids, so they do not set seeds. They also do not produce much nectar or pollen but are still highly attractive to bees. Where large numbers of sterile hybrids exist (such as in agricultural monocultures) bees can literally starve to death, visiting flower after flower with nothing to feed on. Leucaena is not just a great fodder plant, bees love it too.

If you have a paddock full of weeds, find out what they are before you confine stock to the paddock. Cows, sheep, horses and goats will be poisoned by eating certain weeds. As mentioned, this is most likely to happen in paddocks which are in poor condition where choice is limited. They will happily eat some of the stronger tasting weeds like wild brassicas, but you may end up with tainted milk. Most animals will select the superior feed first and leave behind what is less palatable. Make an effort to get to know the weeds in your paddock and also the local weeds which are likely to be toxic to your livestock. Avoid putting stock into paddocks dominated by a small diversity of weeds as this reduces their ability to avoid toxic weeds. Even fireweed (*Senecio madagascariensis*), a problematic and highly toxic weed, will be avoided by stock if they can eat something else. If you have toxic weeds in your paddocks, don't cut hay from them because animals won't be able to avoid them when feeding. Fireweed is an indicator of overgrazed paddocks. It grows fast and will seed prolifically, colonising bare soil quickly.

Paddocks that are overgrazed are at high risk of becoming weed infested. As the wanted feed plants and grasses are eaten beyond the point of recovery, gaps appear, which allow weeds to colonise. Given that the preferred pasture plants have been eaten to the point of exhaustion, we can safely assume that there is a certain degree of exhaustion in the soil too. This creates a perfect environment for weeds. When weeds start appearing in your paddocks, it is time to rest them and allow recovery.

If you are borrowing your neighbours' stock to graze a paddock and save the need for slashing, be aware that they will selectively graze and therefore control only the palatable plants. What they don't like can then become dominant. Goats would be a preferred option as they have a much broader palate than cows, horses and sheep. Whichever animal you use, it is a good idea to allow the field to rest and recover. Allowing the pasture grasses to mature and set seed before they are eaten again will allow for seed of the plants you want to take hold in any gaps, rather than leaving the gaps to be filled by weeds.

The notion of overgrazing as a means of exhausting the fodder plants is a principle which we can apply to our advantage in garden situations. Over grazing involves removal of the top of the weed more often than the roots can support. The plant becomes exhausted and dies because without the ability to photosynthesize (which requires leaves) it cannot feed itself. When we talk about exhausting a plant this is exactly the same principle. Keep taking off the tops and the plant will eventually die. Even the most tenacious of weeds can be controlled this way.

Compost Weeds

Much loved Australian author Jackie French once wrote that "nothing grown is ever wasted". It is one of my favourite quotes! If there is nothing left to do with the weeds you have, compost them.

All plants take nutrients from the soil as they grow. Many weeds are able to extract minerals from the soil that other plants cannot access. By composting we are returning those minerals to the garden. By composting in situ, we save work for ourselves but also return those minerals to the same soil they were extracted from, allowing those weeds to continue their important job of soil repair even after they are dead. It can be so much easier to quickly pull a weed or two as you go by, rather than thinking of the weeding as a big job that you need to psych yourself up for. If the job becomes so big that the garden starts to disappear under the pile of pulled out weeds, you may need to move the weeds elsewhere to compost. Mind you, if you have pulled a huge pile of weeds out of the garden it is likely that you now have lots of bare patches where those weeds can indeed compost in situ.

There are so many different ways to compost weeds. The key is to find what works for you and will ensure your weed can compost rather than regrow. Composting may include throwing the weeds into the chook pen for the chooks to compost (or eat) for you, leaving them on top of the garden bed as green mulch, adding to the compost bin or heap, feeding the worm farm or even making weed tea.

Weed tea is particularly good for those real nasties that are hard to kill – anything that will regrow from seeds, runners or tubers. Soak them in a bucket of water for a few days and then strain and use as a foliar feed. All the wonderful nutrients they contain will be returned to the garden this way, and the stinky rotten weeds that remain in the bucket are now ready for the compost bin.

Other very difficult weeds can be *solarised*. This means filling a plastic bag (black is particularly good as it gets hotter) and leaving it in the sun for a few weeks. The weeds inside literally cook, often killing the seeds as well. The rotten mess can then be used as compost.

Many of the ways of dealing with weeds that we discussed previously result in weeds being composted one way or another. All methods work to return the nutrients that were drawn up from the soil in the first place, improving the soil along the way which is a key ecological role of weeds. However, you choose to deal with weeds, don't miss the opportunity to compost these hard-working plants.

Weeds as Companion Plants

Using weeds as valuable companion plants within a garden or indeed a farm is not a new idea. It is however one that struggles to gain mainstream acceptance, despite ample evidence of its success. While we are very open to the idea that some plants assist others to grow better, are we as open to this idea if the companion plants are weeds? There is actually very little scientific evidence that companion planting works, and even less understanding as to how it works. Recent scientific research is finding a huge difference amongst plants in the ways take up minerals from the soil. I suspect as this area of understanding grows, we will see the science of companion planting emerge. Most gardeners are not asking for any scientific evidence as the results speak for themselves. Science is making amazing discoveries in the field of plant interactions. They have found that plants communicate through chemical and electrical signals, and that much of this communication happens via the network of fungal mycelium in the root zone of the soil. These fine fungal hairs allow plants a greater ability to absorb nutrients, and via these pathways to share nutrients with each other. Inter specific plant relationships are being found to be very real. Plants do work together for optimal growth.

As much as 70 years ago it was found that growing nettles amongst peppermint and tomato crops could very significantly increase the yield while also keeping many pest problems at bay. In the case of the peppermint, the fields which were interspersed with nettle showed a significantly higher return of oil from the leaf than those fields without nettle.

Less mysterious is the way in which deep rooted plants open up the soil structure and allow the roots of nearby plants to penetrate more deeply into the soil.

Traditionally weeds were considered as garden "robbers", taking valuable water and nutrients away from other plants. If we instead consider that plants grow better in a community that helps each other, the idea of weeds as robbers hold less water. In fact, many weeds are important soil improvers. As we have already discussed, they are able to colonise and exploit soil conditions that other plants cannot. They can do this as a cover crop of weeds alone, or they can be useful soil improvers interspersed with the crops or flowers. As many of the weeds are deep rooted, their roots are not operating in the same soil space as the garden plants (or crops) and therefore there is no competition for resources.

Whilst an overly crowded garden may lead to reduced performance of individual plants, an overly sparse garden will do the same. As we now know, plants can share nutrients, not only by way of natural leaf decay at the surface, but also through root exchange mechanisms which rely on interactions with soil fungi. Many weeds have the ability to extract minerals from poor soil. They are able to make these minerals more available to the plants around them via this soil network, which is a real bonus for those nearby plants. In his 1950 book, "Weeds, Guardians of the Soil" Joseph A Cocannouer gives numerous examples of farmers all over the world seeing massively increased crop yields by allowing some weeds to remain in their fields. In all cases, allowing the weeds to be too dense caused reduced crop yield, but no weeds at all also resulted in a lower yield than a field with an even distribution of weeds, especially deep-rooted weeds.

When I was working on restoring Sue's old weedy garden, I found roses that were smothered by weeds. In uncovering the roses, I found one had a false mallow growing at the base of the rose. This weed was allowed to stay. It is a low growing plant which shades the soil around the rose, acting as living mulch. It flowers well and helps bring in beneficial insects to the rose. It also has very deep roots, which help forge a way down for the rose roots, in doing so maintaining a living soil biota deeper into the soil. This particular rose plant was not just the healthiest of all the roses in this patch, it was at least 5 times the size of the others and is never without a flower. Even if you can't agree that the weed growing at its base is helping the rose, it is clear that it is not doing any harm at all.

In using weeds as companion plants there are a few considerations. Get to know your local weeds. Both annual and perennial weeds can be good companion plants, and in fact both have something different to offer. Annuals tend to live short life cycles and produce a lot of organic matter rich in minerals in that short life. Perennials tend to produce deeper root systems and can provide soil cover and protection during very harsh times of year.

Jackie French has found that once vegetable seedlings reach approximately one third of their mature size, they no longer complete with weeds and therefore is fine to allow the weeds to grow in the vegetable patch beyond this point. Using the above logic, allowing these weeds to grow will not only be ok, but it will also be highly beneficial.

Weeds as Environmental Repair Agents

We have discussed at length the idea of weeds as soil improvers. We can learn to read the weeds to see what might be happening in the soil and how to fix it. This is very useful in a home garden or even in agriculture, but how does this help in public or disused spaces? Weeds are true survivors, as spontaneous urban plants they are able to grow in some extremely harsh localities, places completely unsuitable for most plants to grow at all. The option for green life in these spaces is often weed or nothing.

We too often forget the valuable role these weeds are playing. As I travel around and see weeds, I try to appreciate why the weeds are there. In almost all cases, the weeds are surviving on abused land, land that is in need of care and repair. In most of these cases there is not a loving gardener in residence to help with soil care, so the weeds are the only soil repair agents at work.

Within these harsh environments, whether that be cracks in the footpath, the roadside verges, industrial wasteland, along railway lines or drains and creeks, the weeds are there because nothing else is, and they are doing good work. Small and large, they are absorbing carbon dioxide and producing oxygen. They are providing soil stability, reducing erosion and slowing stormwater flows. Living green matter assists with reducing the urban heat island effect through reducing reflected heat. They are providing habitat for insects, birds, reptiles and mammals where there otherwise was nothing. Many weeds are also extremely good at extracting pollutants, from both the air and the soil. Long term weed growth can be highly beneficial for cleansing contaminated sites. Weeds such as sword fern, and others, have been found to be very good at accumulating heavy metals from soil, although in these cases the green material of the weeds now does need to be treated as contaminated waste.

Many Brassica weeds have been found to be able to absorb salts from moderately saline soils and be able to return those salts in safe organic forms as they decompose.

Weeds are agents of soil repair, leading to long term change. As we mentioned previously, if a field of weeds is left alone for many years, it will be a link in a natural succession towards a more permanent ecosystem. As the soil improves, the weed community will change. Trees will establish and native vegetation will slowly return in some form. We discussed earlier in this book, the role of Cinderella ecosystems, in which weeds pave the way for a more desired ecosystem to be able to become established. Cinderella ecosystems are all around us.

Lantana is a highly controversial weed here in Australia, but could it have some benefit? Research by Humphries and Stanton (1992) found that lantana is unable to invade dense rainforests or dry vine thickets. It is however able to establish itself around the disturbed perimeter of the rainforest where it forms dense stands preventing other weeds, especially grasses, from entering the rainforest. Other research has shown that this pairing may also help to protect the rainforests from fire damage in the dry season (Stocker and Mott, 1981). When we feel lantana is invading a rainforest, look closer. Is the lantana really invading pristine rainforest, or is the rainforest dying back due to other environmental or human factors, and the lantana filling the gap left behind? This is not a question that can be answered at a glance. In the case of damaged land, what have we to lose by allowing the weeds to perform this valuable work for us?

Weeds as Habitat

We have mentioned already that weeds tend to fill empty spaces, that they are spread by birds eating the seeds and we have mentioned the value of a mature tree, regardless of the species. All of this matters, not just as earth repair, but to host animal life, large and small, in places where their natural habitat has been degraded or destroyed. Weeds act as attractants for many insects, good and bad. Many weeds are insect pollinated, and in order to ensure reproduction in a short lifespan, will be very good at attracting those pollinators. Many of the most predatory insects, important in keeping down the populations of problem insects, are the juvenile stages of pollinating insects. A healthy weed population will maintain a constant supply of food for pollinators to not just visit, but to set up permanent camp and to be there when needed to keep the leaf chompers and sap suckers under control. This means that your crop, or vegetables or flowers will have pollinators nearby to ensure seed set and fruit production. In an amateur entomology group that I belong to, a member has recently shared a series of photos of numerous species of bees and wasps, all visiting the flowers of cobbler's pegs. Within entomology circles this plant is appreciated for the enormously rich insect diversity it attracts.

With knowledge and understanding of the role of beneficial insects in the garden, gardeners are planting more flowers to attract these beneficial insects. At the same time, they are still destroying weeds, especially in their lawns, and harassing their local authorities to do the same. Insects have a highly varied ability to cover large distances, and like other animals, they do follow habitat corridors. The lack of flowers and the overuse of pesticides in modern gardens has seen a massive decline in insect numbers, and in particular insect biodiversity. Scientists are reporting shocking numbers when it comes to insects in decline around the world. We hear about the loss of bees, but the fate of the bees is also the fate of many other very important but less well-known insects. Weeds are becoming more and more valuable as remnant insect habitat.

Weeds tend not to cause a build-up of pests which can then move on to your garden plants unless you have a badly out of balance garden. More often you will find the weeds have been a very successful decoy plant and have allowed the good bugs to also set up camp and deal with the bad bugs. That remnant weed habitat acting as insect corridor will play a major role in bringing those good bugs into your garden. The bad bugs will be less dependent on the corridors and will usually arrive first. If you have encouraged your neighbours to "deal with their weeds" you may find the good bugs take longer to arrive, and in fewer numbers and as such are less available to help you deal with the insects you don't want in your garden. Successful habitat of any sort within your garden will rely to some extent on connections to habitat outside your garden – even if that habitat is your neighbour's weeds.

I love finding neglected fields full of weeds. Apart from how pretty they are because they are filled with flowers, they are also very alive places. The obvious insects are always there – bees, wasps, butterflies, dragonflies but there are so many others as well. Sit a while and just watch. You will be surprised how many different insects you see. In addition to the insects are the birds. This place is paradise for small insectivorous birds like wrens, willie wagtails and swallows, all of which are becoming much rarer in suburban gardens. Weed fields have an abundance of seed on both the weeds and the grasses, providing a valuable food source for an entirely different group of birds and small mammals. Grassland ecosystems are some of the worlds most endangered ecosystems due to agricultural pressures. A field of weeds can support many of the same animals as the native grassland once supported.

The value of any ecosystem lies in its diversity. Monocultures of any description will have very little habitat value, and this includes weed monocultures. In any area where weeds are contributing to increased biodiversity, they will be providing habitat value. In many degraded and urban environments, the weeds are the only plants there at all, and as such are important contributors to local habitat for critters large and small. It has long been suggested that weeds rarely invade healthy natural habitats. More commonly they are invading human influenced landscapes which are no longer ideal conditions for the original native vegetation. In more recent times I am certainly not the only ecologist to suggest that given the tendency of weeds to colonise damaged landscapes, they are most often increasing rather than decreasing the biodiversity of an area and in doing so, providing multiple layers of valuable habitat.

Other Weed Ideas: Be Creative!

If weeds are there in your garden, use them. By putting them to use, you are making the task of weeding a little more meaningful and less of a drag. You will be surprised how many uses you come up with for bits of plant – weed or otherwise. When using weeds for any purpose, be aware of spreading unwanted seed or propagating material, not just around your own garden but also around other people's gardens or natural areas. By using weeds, we no longer see weeds as just an enemy, an attitude which has only led to frustration and reduced our enjoyment of gardening. This being said, spreading weed seeds and therefore weeds, is not going to make us feel like better gardeners and our responsibility as environmental stewards should not be forgotten. Use them, enjoy them, but do not spread them.

Weaving

Use vines and long thin branches for weaving. These are best used fresh so they are still pliable, but if they do dry out, you can usually soak them for a few hours in water to soften them again ready for weaving. Baskets are the obvious weaving project but be creative. A simple Christmas wreath is a good place to start. Why not try making birds' nests as garden art? Baskets can be a little tricky. I have yet to get one to hold any shape and not fall apart. On my bucket list is to do a basket weaving workshop and learn how to make one that stays together. Even thin sticks can be woven when they are green and pliable. Woven sticks can be used to make a rustic tray. I also like using weeds to weave rustic trees for Christmas. To do this I begin with 7 sticks of equal size, tied together at the top. Semi-hardwood branches of Duranta (yes, another weed!) work well for this. Then weave any vine you have available, starting from the top where it has been tied together. Allow your weaving to gradually loosen and you will end up with a woven cone shape. Orange trumpet vine, a local weed which produces semi-woody stems, works well for this weaving project. Make a star out of sticks for the top and decorate with seed pods (free of seeds if you are using weed seed pods) or anything that appeals to you.

Try using canes of weeds like willow or lantana. Obviously if using lantana, you may want to use gloves as the stems are rather prickly.

I like using the stems of cat's claw creeper to make Christmas wreaths, but like lantana, they do come somewhat armed. The claws which give the vine its name help it cling to trees, and to fingers as we try to weave with it, but they also help our creation stay together after it has been woven. The cats claw creeper I refer to is *Dolichandra unguis-cati* a subtropical vine in the Bignoneaceae family – do not confuse it with the cat's claw creeper used in herbalism which is the unrelated *Uncaria tomentosa* in the Rubiaceae family, also a tropical vine from South America but completely unrelated.

Plant Ties

Use strong but not woody vines as plant ties. I like using fresh morning glory vines for this. Choose a lengthy piece of vine and strip the leaves off it. As the vine is pliable it works well to gently tie up soft plants, for example staking tomatoes or tying back lanky perennials. You do need to choose a long piece of vine because if you are too rough it will break, and you will be grateful for the extra length. The vines do not last longer than a season, but for this use they do not need to, and you do not have a rubbish problem with plastic ties when cutting back the tied-up plants when they are finished.

Garden Stakes

Use woody weeds to make garden stakes. Branches of cestrum, Chinese elm, Mickey Mouse bush, lantana and crepe myrtle are good for this. Choose branches which are reasonably straight and at least 1cm thick. Thicker branches are better for longer stakes; thinner branches will need to be used as shorter stakes. Strip off the leaves and small side branches to give a neat stake. If the stake is to be used to support vines you might like to trim the side branches but leave the branch stubs behind for the vines to cling too. These weed stakes can be used for so many things besides staking plants. They can be used to mark where you have planted bulbs or to create a stick forest to deter cats or brush turkeys from digging in the garden. If you have plenty use the stronger stakes as fence stakes and weave the thinner ones horizontally to create a rustic fence around your garden. If you use thin green branches for the horizontal sections of the fence, as they dry, they will become less flexible and stay in place. You can also use some weed vines to tie the horizontals in place if they need some help. I once used some lovely straight crepe myrtle sticks as garden stakes. They made lovely strong stakes, until they all grew! If you do not want them to grow (and make a lovely living fence perhaps?), it is best to let them dry out before using them.

Flower Garlands

Make daisy chains. The name may suggest that you need to use daisy flowers, but in truth, any flowers with a stem will work. Like so many others, I grew up making daisy chains with clover flowers. Clover flowers make a great daisy chain to wear as a necklace or headdress thanks to their delightful perfume. There are so many weeds that could be used to make fun daisy chains. Try dandelions, billy goat weed, or nasturtiums. To make the daisy chain, cut the flowers with as long a stem as you can. Use your fingernail to make a slit in the stem at the opposite end of the stem to the flower head. Poke the stem of the next flower through the small slit and pull it through until the flower head of the second flower comes to the slit and acts like a button in a buttonhole. Make a slit in the stem of the second flower and add another flower to the chain. Make the slits carefully, if they are too large the flower head will pull through and the chain will fall apart.

Make A Wish

Blow on dandelion (and related) seed heads and make a wish like we did as kids. A world without dandelion wishes does seem sad. Why not collect up lots of seed heads and place them carefully into a pretty jar. This makes a "jar of wishes" and makes a rather magical little gift for adults and children alike. To make your weedy gift even more weedy, maybe you could use weed fibres to make paper to make cards for the jar. Yes, blowing wishes does spread seed! Do this in an area where the weed is already growing and there is already a significant seed load in the soil. Or do it in your own garden where you are able to create dense conditions where seeds cannot grow.

Plantain Pop Guns

Stage wars with the kids shooting plantain seeds at each other. Pick the seed heads with a long stem. Fold the stem over itself and wrap the top of the seed head through the V shape. Hold tightly and pull firmly and swiftly. The seed head should pop off and fly forward. Lots of fun for kids. Again, this one does spread seed, so should be done where the plant is already growing and there is already a seed load in the soil. Or in my garden where I am happy for the seed to grow as plantain is such a valuable plant to me.

Fibre Art

Try investigating weeds for fibre art. Fibre art takes so many forms. Make string or even rope from fibrous weeds. Many grasses are good for this, as are things like canna leaves torn into strips. Some of the weeds in the mallow family are known for their strong fibres and would be worth experimenting with in fibre making activities. Fibre artists use plants to make string, but also to make paper with incredible textures. Start with using the tougher plants so you have strong fibres for your finished product. You can even make paper out of the fleshy fibrous roots of snake plant. Other leaves and flowers can be dried and pressed into your homemade paper to give lovely results. A Detroit artist, Megan Heeres, runs the Invasive Paper Project, which features workshops and art installations using handmade paper made from invasive weeds. In these workshops she not only teaches people to create handmade paper from weeds, but also encourages participants to explore the idea of 'invasive' through "find(ing) new solutions for unwanted plants and seeking connections between our horticultural and anthropological languages." www.meganheeres.com 2018.

Make Weed Dyes

Weeds can be used as a source of dye for natural dying projects. The orange root of sanserveria can be used to make a yellow dye. Other common weeds that will give a yellow dye include mullein, yarrow and goldenrod. Try using the berries of poke weed (*Phytolacca americana*) or coral berry (*Rivinia humilis*), both of which have cultural uses for making red dyes. Both of these berries are also poisonous, so have fun but don't eat them. Interestingly, both also have medicinal uses, again a case of having great respect for plants and an even greater respect for plant medicines.

By using the berries and roots of weeds, not only do you get to have fun creating beautiful natural dyes, but you are also making use of the propagative part of the weed and therefore reducing its spread. Many other weeds will give a range of green and brown shades using barks, roots, stems and leaves.

You will be able to get shades of blues from morning glory flowers and purples from elderberries, canna seeds or lantana berries.
Dandelions, sorrel and cleavers will give shades of pink and red.
Dock, nettles, plantain and amaranths can give shades of green.
Using different mordants to fix the dye will give different shades. It is easy to see how artists could get completely absorbed into the world of plant textiles and dyes, as the variety of results is not only beautiful but infinitely diverse. While we may not all aspire to be textile artists, there is no reason we cannot have a little fun with those weeds we are pulling out anyway.

Making Weed Paper

After experimenting with making paper from plants, in particular snake plant (*Sanseveria sp*), I have a new-found respect for this incredibly tough plant! Any plants suitable for making paper will have strong fibres. When it comes to the snake plant it is certainly strong. I boiled the chopped pieces of plant for six hours and it still did not fall apart. I now not only chop the roots and leaves into small pieces, I also smash them with the hammer first. The root fibres made a very rough paper. I found the leaf fibres made a paper which was still leathery and tough, but not as course at the leaves. Fibres of the leaves of canna made a rich dark green paper and were much softer to work with. You will get dark earthy colours to your paper when using plant fibres without any bleaching. A simple recipe for plant paper is as follows:

Place chopped pieces of plant into a large pot and cover with water. Add a tablespoon of bicarbonate of soda (bicarb), and boil for 2 hours. Let it sit for a few days. This allows the plant material to start breaking down. Drain the water off and use it in the garden, afterall it is a version of weed tea. The bicarb will have broken down in the boiling process and will not hurt the garden. Rinse the plant matter a few times to reduce the amount of colour in the water. This is the digested plant material, the part which contains the goodness for the garden, and the part which is of no use in making paper. What you are left with are the fibrous parts of the plant. You can make paper without this washing process, but the result is a courser paper.

Add fresh water to just cover the fibrous plant material and pulverise with a blender until you get a fine mix. The fibre can wrap around the blades and burn out motors, so it is best to do this in small batches.

Scoop or pour the fine mixture (paper slurry) onto a paper making decal. Spread the slurry evenly over the area of the frame. You can make it as thick or as thin as you like but try to get good coverage or you may end up with holes in your paper from too thin patches. If you make your sheet too thick, it can be difficult to get it to dry thoroughly.

If you want to embed pressed flowers or seeds into your paper, sprinkle them over your slurry layer now.

Place an old tea towel over the top of the paper slurry on the decal and press to squeeze out some of the excess water. Flip the entire thing upside down so the paper is released from the decal and onto the tea towel. Lay this down flat with another tea towel or cloth on top. Add a weight to the paper sandwich. This helps to compress the fibres into a well-formed sheet of paper. Check and change the tea towels daily to aid with drying the paper. When you feel it is well compressed you can leave it open to dry thoroughly. When it is completely dry it should peal easily off the tea towel.

Enjoy the Flowers

Enjoy the abundance of flowers many weeds offer in otherwise difficult parts of the garden - without letting them escape beyond the fence. Even the less showy weeds provide a nectar source for bees and insects when in flower, and sadly are often the only flowers in many gardens, making them valuable habitat plants. I find that some of the weedy Ruellia species fill empty spaces in the garden very well, especially those dry shady spaces under trees. They can give masses of colour in Autumn and Spring, and spot flower all year. I get visual appeal in an area of the garden that would otherwise be bare. Cutting back promptly after flowering can help limit seed spread and help keep the patch tidy. Cutting back gives me prunings to compost in situ, improving the soil and ensuring there is no opportunity for propagative material to spread.

Living Mulch

Let weeds act as living mulch, protecting the soil underneath. Callisia, Commelina and Tradescantias can be a nuisance but do make an excellent living mulch, growing densely and protecting the soil. The dreaded Singapore daisy can do this too. Their succulent leaves actually help to keep water in the top of the soil so they can be very effective around shallow rooted plants such as citrus and azaleas. They also flower well and are very good bee and butterfly attractors. Throughout a recent extreme hot and dry summer, *Callisia repens* has done very well spreading through my garden. Although I do not want this plant, for now it is on my side. It is forming a dense carpet to protect the soil and help to keep roots of other plants cool. It is also trapping any tiny amounts of rain and keeping moisture available in the surface of the soil.

Party Decorating

Ivy is a fairly common weed that can be very popular used as decoration for weddings, Christmas and other events. Cissus is another weed vine which is prolific in warm climates but can make a good ivy substitute when decorating. The leaves of cissus turn red in Autumn, so it can have added interest at that time of year. In reality, most vine weeds will work as an ivy substitute for decorating purposes. Choose a vine that has smallish and tough leaves. Large floppy leaves such as those of the ipomeas are likely to wilt too quickly to work for wedding or event decorations. I once used cats claw creeper and balloon vine quite successfully to dress tables, a marque and an arch for a wedding. It looked great and the guests, who were not avid gardeners, did not notice that it was all done with weeds. On the topic of weddings, I know of a lady who collected a large number of lantana flowers to use as confetti at a wedding. It was a great success, was fully biodegradable and stopped the lantana from setting seed.

Fairy parties, fancy dress or Halloween parties – weddings aren't the only occasion improved by some green decorating. What little girl doesn't want a fairy party at some time in her life? Fairy parties usually entail a lot of plastic and glitter, none of which is good for the environment. Instead, why not create a magical theme using whatever weeds you have available? Some of the Thunbergia and Ipomea weed vines are highly ornamental and would make great decorations or even fairy head dresses. By pulling out and using these vines in flower you will be enjoying the flower but preventing seed set.

I once used large bunches of ivy hanging in a doorway to create an entrance to a magical fancy dress party. This does not have to be just for fairy parties, cardboard bats or spiders would turn this into a Halloween theme. If you were to use large bunches of cat's claw creeper instead of ivy, the little claws would grab at unsuspecting guests, adding to the Halloween fun. Add edible weed flowers like dandelions, soursob and clover to the food table as flower confetti instead of glitter. Use dandelion wishes instead of glitter wishes, and perhaps instead of pass-the-parcel you could get the little fairies to pick a bunch of weed flowers to take home. Being weeds we are not worried about the children decimating our precious flower gardens, but we are still allowing the kids to interact with nature in a joyful way.

Harvesting weeds in abundance for things like decorating can be a good way to remove flowers to reduce seed set or to keep rapid growth in check. And it makes for fully compostable decorations.

Appreciating Trees

Chinese elms (*Celtis sinensis*) and camphor laurels (*Cinnamomum camphora*) are two trees that are much maligned in the subtropics and indeed are weeds that seem to produce endless seedlings. Pull them out as compost when they are small but appreciate them as magnificent trees if you have a large one – they offer shelter, homes and food for wildlife, erosion protection and valuable shade, in addition to being beautiful trees. Any large tree is not easy or quick to replace so appreciating it instead of rushing to remove it may be somewhat controversial but worth considering.

Plant a native alternative nearby so that in 10 years' time you can remove the weed tree and not be left without a tree. When it is time for the weed tree to go, consider instead of removal, kill the tree by ringbarking and let the dead tree frame provide nesting hollows for wildlife. If you are doing this, you will need to remove the excess branches for safety reasons, giving you branches to use for rustic furniture making, kids play, rustic fence building or even just firewood.

You could also try planting a native strangler fig into a fork in the weed tree and let nature gradually replace a weed with a native, all the while retaining a mature tree.

Willow Rooting Powder

Willow trees (*Salix sp.*) are a problem weed in southern Australia but not so much in the warmer parts. If you have access to willows, cut the soft tips of the branches and soak them in water for a few days. The resulting liquid apparently makes a good rooting stimulant for striking cuttings. Willows also make wonderful branches for weaving to create cane furniture and the like. Cut the branches before their autumn leaf drop and take them home so the leaves can drop into your compost. This prevents the substantial leaf drop from contaminating our fragile waterways.

Cubbies for Kids

Make cubby houses with any weeds large enough. I remember as a child that we made straw huts in the tall grass growing behind our back fence. We broke off some strips of grass that we could use to tie the bunch together at the top then climbed into the middle and squashed the inside flat enough to sit down. Each hut only had room for one child, but that was fine as we could each have our own space. These were living cubby houses. We squashed the middle of the clump of grass, but it was still rooted into the ground. We often got a couple of weeks use before someone came and slashed the long grass.

Any weeds that have bushy branches, palm fronds or long vines can be fun building materials for children. The nature play movement has been created in recognition of the fact that children are interacting with nature less and less these days. A landscaped garden offers little in the way of interaction. Give kids free reign on a patch of weeds and see what fun they can create, especially when they know they do not have to be precious about picking flowers and breaking branches. It seems ironic to me that we see patches of weeds cleared to create highly designed nature play areas for kids, with tough plants carefully chosen to bring the nature aspect back in. Our local school recently received a grant of $30,000 to create a nature play area. The money was spent on clearing the area of weeds, plants, rocks etc and then bringing in large sandstone boulders and cementing them in place. Oh, and adding a tap. If we had let the kids loose on the weed patch to begin with, we would have saved a lot of time and money, and the kids would have been just as happy.

Christmas Trees

Radiata pines are a problematic weed in Australia, and our favourite real Christmas tree. Perhaps instead of buying a weed tree each Christmas, you can find and remove one from where it shouldn't be. Obviously, you need permission to cutting down trees on land you don't own, even if they are weeds. There are fines for cutting down pine trees in state forest, even if they are on the outside of the plantation. There are several species of pine that can be used as Christmas trees and are considered weeds here in Australia.

Australian native pines do not have the distinctive pine fragrance to their needles which will help you to ensure you are not removing native trees by mistake. In other regions of the world, find out which local weed trees might make a good Christmas tree. The radiata pine is rare in its native California and Mexico, so do not go cutting one down there thinking it is a weed.

Instead of cutting down a tree, why not use weeds to create a Christmas tree? I use weed vines to weave a small tree each year. This works well as a table centrepiece or a floor decoration, depending on the size. You will need to gather rather a lot of vines, and the vines need to be used fresh. As they dry out, they are less flexible and more prone to breaking. Begin with seven branches. The length and thickness are up to you but as a starting point try the thickness of your little finger and approximately 800cm long. Tie them together at the top. Using the vine, start weaving from the top, tucking the end of the vine into the centre. There is no need to tie off the end, just tuck it in. As it dries out it will hold in place. As you weave remember to compress the vines you have woven to keep the weave tight. Don't pull too tightly as you weave however, or your tree won't flare out at the bottom. Once you have woven your tree, trim the feet to ensure it sits evenly and add some decorations that appeal to you.

Weed Profiles

Cobbler's pegs (*Bidens pilosa*) are exceptionally good plants for pollinators.

In this section I have profiled 42 weeds to help you see them in a different light. You will be familiar with most, if not all of these weeds, but you might not be familiar with their more interesting characteristics. It is through knowing a little more about them that we can stop hating these weeds and instead appreciate them as the amazing plants they are. This additional understanding also helps us to better manage them without turning to poisons as a first resort.

This isn't a comprehensive list and you might not find the backyard weed that you're most interested in here. There are usually a few hundred weeds listed in each local council area, which means that there are *thousands* of weeds around the world – far more than one book can hope to include.

This section is also not meant as an identification guide. Please use the scientific names given in this section to do more research of your own and look at multiple pictures for certain identification. It does, however, include common weeds that are found all over the world and in particular, the subtropics of Southeast Queensland.

I hope you find this section fascinating and I hope it encourages you to find out more about the weeds that have until now been a bother to you in your garden.

Asparagus Weeds

Asparagus sp

Wild forms of asparagus were sought out and eaten by peasants in the Middle Ages. They are still keenly foraged for in Southern Europe. All asparagus species produce edible shoots, which includes asparagus weeds – apparently. They all taste like cultivated asparagus, more or less. I have tried a couple of the weedy asparagus that grow around here: the ground asparagus, *A. aethiopicus* has a very strong bitter aftertaste that is hard to get rid of and I *do not* recommend eating it; the shrubbier *A. virgatus* however is quite pleasant to eat, even if the shoots are ridiculously slender; and the climbing asparagus, *A. setaceus syn A. plumosus*, which produces larger more worthwhile shoots that are delicious (the tip of the shoot is worth eating even as the shoot reaches for the sky, so long as it is harvested before the ferny leaves open). Given that this genus contains up to 300 species spread all around the world, I suggest you give your local variety a try. Do nibble carefully before taking a big bite in case you end up with one of the bitter varieties.

Climbing asparagus, (*A. setaceus*) has delicate ferny foliage but sharp barbed thorns on the main stem. The leaves are actually cladodes, meaning they are modified stems capable of photosynthesizing.

The identification of certain asparagus plants can be confusing. Names have changed and the different species hydridise readily, adding to the confusion the lack of certainty over the number of species that exist. Misidentification is rife, even amongst weed control professionals.

The wild asparagus species tend to have shoots are much smaller than the cultivated edible asparagus, making it difficult to harvest enough for a meal. If you have a patch of asparagus weed, I suggest slashing it to encourage the new shoots for harvesting. The rest of the plant is too fibrous to eat, and the berries of all asparagus species are toxic - never eat them. Many of the asparagus species flower and fruit readily and the red (or black for some species) berries can add to the ornamental value of these plants. Those that have spread as weeds have done so through the dumping of unwanted house plants, or via birds eating the seeds. Currawongs are rather fond of asparagus seeds. Even as declared weeds, many of these asparagus plants are still enjoyed as houseplants, or used in floristry. If you are enjoying any variety of asparagus in your garden, be it weed or ornamental, please do not let it seed. Cut it back as the flowers finish. Bees will be attracted to the perfumed flowers, but many asparagus species are self-fertile and can produce seed without pollination.

For those looking for an asparagus substitute whilst foraging, keep an eye out for the very young shoots of bulrushes (*Typha sp*). There is a myriad of edible parts to the bulrushes, including protein rich pollen. Apparently the very young shoots, harvested before they develop a dark green colour, can be used as an asparagus alternative. Similarly, Japanese knotweed shoots are a good asparagus substitute and very good eating apparently.

By constantly cutting asparagus (or any) plants back to harvest new shoots, not only will you keep this weed in check, but you will also eventually weaken and exhaust it. A plant that cannot photosynthesise will eventually weaken and die. If you are trying to eradicate this weed, you will need to dig out the crown. This is the section where the roots and stem join. The roots of the plant will not regrow but there is likely to be a network of underground rhizomes, which will reshoot if left in the soil. Those varieties with tubers on the roots can be cut at the base with the roots left behind. These are water storage tubers and will not regrow, contrary to what some sources say. Any regrowth will be from rhizomes left behind, not from the tubers. If the crown is underneath other plants in the garden, which it commonly is because all of the asparagus weeds prefer to grow in semi-shaded locations, try constantly cutting the tops off to exhaust the plant.

Asparagus weeds, particularly those with underground tubers, like free draining soils and are often found growing on steep sites where the roots are helping to control erosion. In these situations, the use of herbicides is recommended so that any soil disturbance is minimised (cut and dab method only, so you are keeping the herbicide contained within the plant tissues only).

Asparagus species feature prominently on the WoNS (Weeds of National Significance) here in Australia. *A. aethiopicus*, *A. africans*, *A. plumosa*, *A. scandens*, *A. declinatus* and *A. asparagoides* all make the list. They are extremely hardy plants tolerant of a wide range of soil and climatic conditions, which is why asparagus weeds can be found all over the world.

Basket Plant / Purple Succulent Weed

Callisia fragrans

This plant is edible and is a popular medicinal plant in many areas of the world. It is also a nuisance weed in warm climates. I have seen it for sale at high prices on websites touting its medicinal benefits. I have also attended garden club talks promoting this plant as a medical wonder plant, without referencing the fact that it is a weed. It grows and spreads so very easily, and while it might be useful, it is a weed and should not be marketed or bought without due regard for the harm it can cause in the environment. Basket plant has largely been spread through the dumping of garden waste and is a clear case of gardening habits contributing to the spread of weeds. Now that it is well established as a weed, broken pieces continue to be spread by animals and stormwater runoff, enabling it to continue spreading.

Basket plant (*Callisia fragrans*) has fleshy leaves that turn purple in the sun. The fleshy stolons appear jointed. Plantlets will form at the tip of the stolon and will root when they touch the ground. The flowers are white and highly fragrant, borne on long inflorescences.

Should you find this weed growing in bushland near you, weed it out and take it home. Grow it where you can control it. In cold climates it is a popular indoor plant for hanging baskets, hence the name *basket plant*. Being a succulent weed, it is exceptionally hardy and will happily grow in poor soils with limited water. The leaves will turn purple when grown in the sun but remain green in the shade, hence the name purple succulent weed.

Basket plant, and its miniature cousin, creeping inch weed (*Callisia repens*) have shallow root systems. They are both capable of forming dense mats which smother nearby plants. These dense mats can be effective as living mulch under trees. The moisture in their leaves helps to keep soil beneath moist and encourages an active humus layer beneath the plant. They are easy to remove, however you will find your humus layer will be lost with the plants as they are pulled out. The Callisia weeds are good candidates for solarisation, weed tea or deep smothering. My chickens will happily eat both species of Callisia weeds. Creeping inch weed is a huge garden pest here in the subtropics. Every tiny piece left behind will regrow. In wet weather it grows vigorously, smothers the garden and needs to be controlled. I don't try to eradicate it however, because when the weather is dry it will provide valuable soil protection and help trap moisture in the soil, which is good for nearby plants.

Callisia weeds will grow in a wide variety of soil types. Their very shallow roots will trap and create a humus layer which allows the plant to thrive independently from the soil below, also allowing them to grow over rocky sites such as steep, shady embankments. In this situation they are gradually helping to build soil and to protect those shallow soils from erosion.

Although it is edible, basket plant is not considered a desired food plant, and I cannot find any record of it being a diet staple even in its native Mexico and South America. There is however plenty of information about its value as a medicinal plant, with some even referring to it as the *home doctor plant*, or *home ginseng*. It is widely used as a medicinal plant in Mexico, but it is in Russia and Northern Europe where this plant has achieved hero status. It is too cold there for it to grow outside so it is used as an indoor plant only. This plant is sometimes recommended for absorbing indoor air pollutants (such as volatile organic compounds given off by paint, new carpet and other synthetics used in indoor decorating) and helping maintain indoor air quality. Personally, I would be cautious about using any plant to absorb pollutants if you are planning on consuming it. Perhaps keep a second pot elsewhere for harvesting and always harvest weed plants from areas free from major pollutants. Roadsides and industrial areas are definitely not suitable foraging places for most plants, especially plants like these that easily absorb pollution.

The medicinal uses of *Callisia fragrans* are many and varied. Chewing a leaf directly from the plant helps relieve stomach-ache and digestive troubles. I have found that chewing just one leaf can be very effective at relieving headaches (and hangovers). The leaves are very fibrous. Chew it until all the juice is extracted and spit out the fibre. The entire plant is a useful antibiotic, antioxidant and anti-inflammatory. The easiest way to use it medically is by making herbal tea.

One of the most popular uses for basket plant is to infuse it in oil to make a joint rub to treat sore muscles, sprains and bruising. Gardeners have appreciated this plant as an after-gardening remedy, not just for the muscle relief, but as a valuable skin repair herb. Other uses for it include to treat skin problems, asthma, arthritis, colds, cancer, thyroid problems, uterine fibroids, heart problems and many other conditions. In these circumstances it is usually made into a herbal tincture. In Russia, vodka tinctures of this plant are common in Grandma's medicine cabinet. It has strong immune supporting properties due to its high content of vitamins, steroids and flavonoids. Like all herbal tinctures, tinctures of basket plant should be taken in small doses and the supervision of a naturopath is advised.

Research suggests that small amounts of this herb are highly effective but there are no indications of problems from using too much. Vietnamese studies have reported no toxicity and no side effects. In making infused oil or tinctures, use the stem joints from plants with more than nine joints per stem for stronger medicinal properties.

While *Callisia fragrans* has been found to be highly medicinal, there are no reported medicinal uses for *Callisia repens*.

Although this plant is a popular indoor plant in cold climates, it prefers to grow in warm climates. It becomes a weed in subtropical and tropical climates.

Billy Goat Weed

Ageratum conyzoides

Billy goat weed (*Ageratum conyzoides*) has hairy leaves with a pungent odour. The fluffy flowers can be white through to purple.

What a pretty pest. Billy goat weed is one of the worst weeds of farmland in warm climates and is therefore much studied. It has a short lifespan and the ability to produce enormous amounts of easily dispersed seed. It is also highly adaptable to different soil conditions. Over grazing and overuse of fertiliser have been found to contribute to the success of billy goat weed. It has allelopathic properties which can encourage this weed to become dominant in the short term. It has also been shown to act as a highly effective coloniser and allows for the establishment of other plants within a couple of years. Studies have found that soil carbon and soil nutrients were significantly improved after a crop of billy goat weed had been allowed to grow for a period of time. This is a classic example of a weed species proliferating as a natural solution to poor soils where human activity has led to degraded environments.

Billy goat weed originated in the tropical Americas and was spread as an ornamental plant with European exploration in the late 1600s. The common name refers to the smell of the crushed leaves which apparently smell like a male goat. The leaves are sometimes listed as edible, although not regarded as particularly appetising. Many references refer to toxins, including a mass poisoning incident in Ethiopia where grain was contaminated with billy goat weed, so I would steer clear of eating this one. The leaves are however useful in rubbing on insect bites to relieve the itch and sting quickly. I have used it on both paper wasp stings and green ant bites and found almost instant relief from extremely painful stings. On this basis alone, I like to have some growing in my garden! It has been shown to have some anti-inflammatory and antiallergic properties, which is why it is so beneficial in relieving insect bites. These properties may also be why it has been considered useful as a scalp wash for dandruff. This plant has been attributed many different medicinal uses, however with the presence of toxins, I would recommend it for external use only.

The pretty flowers are much favoured by bees and beneficial insects. They are also good for attracting and providing habitat for predators of citrus mite, making it a beneficial companion plant for citrus.

If you have a problem with billy goat weed, I suggest chop and drop to exhaust the root system while allowing the plant to compost in situ and improve the soil. Mulching the garden will also be important in the control of billy goat weed to reduce the chance of new plants establishing from seed.

Billy goat weed prefers warm through to tropical climates and is a serious weed in Australia, the USA, Africa and Asia.

Bindii / Lawn Burrweed

Soliva sessilis

One of the most undesired lawn weeds is synonymous with summer in Australia, but it can be found upsetting feet in lawns in all warm climates. This low growing weed with the nasty prickles that stick into our delicate bare feet, making us hop and complain, is telling you that your lawn needs more attention. Apply all of the previously discussed lawn care and bindii will no longer be a problem. Bindii (and dandelion, plantain and clover) like slightly acidic soil, so an application of lime can adjust the pH of the soil and reduce its competitive advantage. This weed also prefers compacted, damaged soil which is low in magnesium. An application of dolomite or Epsom salts will help with the magnesium deficiency, but a good quality rock mineral product that is high in silica will be far more beneficial here, as it will help to open the compaction at the same time. Soil improvement efforts will help give the competitive advantage back to the lawn grasses. Bindii will not invade a healthy, thick lawn.

Bindii (*Solvia sessilis*) grows as a small rosette of feathery leaves which surround (and hide) the rosette of seeds in the centre. Seeds have a sharp upward pointing spine.

Bindii is an annual weed which sets sharp seeds, hence the reason it is so disliked. Regardless of the soil improvement you do, you still need to consider the seed bank in the soil. Use the plant's seed dispersal mechanism to your advantage. Mow using a catcher to expose the seeds and then walk over the area repeatedly wearing an old pair of thongs (for my international readers – jandles or flip flops). The seeds will stick into the bottom of the rubber, and when the thongs are full of seed they can be disposed of, taking the seed with them. You could also do this with an old paint roller or anything that the seeds will stick into. For large lawns try wrapping a turf roller in old carpet and rolling over the lawn. The grass clippings in the catcher of the mower are likely to contain bindii seeds as well, due to mowing low, and so should be dealt with appropriately. Use them to make weed tea so that the seeds break down but goodness in the clippings can be fed back to the lawn as a liquid feed. Keep the lawn healthy and thick and any seed still in the soil will not receive enough light to germinate the following year. After you collect the bindii seeds, adjust your mower to a higher setting to ensure you do not scalp the grass in future. You should also check that bindii seeds are not stuck in the tyres of the mower.

Bindii can be hand weeded easily in small areas. This is especially effective with a hand weeding tool or after rain when the soil is soft. Boiling water or steam are also effective on bindii, as is flame weeding, but will also kill the nearby grass, slowing it from covering the bare patch left behind by the dead bindii.

This plan also applies to any lawn weed with prickly seeds – yes there are others! Caltrop (*Tribulus terrestris*) and spiny emex (*Emex australis*) are two very unpopular weeds due to their ability to grow low in lawns and produce awfully sharp burrs. Both have at times been called puncture weed due to the ability of their burrs to puncture bicycle and wheelbarrow tyres. Both are ground hugging weeds with long tap roots, a great indicator that our lawns are suffering from compaction, nutrient deficiency and we are mowing too low. Spiny emex has leaves resembling ground hugging spinach, and is edible, so if this one troubles your lawn, weed it out by hand, eat it and then look to improve the conditions in your lawn. Bindii, on the other hand, is not edible – yes, I have been asked if it is! I even know a lady who once served it as garnish on an omelette because she mistook it for parsley. It is not known to be toxic, but that does not make it edible or palatable.

Yet another prickly lawn weed with a tap root is khaki weed, *Alternantera pungens*. This one seems to have spread enormously since the millennial drought here in Australia. Khaki weed goes dormant in dry times and the seed is able to embed itself, not only into our feet, but also the soil where it can wait for the return of wet weather. It propagates vegetatively (by stem cuttings and layering) as well as seed, so is easily spread by mowers. It cannot take hold in a think healthy lawn, so once again, good lawn care is vital to weed control in lawns.

Blackberry Nightshade

Solanum nigrum

Blackberry nightshade can be an indicator of moist, high nitrogen soils with low calcium and phosphorous. It also likes soils high in potassium, manganese, magnesium, boron, iron, sulphate, chlorine, and selenium and low in humates (which are sourced from organic matter, so equates to low organic matter). It will tolerate a wide pH range and a wide variety of soil types. The origin of this weed is uncertain with various sources stating it originated in the Americas, Europe or Asia. Given that seeds of the blackberry nightshade have been found in association with the earliest humans in British archaeological sites, the origin is most likely

Eurasian. Regardless of its origin, it has a cosmopolitan distribution and a very long history of use around the world.

Blackberry nightshade (*Solanum nigrum*) has flowers and berries that point downwards. Flowers have white petals that recurve with age, and bright yellow anthers. Berries are borne in clusters. Leaves are ovate to heart shaped and may be wavy or toothed at the edges.

It took me a while to get past being told as a child that this was deadly nightshade (it isn't) and to actually try eating it. Deadly nightshade (*Atropa belladonna*) does not occur in Australia at all but is common elsewhere. What is surprising is that deadly nightshade makes it onto weed lists here, including the Brisbane City Council weed website, and yet no locations of the weed have been identified. There are no observations of this plant at all in Australia listed on iNaturalist (which is a great tool for recording sightings of all plants and animals and is collecting very useful data). Deadly nightshade, also known as belladonna, is a weed in many parts of the UK, Europe and North America. It is a showier plant than either the blackberry or the glossy nightshades, with larger purple or yellow (not white) flowers and larger berries which are borne as single berries, not in clusters. Deadly nightshade certainly can be deadly, so it is worthwhile knowing what it looks like. Confusion between these plants is not new. In 1653 Nicholas Culpepper wrote: "Take care you mistake not the deadly nightshade for this: if you know it not, you may let them both alone, and take no harm, having other medicines sufficient in the book." This is good advice even today! It can be applied to any weed or herb; if you are not sure of the correct identification, leave it alone. It is likely that there are other plants with similar medicinal properties that are equally suited to your conditions.

If you are in Australia, the black berries on your garden nightshade weeds are fine to eat, but in time we may find new and more toxic nightshade plants entering our world of garden weeds, so always ensure you have the correct identification to be safe. In Hawaii there are several other Solanum species which are similar but do not have edible berries.

The berries of both the glossy (*Solanum americana*) and the blackberry (*S. nigrum*) nightshades are quite palatable when fully ripe and black. I find they make a refreshing little snack when I come across them while gardening. They should not be eaten unripe as they contain the same toxins as in green potatoes - solanine. This plant is in the Solanaceae family - a family which includes some of our favourite vegetables, including potatoes, tomatoes, chilies, eggplant and capsicum, but which is also well known for being highly toxic. Young leaves can be used as a potherb when cooked (boiled twice and the water discarded - not raw) and are a sought-after vegetable from Africa through to India and Asia. It has a high vitamin A content and numerous medicinal uses.

Solanine levels will vary according to the variety (there are numerous varieties of *S. nigrum* grown around the world) and growing conditions, including soil type, climate and the age of the plant. This may help to explain why it is a highly valued potherb is some cultures but not others. The solanine level is usually highest in the green berries, making them unsuitable for eating. It is the toxicity of these green berries which makes this weed a highly problematic and closely managed agricultural weed. Modern picking and sorting machines cannot distinguish these berries from green peas, which has led to rare and isolated cases of poisoning from green berries being found in frozen pea packets. While the solanine needs to be removed for eating, this is the source of many of the medicinal properties of blackberry nightshade. There is a long folkloric history of this plant's medicinal uses. Modern science is now looking more closely at this plant for possible new medicines and are finding that many of these folkloric uses have merit.

The leaves can be crushed and used externally on sores, ringworm, ulcers and skin conditions. Externally it is useful as an anti-inflammatory and antimicrobial and may have mild analgesic properties. Preparations of the whole plant have been found effective in preventing cancer and protecting the liver, but before you start trying to treat yourself, familiarise yourself with the symptoms of poisoning. This is considered a rather dangerous herbal remedy, best left in the hands of experts! It will be great to see modern medicines derived from this plant in the future. For now, you can make a medicinal skin cream with it using the skin cream recipe later in this book – for external use only!

I personally never eat the leaves. There are plenty of other weed greens to eat which don't pose a risk and don't need to be cooked first. I avoid almost any plant which needs to be cooked significantly to neutralise toxins – I don't trust my own cooking and don't particularly enjoy it, so I prefer to eat things that are safe when under cooked.

I enjoy the berries of both the blackberry and the glossy nightshade regularly. Only eat the fully ripe berries. If you find one that is a bit bitter spit it out – it is not ripe. Simple. Once again, our own bodies are protecting us from any toxic effects. I like the berries as a gardening snack straight from the plant, or with yoghurt or on pavlova - yum!

The closely related glossy nightshade (*S. Americana*) also has edible berries but I have not found reference to using its leaves. Interestingly, although the species name is Americana, it has been suggested that it actually originated in Australia, which is a big part of this *weed issue*. Tracing their origins is not always simple because they have travelled so widely with humans. These two nightshades can be distinguished by the fruit. The berries of blackberry nightshade face downwards on the stalk, while those of the glossy nightshade are held upright on their stalks.

Like all Solanaceae, the nightshades will attract the foliage-munching 26 and 28 spotted ladybugs. They can work as an excellent decoy plant but don't grow them too close to the vegetable garden – you want to draw the pests away not show them the way in.

The seeds prefer to germinate on bare ground, so a well mulched garden is far less likely to have this weed growing. It is usually easy to control with hand weeding or by repeatedly cutting the tops off to add to the compost. Both blackberry and glossy nightshades are common throughout temperate, Mediterranean, subtropical and tropical climates.

Brazilian Cherry, Surinam Cherry, Pitanga

Eugenia uniflora

Brazilian cherry (*Eugenia uniflora*) has ribbed, bright red fruit. Leaves are ovate, glossy and arranged in opposite pairs. Leaves smell spicy when crushed.

This small tree has become a weed of most tropical and subtropical parts of the world and is even establishing itself in the Mediterranean. It is not fussy about soil conditions, will grow in sun or shade and will tolerate occasional waterlogging. I've seen it survive and thrive after major flooding.

It is an attractive tree with glossy leaves and white flowers, producing abundant edible fruit which are much enjoyed by both humans and animals. If you have a tree, keep it pruned to a manageable size. This will allow you to reach and enjoy the fruit, in turn helping to keep the spread of this weed in check. Without pruning and management, Brazilian cherry will form a small tree with all the fruit well out of your reach and right where the birds will love it and spread the seeds. The seeds germinate easily, even without the help of birds.

The fruit is tart but high in vitamin C, vitamin A and antioxidants and makes great jams. I like eating the ripe fruit straight from the tree, but for some this is a little too tart. The fruit can also be used in relishes and pickles or used to make wine or vinegar due to its high sugar content. The darker red the fruit, the sweeter it will be. Use the slightly underripe orange berries for relishes and pickles, and the riper red berries for jams and sweets.

Studies have found it to have medicinal properties. In its native South America, it is used to treat stomach complaints. In Java the fruit is used to lower blood pressure.

It makes a good privacy hedge but if it is kept too tightly pruned you won't get the edible fruit. Pruning will help it form quite a dense hedge or shrub, and in doing so can be a great place for small birds or ringtail possums to nest. New growth is a coppery-pink colour which is quite attractive. I have managed trees in the garden as large lollipop standards very effectively with regular light pruning. This allowed me to turn existing weed trees into instant formal features when overhauling a garden. The regular light pruning meant that the colour of the new growth was a regular feature, but the tree was never allowed to flower or fruit.

While pruning the tree helps with preventing future seed set, be aware that past seed may still be viable in the soil and keep an eye out for and pull out seedlings before they can establish. Despite its weed status, the Brazilian cherry is still sold by specialist fruit nurseries and is still a desirable fruit tree. Personally, I would not pay money for one, they grow remarkably easily from seed and there are plenty of weed trees around to harvest seed from for free. Even better, I can harvest fruit from weed trees without needing to grow my own.

Brazilian cherry is a common weed throughout subtropical and tropical regions of the world, including northern Australia and southern USA. This is another weed that is seeing its range increasing with climate change. Given that it is commonly spread by fruit eating birds, consider removing this small tree from your garden and replacing it with local native trees that will provide a native food source for these birds. You may well find that in doing so, you too get to enjoy some local bush tucker – but be careful, not all fruits enjoyed by birds are safe for humans, so do your research.

Burr Medic

Medicago hispida syn M. polymorpha

Burr medic (sometimes known as burr clover) is a common lawn weed. In abundance it can indicate compacted alkaline soils which are low in nitrogen, calcium, phosphorus and soil moisture. If you have a lawn full of burr medic, refer to the section on lawn weeds to review your lawn management practices. The root system of burr medic is deep and spreading, so it is working at breaking up the compacted soil for you. It is an annual legume, which means it fixes nitrogen in the soil and is great for compost. It is closely related to lucerne (*Medicago sativa*), a well-known soil improver, excellent fodder plant and food for us by way of alfalfa sprouts. Burr medic also makes a good fodder and is regularly eaten in China. Cultivars of burr medic have been developed for use in agriculture due to their tolerance of a wide range of soil conditions, together with their value as fodder and as a soil improver.

Burr medic (*Medicago hispida*) has tripartite leaves (divided into 3 sections) that resemble clover. The tiny yellow pea flowers are clustered in the leaf stems. The seeds form inside a tightly coiled pod covered in prickles, forming a burr.

I like to leave this one alone in a lawn as I work on general soil improvement measures. It is a real ally in the soil improvement process, as is another deep-rooted, low-growing legume common in lawns, creeping indigo (*Indigofera spicata*). The flowers of both plants are appreciated by pollinators, but the seeds of both are rather prickly, so I find it best to chop the tops off before they go to seed. One of my dogs is rather fond of rolling in patches of burr medic and comes out covered in the burrs. It is easy to see how this plant spreads! The tops make great compost, and by leaving the roots behind and allowing the plant to continue to grow, I am allowing it to continue the important work it is doing in improving the soil. Burr medic is comparable to lucerne as a soil improver, so if you like to buy lucerne mulch for your garden, check the lawn first, you may already be growing a great alternative!

This is a much-hated weed by lawn lovers, but if they realised the good it was doing underground, they may see its emergence as a warning that soil care is needed and be grateful for the chance to fix the problem before the lawn is degraded any further. Unlike burr medic, creeping indigo is a poisonous legume, so avoid eating it, or allowing horses in particular to eat it.

Burr medic is a Mediterranean plant hardy in warm temperate to subtropical climates. It has however, been recorded across a vast range of climatic conditions, and so is likely to have a much larger tolerance range.

Canna Lily

Canna indica syn. Edulis

There is much confusion regarding the name of this plant due to the history of where the plant was found by modern botanists. This plant had already spread around much of the tropical world as a food plant before modern European botanists discovered it in India and gave it the species name *Indica* (meaning from India). It has since been established as being of South American origin and has been a food plant there for thousands of years. The confusion continues as another canna species known as achira, *C. discolor*, is also often referred to as *C. edulis*. Some taxonomists suggest that *C. discolor* is a variety of *C. indica,* others disagree. If taxonomists cannot agree if these are the same or different species of plant, then how are we to work this out? Both plants are often referred to as *C. edulis*, largely because both are edible. It may well be that the distinction between the species, if there is one, is not important here. For those who are keen to distinguish these plants from each other, *C. discolor* is more likely to have red edges to the leaves and stem and produces far less abundant seed. Less seed does mean this plant, whether variety or species, is less likely to become a problem weed.

It is also not a lily. Cannas are in the ginger family, not the lily family. This weed is commonly called Queensland arrowroot in Australia, as it was grown commercially in Queensland in the 1800s, to produce arrowroot flour.

Most of the showy garden cannas with large flowers are cultivars of this plant, but the weedy canna has small red or yellow flowers. It seeds prolifically. The hard seeds can be dormant for a long time. This one tends to be a bigger weed problem during wet summers, with storm water runoff being a major seed dispersal mechanism. It prefers moist soils and damp conditions, even growing in shallow ponds and waterlogged soil, but can store water in the stems and tubers, making it surprisingly drought hardy.

Canna (*Canna indica*) has a fleshy, branched rhizome. The upright stem is unbranched. The overlapping leaf sheaths can form a pseudo trunk. Leaves are large and simple. Flowers are tubular, formed by a fusion of sepals and petals. Flowers can vary in colour from green and yellow to red.

The tubers can be eaten as a starch, similarly to potatoes, or ground into flour. As a starch source, arrowroot is easy to digest, and therefore is excellent for infants or anyone with delicate tummies. This is why we were given arrowroot biscuits as children if we had a sore tummy. Sadly, these days commercial arrowroot biscuits contain almost no arrowroot flour at all and there is no longer an arrowroot industry in Australia. If you would like to eat arrowroot flour, you will have to grow your own.

The seeds are sometimes called Indian shot as they were used for bullets during the Indian Mutiny when bullets became scarce – yes, they are hard! They also make good beads for jewellery, are used in making instruments such as gourd rattles, produce a purple dye, and have even been ground and eaten. Apparently, in some remote areas the seeds are fermented to produce alcohol. The tubers can be used as you would use a potato, although tend to be a little blander. The tubers do not keep well so are best dug as required for eating. Choose the young tubers for eating, because like most root vegetables, they get woody with age.

The young leaves and shoots can be used as a cooked vegetable. The older leaves can be used for making food plates and wraps similarly to banana leaves. This plant tends to produce an abundance of leaves, more than most of us can eat. Luckily the leaves are excellent for compost and the entire plant is great fodder for animals. In warm and wet conditions, it is a very fast growing and dense plant. It can work very well as a border plant around vegetable gardens to provide shelter from wind or marauding animals. When it is no longer required, it can be cut for compost. As it is fast growing in warm climates, it can be very useful there as a source of biomass for composting. It is considered a useful alternative to comfrey for composting in warm climates. This fast-growing plant is useful for soil improvement, not just for being dug in as a green manure, but while it is actively growing. It is common to find that the soil is richer and has more worms under the tubers of canna then elsewhere in the garden. If you do not want this weed, you will need to dig out every bit of the tuber, which is not easy in heavy or waterlogged soils. You may find that by constantly cutting off the tops for compost, you can at least keep it under control until it eventually dies from being unable to photosynthesise.

Be aware that cannas have a high tolerance for pollutants, and so should not be wild foraged from areas which may be contaminated.

Canna is a weed of subtropical and tropical climates worldwide.

Chickweed

Stellaria media

Chickweed is an indicator of moist, fertile soils. This weed tends to appear in the cooler months here in the subtropics and then disappear as soon as the weather gets hot. In temperate climates it can grow all year round. In cold climates it is a spring and summer weed, dying down as conditions get too cold. If you don't have much of it, leave it be and let it die away naturally. If you have a lot of it, it is easy to pull out and compost as it is shallow rooted, but you may find that as you get to know this weed, you might just want to keep it around.

Chickweed (*Stellaria media*) is a low growing annual plant with tiny white flowers. Flowers have 5 bifid (divided into 2 lobes) petals nestled inside green sepals with fine hairs. A row of hirs also runs down the stems, alternating sides at the nodes. The leaves are hairless and have a hydathode at the tip (a pore for excreting excess water) so will often be seen with a drop of water at the end of the leaf when growing in wet conditions.

Chickweed is rich in minerals, so it is a great idea to let it act as a natural ground cover and return those minerals to the soil as it dies.

It is well known to be highly nutritious and has many wonderful medicinal benefits, so eating it is the best thing you can do with this wonderful weed. It is a valuable medicinal plant for skin complaints and can be used topically as well as internally. Chickweed is one of the supreme healers amongst herbs. It is very high in vitamins A, B and C and in chlorophyll, fibre, protein, minerals and other valuable phytochemicals.

Chickweed has a long history of use for both food and medicine. Modern science has supported ancient uses and found the plant to have many beneficial phytochemicals, supporting its use in wound healing, treating inflammation, eczema, and other skin conditions and as a general health tonic.

Chickweed is very soothing to apply externally to irritated skin. Rub leaves directly onto inflamed skin for almost instant soothing. Chickweed tea can be added to the bath for relief of inflamed skin, eczema, even shingles and varicose veins. It works internally for wound healing as the rutin in it strengthens blood vessels. It has been found to be useful in reducing inflammation, making it beneficial for joint pain and swellings. It is soothing for the digestive and respiratory systems. Other phytochemicals support its use as a gentle detoxification and have shown it to be helpful in slimming as it reduces the absorption of fats and carbohydrates. To get significant medicinal results with chickweed, as with any herb, you will be best served by creating herbal teas, tinctures or tisanes, however even if you are not getting a therapeutic dose, by adding it to your diet, you can be assured that you are getting valuable health benefits simply by eating as much of it as you can. As a herb that is so easy to eat, and with nutrients which are so readily bioavailable, chickweed is a weed that can benefit us enormously by adding it to our diets.

It has a mild pleasant flavour which works well in salads and on sandwiches but can also be used as a pot herb and added to any dish you would put green leaves in. I use it as a lettuce replacement to form the basis of a salad, add it to all sorts of dishes including a delicious chickweed, potato and leek soup, and on pizzas. If you have too much to eat it all, feed it to animals or compost it rather than waste the valuable nutrients it contains.

Take care with identification. Once you know it you will not mistake it, but if you don't there are a couple of *look-a-likes* which are not edible, including radium weed and scarlet pimpernel. Mouse eared chickweeds (*Cerastium* species) are edible but are not considered palatable. They have the same tiny white star shaped flowers, but the entire plant is hairy. Another of the look-a-likes is tropical chickweed (*Drymaria cordata*), which has slightly sticky stems and sticky seeds, making it easier to identify. This one also likes shady moist areas and can spread over large areas. The sticky seeds can be very annoying, especially if you ever wear socks near it or have pets. It is edible, although not as easy to eat nor as valuable a food as true chickweed. To help you be sure that you have identified true chickweed correctly, gently break the stem and pull the two sections apart. You will see numerous tiny fibres holding the stem together.

Chickweed and its look-a-likes are short lived annuals in warm climates, which set plentiful tiny seeds. If you don't want them to return next season, mulch over the area to prevent the seeds from germinating or grow a dense array of plants in that area to keep light from reaching the soil and allowing the seeds to grow.

Chickweed is hardy across all climate zones except the Arctic/Antarctic, the true tropics and arid climates. It is an exceptionally widespread weed.

Clover

Trifolium repens

Clover is a legume, so it likes nitrogen deficient soils where its ability to fix its own nitrogen gives it a competitive advantage. It can be an indicator of soils which are low in calcium, high in magnesium and compacted. The dense root system of clover makes it a good soil protector and it can be valuable for breaking up compacted soils. It is an extremely good fodder plant, wonderful compost plant, very popular with bees and beneficial insects, adds nitrogen to the soil and is fun to make daisy chains with – in addition to being edible. Clover and some of its close relatives are nuisance weeds in lawns. If you see a lawn full of clover, ask the owner if you can mow it for them and keep the clippings for your compost. It tends to be a bigger problem in winter and spring and dies back in hot weather. As with all legumes, treat it with low doses of a nitrogenous fertiliser and mow often to eradicate it. Or simply mow it often without the catcher. The grass and clover clippings will be high enough in nitrogen to feed and strengthen the lawn.

Clover (*Trifolium repens*) is a legume and on close inspection each flower head comprises many tiny whitish pea-like florets The leaves are trifoliolate with long petioles (leaf stalks).

Lawn care websites will promote the use of herbicides to deal with clover in lawns. As with most herbicide use, it ignores the underlying reasons that the weed is there, and a valuable opportunity to improve the growing conditions for the lawn is lost. Sadly, these herbicides are toxic to bees and other pollinators. You may see a warning in the fine print on the bottle of herbicide to only spray in the early morning or evening when bees are not active. If your clover (or other weed) has flowers, the bees will still come into contact with the residual poison when they visit the flowers. If you must use herbicides (and in this case I am sure you won't be, but will know someone who will), mow the lawn with the catcher on to remove the flowers and reduce any contact bees may accidentally have with the herbicide.

Clover is edible and has a high protein content but is not considered particularly tasty. It surprises me that this weed is one that fancy restaurants are using for wild garnish. Of all the weeds they could have chosen, this is not the tastiest nor the easiest to eat, being quite fibrous. Care should be taken if you wish to eat clover because in certain conditions it can accumulate cyanide compounds in the leaves, making the leaves (not the flowers) poisonous. This phenomenon is currently being investigated further but as yet there are no fail-safe ways of knowing if the clover you have is safe to eat – except by experience.

The perfumed flowers can be used for making a soothing, relaxing herb tea with a mild pleasant flavour or can be added into edible flower mixes.

The related red clover (*Trifolium pratense*) is a valued medicinal herb but is much less common as a weed.

Clover is common in all climates.

Cobbler's Pegs

Bidens pilosa

Amongst the most disliked seeds in the world are cobbler's pegs and its relatives! They have a lot of different common names, including beggar's ticks, jumping jacks, sticky beaks, farmers friends and burr marigold.

Cobbler's pegs do not like sandy soils and prefer areas of high rainfall. They can be an indication of soils low in calcium and phosphate, and high in manganese, magnesium, boron and potassium. Cobbler's pegs are found throughout temperate and subtropical regions of the world, with folkloric uses covering all regions. They like sunny positions, reasonably dry soil and are capable of producing thousands of seeds per plant. No wonder it has succeeded as a weed.

Yes, this one is edible, and highly nutritious too. Young leaves are best. Use it as a pot herb or in green smoothies. Or feed it to chooks and guinea pigs who love them. They make an excellent green manure crop if not allowed to reseed. The leaves and flowers can be chewed to relieve toothache. Research has found that they have a strong antibacterial action against dental pathogens. Many other medicinal uses have been ascribed to cobbler's pegs, making them a useful weed to have around, with research into their medicinal benefits ongoing. They have been found to be highly antimicrobial, anti-cancer, anti-inflammatory and even useful in treating diabetes. Their use against antibiotic resistant superbugs is also being investigated. During the 1970s the United Nations Food and Agriculture Organisation promoted cobbler's pegs in Africa as a starvation food. Research has proven that they are indeed highly nutritious, containing over 200 phytochemicals (some sources suggest over 300) which have value to human health. They are now being promoted as a safe and reliable source of nutrition to be valued even when other food is plentiful.

Cobbler's pegs (*Bidens pilosa*) can grow to 1.8m tall. It has leaves which are oppositely arranged and can be simple to pinnate in form. The upper leaves have 3 to 5 dentate, ovate or lanceolate leaflets. The flowers have 4 or 5 white ray florets surrounding tubular yellow disc florets in the centre.

With their strong antimicrobial properties, cobbler's pegs are great for boosting winter immunity. I like to add loads of the fresh leaves to our winter diet, and if colds start, I make a herbal tea using cobbler's pegs, plantain and paddy's lucerne. I will also add chickweed stalks to this brew after taking the leafy tops for the salad. As a herbal tea it has a mild flavour similar to green tea, so is easy drinking, even for children. A stronger herbal tincture can be made using the entire plant, seeds and all, steeped in vodka. A little added pepper and ginger have been shown to increase the effectiveness of cobbler's pegs. If you are interested in making herbal tinctures, it is best to do a short course in herbalism or invest in some good books on the topic. Tinctures are much stronger and should be made and used with knowledge of what you are doing.

Young leaves and flowers of cobbler's pegs are great in salads, and we eat a lot this way. The flavour is probably too strong to use as the basis of the salad, but a large handful in with other salad greens works very well. I use the older leaves anywhere that I would otherwise use spinach. They make great microgreens when large amounts of the seed come up in a garden, but this is far less likely once you start eating them as they do not get the chance to set seed. The seeds stick to skin and clothing and are a huge source of annoyance to gardeners. I like to let the seeds stick to me, and then brush them all off in a patch of gravel near the back stairs. This way the seeds all grow in one place where I can easily harvest them when young for the kitchen.

Be careful if harvesting cobbler's pegs in potentially contaminated areas. This weed has the ability to hyperaccumulate cadmium, so much so that it has been studied for use in cleaning up contaminated sites.

This wonderful weed is not only much appreciated by me; Bidens belong to the daisy family and as such are much favoured by bees and other pollinators. Unlike most other members of this family, cobbler's pegs still have an abundance of nectar and pollen once the plant is pollinated, and the petals have dropped. It is not uncommon to see bees happily foraging on what appear to be spent flowers. If you are keen to find pollinators, find the patch of cobbler's pegs and there they will be!

Cobbler's pegs are easy to eradicate through hand pulling. Lay the plants back down to compost in situ. This prevents seed spread and is also wonderful for building fertility into the soil. You will have to come back to the spot and keep pulling the new plants out as the seeds grow, but it is possible to eliminate all the seeds in the soil simply by letting them grow and pulling them out before they can reseed. I have done this very successfully on a large scale. The cobbler's pegs were completely eliminated as a result and the soil fertility was hugely increased as well. You can prevent the seeds from growing by mulching over them or filling the garden with plants. The seeds will not grow if there is no sunlight reaching the soil.
Cobbler's pegs are a serious tropical weed but are found throughout warm temperate through to tropical regions of the world.

Dandelion

Taraxacum officinale

Have you ever noticed how many weed killer adverts feature dandelions? This tends to upset weed lovers as dandelions are the posterchild for wonderful weeds.

Dandelions like acidic soils (pH below 7), so raising the soil's pH will help make it less suitable for them. They also grow well in soils deficient in phosphorous, potassium, calcium and iron, and which are compacted, as does its look-a-like, false dandelion (*Hypochaeris radicata*). Both plants can absorb huge amounts of minerals from deep in the soil, making both of these plants excellent for compost. Dandelions emit ethylene gas which inhibits the growth of nearby plants, helping them to become the dominant weed where they are growing. Use this to your advantage. If your pineapple plant is not fruiting, put some dandelion flowers in the centre of it.

True dandelion (*Taraxacum officinale*) always has a single flower per stem. The leaves are deeply lobed or toothed, which gives rise to the common name; "dent de lion", meaning lions tooth in French. It is also sometimes called "piss-the-bed", referring to its medicinal uses as a diuretic.

Weed it may be, but a world without dandelion wishes would be a sad place. Over the centuries gardeners have had a love-hate relationship with dandelions. At times they were valued and revered and at other times (including recent times) dismissed as a nuisance weed sent to ruin the perfect lawn. They came into widespread use in the eleventh century amongst the Arabs. By the Sixteenth Century dandelions were listed as an official drug in the European Pharmacopoeia. The Chinese and Indians have been using dandelions much longer.

True dandelions are much less common in the subtropics, preferring cooler climates, but they can be found and grown here. In warmer climates false dandelions are far more common. Dandelion leaves are not hairy like the false dandelion (which is also known as cat's ear or flat weed), and they have a single flower stem, never branching. The smooth cat's ear (*Hypochaeris glabra*) is also common in Australia. It has smooth leaves which might initially suggest dandelion but has a branched flower stem. False dandelion is also edible and has similar, if not as potent, nutritional and medicinal benefits, and for that reason is included in this profile. As the false dandelion tends to be a little less bitter than true dandelion, some foragers prefer them for eating. This bitterness is associated with the amount of phytochemicals in the leaf, so the more bitter the leaves, the greater the nutritional and medicinal benefit.

Dandelions have been valued as a pot herb and medicine for centuries. Due to that bitterness younger leaves are preferred, and if you are new to eating weeds you may prefer to eat them lightly cooked rather than in salads. Bitterness indicates that they are good for digestion. With their high levels of minerals, vitamins and enzymes, they are a good tonic herb. They are a renowned herb for the liver and kidneys, and a safe diuretic. The wonderful health-giving properties of dandelions is attributed to the fact that this humble plant is rich in vitamins A, C, and E as well as B-complex vitamins, iron, magnesium, phosphorus, potassium, biotin and calcium, and is high in antioxidants, healthy fatty acids and phytonutrients that fight free radicals, provide anti-inflammatory and immune system benefits. Not enough? The root contains inulin, a natural probiotic. It can be incorporated into both sweet and savoury dishes, and in a multitude of beverages. A multi-talented weed indeed.

The very young flower buds can be pickled and used as capers. To do this you must use the very young flower buds, which will likely be on a shorter stalk. Once the bud is close to opening, it is much less pleasant to eat.

Studies of false dandelion have found it to be a beneficial weed of pasture as it is eaten by livestock, and in the case of sheep it is eaten preferentially. It is superior to most grasses nutritionally, being high in protein, calcium and copper but low in fibre. It is commonly found in overgrazed paddocks and serves to increase the carrying capacity of those paddocks, especially in winter when other fodder plants are less prolific. In Australia false dandelion has been shown to be allelopathic (meaning that it produces chemicals which retard the growth of nearby plants) to itself so it does not form large patches to the exclusion of other plants as it can do in Europe. The rosettes of the plant are usually spread over an area with little if any overlap between plants, allowing other plants to grow between them.

False dandelion (*Hypochaeris radicata*), also known as cat's ear for the furry texture of the leaves, or flatweed as it grows flat to the ground, always has a branched flower stem.

The roots of both plants can be dried, roasted and ground as a delicious coffee substitute in the same way that chicory root can, and both are considered highly valuable as edible greens. Both plants have flowers that are highly attractive to bees, butterflies, beneficial insects and small children. The flowers are high in both nectar and pollen so are valued by beekeepers. To add the flowers to a meal, pull off the petals rather than trying to munch the entire flower head. The yellow petals are a good source of lecithin - should you need another reason to enjoy them.

Dandelions are anything but a reason to spray herbicides. If you are keen to eradicate them from your lawn, revisit the chapter on lawn weeds and change your lawn management practices. As your soil improves and your lawn becomes healthier, it will easily outcompete the dandelions. They can be eliminated from cracks in the paving using boiling water or steam, but your paving may be a little less interesting if you do so.

The dandelion group of plants include the hawkweeds, which also have a rosette growth form and similar flowers and so can be confused as look-a-likes. The hawkweeds are all edible.

Some, such as the white hawkweed (*Hieracium albiflorum*) are only a slight nuisance to gardeners, others are more invasive. Three hawkweeds are considered problematic and are prohibited weeds in Victoria (*Pilosella piloselloides, P. officinarum* and *P. aurantiaca*).

Dandelion is hardy in very cold through to warm temperate climates. False dandelion is also very cold hardy but is hardy in subtropical climates as well. False dandelion is more tolerant of both heat and humidity than is true dandelion and is therefore more common than true dandelions in warmer climates. Dandelions are weeds in all temperate to cold regions of the world.

Dock

Rumex spp

Docks can be an indicator of soils which are periodically waterlogged, indicating drainage problems. The various Rumex species are all edible but can be very different indicators of soil conditions. The common curled dock (*R. crispus*) can be an indicator of high nutrient soils, while sheep's sorrel (*R. acetosella*) prefers acidic sandy soil with low nutrients. Broad leafed dock (*R. obtusifolius*) can be an indicator of soils low in calcium and phosphorus, but high in potassium, manganese, iron, copper and salt. The Rumex species tend to have deep tap roots, making them great compost weeds, in addition to good eating. Docks are good accumulators of potassium, so are valuable as compost.

Docks have a slightly tart taste, are high in vitamin C, A, protein and iron and have numerous medicinal benefits. Curly dock is reputed to have four times the vitamin A content of carrots and is a useful leafy green when young. The leaves can be steamed like spinach, and the stems can be stewed with sugar as a rhubarb substitute. The large leaves can even be used as a vine leaf substitute for making dolmades.

The root of the dock is the most medicinal part, being used to support the gall bladder and liver and to improve digestion. I have read that a root can be added to a bottle of red wine, the wine re-corked then allowed to sit for a few days to increase the medicinal quality of the wine. This sounds easy but I have yet to try it.

Dock seeds are also edible. They are used as a grain, being related to buckwheat. They do need the chaff and shells removed first which will be enough to put all but the most serious weed eaters off. I have heard of them being roasted as a coffee substitute but again I have not tried this. The seeds can be sprouted and eaten as sprouts or microgreens.

The slender dock (*Rumex brownii*) has a slender upright growth habit, reaching approx. 60cm when flowering and seeding. Seeds are hooked and are spread by clinging to animal fur.

The seeds of slender dock, *R. brownii*, are hooked and are distributed by being caught on animal fur or our clothing. This dock is one of the most common docks in Southeast Australia, which is great because it is native here. It is often mistaken for an introduced weed because of its ability to grow on disturbed sites with poor drainage and low fertility. It has become an introduced weed elsewhere in the world, with the hooked seeds making it unappealing to gardeners. My Irish wolfhound constantly comes in from the garden covered in these seeds. I don't mind because this plant is as good eating as the other docks. I am happy to collect the seeds from his coat and throw them back into the garden or use them to grow delicious microgreens in the kitchen.

Sheep sorrel makes a good spreading ground cover. It is very high in antioxidants so is worth using a few leaves to add a bit of crisp freshness to a salad or meal.

All of the Rumex species are edible and have a sharp, tart taste. As with all edible weeds, the older the leaf the stronger the flavour, so larger older leaves are better cooked. They range in size significantly between species, but the arrow shaped leaf is common to all Rumex species, as is the three-sided seed. All species contain oxalic acid and tannins in addition to the above-mentioned vitamins. They all have astringent properties, which means they can assist in stopping bleeding (useful when you cut yourself in the garden) and are also well known as an antidote to nettle stings.

While docks have been widely eaten for centuries, they have at times ben rather unpopular as a pot herb. This is because they do not keep their green colour when cooked, they turn a yukky brown colour. A serve of steamed dock may taste great, but it is not visually appealing on the plate.

If you do not want docks growing in your garden, you would do well to look at first at any drainage issues you may have. They are deep rooted and will regrow when the tops are cut off unless you also remove the top section of the tap root. Deep tilling can help. They are perennial plants so will only persist for a few years before the plants die and are replaced by new seedlings. Heavy mulch and dense planting will prevent the next generation of seedlings from sprouting.

There are about 200 species of docks and sorrels (*Rumex sp*), although not all are weeds. Wherever you are in the world there is likely to be a local species with popular local folkloric uses.

Fleabane

Conyza bonariensis

Fleabane (sometimes also known as Canadian fleabane or horseweed) is one of the world's most opportunistic weeds. It produces thousands of seeds per plant, which are distributed by wind to find any empty space to take advantage of.

As a soil indicator, fleabane grows in soils which are low in organic matter and microbes and tend to be dry. It particularly likes silty soils very low in calcium and phosphate and high in potassium, magnesium and zinc. Keep it slashed to prevent prolific seeding and add pulled weeds to the compost.

Fleabane (*Conzya bonariensis*) has small white flowers with wind dispersed seeds. The plant grows in a rosette form, developing a stem when it flowers. Leaves are slightly furry, getting smaller as they go up the stem.

Fleabane can be made into a tea used to bath dogs to kill fleas, hence the name. It is poisonous however and not for eating. It does have significant medicinal properties but is not edible and needs to be used with care.

Externally the crushed leaves and flowers can be used to draw infection out of wounds. The plant is rich in essential oils which have been found to be antimicrobial, making this plant a useful external antiseptic for treating wounds. A tea made from fleabane can be used to wash wounds.

The insecticidal nature of fleabane can be put to use in the garden if you have this weed in abundance. Fleabane tea can be sprayed onto aphid or mealy bug infestations. The dried leaves can also be used in pets bedding to keep fleas away or crushed and sprinkled into the nesting boxes of chooks to keep lice away. I have found it more effective than chemicals for controlling lice on my chooks, with persistent infestations easily dealt with simply by adding pulled fleabane to the pen and nesting boxes.

Fleabane has shown strong antifungal properties, which are particularly useful against soil borne fungal pathogens such as those which cause charcoal rot, a disease most problematic in strawberries here in Australia. A tea made with the leaves and flowers of fleabane can be used in the garden where you have plants affected by fungal issues. Pour the tea directly around the base of the plant. All plants rely on positive relationships with fungi in the soil. Problem fungi tend to arise in situations of poor drainage and a lack of humus and organic matter in the soil. Therefore, use the fleabane tea to treat the immediate problem but also add some of the wonderful compost you have made with fleabane and other weeds to the soil to protect against ongoing fungal problems.

Fleabane does attract pollinators and beneficial insects and can also be valuable in providing erosion control. While it is best cut down before seeding, leave the roots in the ground on sites that are not ready to be replanted to give soil stabilisation. The fine, fibrous root system is able to bind fine silty soil, creating soil structure as it grows. This improves the soil, making it more suitable for other plants to grow there.

Do not use tilling to eradicate fleabane as you will find your fine soil very erosion prone. Instead, cut it down regularly and mulch the soil well to prevent seed germination. This will also help to adjust the soil conditions, speeding up the job the fleabane is trying to do for you. Keep the area well watered, as fleabane prefers to grow in dry conditions.

While it is more common in tropical and subtropical regions, it is also very well established in Mediterranean and temperate regions worldwide, and its range is increasing.

Green Amaranth

Amaranthus viridis

Amaranths can be an indicator of soils high in insoluble phosphorous and nitrogen, which is often caused by over fertilising with poor quality fertilisers. Amaranths are useful in making that insoluble phosphorous available to other plants, so this one is always best to mulch or compost if you are not eating it. It can also be an indicator of high calcium and potassium, another reason to compost it. It has a tap root and can be hard to pull out, but like all the amaranths, it is edible – seeds and all.

Green amaranth (*amaranthus viridus*) is an upright, branched herb growing to around 60 cm. It has terminal panicles (branches inflorescence). The tiny flowers are green and hard to distinguish from the seeds.

There are a variety of different amaranths and many are ornamental garden plants. All are edible. They were valued by the Ancient Greeks, Indians, Chinese and Aztecs as herbs of longevity for their many health benefits. While the leaves are very nutritious, being high in protein, vitamin A, C and iron, it is the seeds where the greatest benefit can be found. The seeds are gluten free, high in protein and tiny. Put a bowl under the flower head and shake. Most amaranths will drop seeds this way, but the green amaranth does not release its seed so easily. For the green amaranth, run your hand along the seed head gently and the seeds will fall off into your hand. You may not get enough to make a cake from the flour, but you will get plenty to put into a meal for added goodness. I eat a lot of green and the more ornamental red amaranth, both the leaves as potherbs and the seeds added to many dishes for an added nuttiness. I love them added to risottos, porridge, curries and even cakes and brownies.

Like all seeds, the seeds of amaranths are high in essential fatty acids and proteins. The seeds can be used to sprout. Sprouts and microgreens are wonderful ways to access nutrients in the seed, but in a leafy form. Amaranth seeds are becoming available in health food stores as we look for healthy alternatives to our modern diet. Before you go ahead and buy amaranth seeds, check your garden, you may already have a variety of them.

With green amaranth, the seeds tend to be somewhat hard to distinguish from the flowers, as both are small and green. I simply take the entire stem tip to add to a meal, using the leaves, stem, flowers and seeds. Unlike other amaranths, green amaranth seeds do not need winnowing to remove the husks before using.

In Vietnam and throughout Asia the various amaranth weeds are used as a diuretic and laxative, and the green amaranth is used to treat dysentery and snake bite.

Like all the amaranths, green amaranth sets large amounts of seed. The small round seeds are easily buried under mulch, so mulch can be very effective in keeping this weed under control. As with all weeds that seed prolifically, your gardening practices will play a huge part in controlling this weed. If you leave empty spaces, the seeds will grow, and you will have the next generation of weeds enjoying your garden. The plants are easily dealt with by hoeing, which removes the top of the tap root.

A. viridis is found in all warm temperate through to tropical regions of the world. In the Americas amaranths are known as pigweed (a name we use for purslane here in Australia), possibly because pigs like to eat the deep tap root.

Ground Ivy / Creeping Charlie / Alehoof

Glechoma hederacea

This herb is native to Europe but a significant pest in northern America and southern Australia and New Zealand. It was one of the earliest plants to be brought to the Americas during colonisation due to its medicinal properties.

Before you attempt to rid your garden of this weed, you may wish to harvest a pile of leaves for drying and using medicinally, although one of its many properties is a high vitamin C content which is lost with drying and storage. Eating it fresh in salads will ensure you get a good dose of vitamin C. Once dried, you will still get many other health benefits associated with the high levels of antioxidants. It makes a bitter tea which is good for digestion and all sorts of tummy troubles but may need to be sweetened with honey. It is helpful for coughs and colds, liver and kidneys, and can be added to your bath to soften the skin and relieve back ache. While once used as something of a panacea, in more modern times the main herbal uses of ground ivy are in treating respiratory and gut conditions. It should be used with caution during pregnancy, however. The name *alehoof* derives from the Saxon use of the herb to flavour and clarify beer before hops was available.

Ground ivy (*Glechoma hederacea*) has slightly hairy leaves which are round to kidney shaped with round-toothed edges. It has square stems that root at the nodes.

This plant is not a weed in my subtropical climate, so when I saw a variegated version of it at the nursery, I decided to give it a go, knowing it would be harder to keep it alive than to stop it spreading. It very quickly reverted to the plain green form and has thrived in a shady spot in my garden over the last few years (which have been very wet). I use a few leaves chopped into salads where it is useful for increasing the nutritional value of meals. I have turned to this weed to add to my herbal arsenal against cold viruses. I have now found that it is becoming smothered by other ground cover plants better suited to my climate, so I will have to intervene if I do not wish to lose it.

Ground ivy is a creeping ground cover in the Lamiaceae family, which includes mints, and this herb does behave somewhat like mint in its ability to spread rapidly in moist shady gardens. It even has a flavour vaguely reminiscent of mint. It likes rich soils high in nitrogen but dislikes high doses of nitrogen, especially in urea form. This weed does not like being weed on! A dose of urea in the form of urine will set it back, so sending the boys out to pee on the plant regularly will do it in.

Ground ivy is soft leafed and although it likes shady conditions, it will tolerate quite a lot of sun in temperate climates. Its liking for growing in the shade rules out solarisation as a control method. Smothering is a good control option with this weed, however as it likes low light, make sure your smother layer is deeper than 15cm to ensure it is effective. As with all soft leaved plants it is susceptible to weed control techniques which involve burning – urine, vinegar or steam. This weed is usually least wanted in lawns. For any shade loving weed to thrive in lawns, it may well be that you are trying to grow lawn in an area that is too shady for grass (even the more shade tolerant varieties) to grow well. Refer to the chapter on lawn weeds for more ways of controlling weeds in lawn. Ground ivy is perfectly capable of spreading into sunny areas if conditions are right, so ensure you are maintaining a strong healthy lawn able to resist invasion. You may also consider whether or not it would be better to convert the shady lawn to a garden bed or accept the ground ivy as a useful lawn substitute for shady areas.

Ground ivy is a weed in all temperate regions of the world.

Henbit

Lamium amplexicaule

Henbit is an indicator of fertile or cultivated soils. It prefers sandy soils low in calcium and organic matter. It is a delicate little weed with pretty flowers. It is edible and good for attracting bees and beneficial insects. As the name suggests, it is good feed for chooks as well. It is high in vitamins, iron and fibre and can be eaten raw or cooked. As this weed stays quite small, it is a good one for leaving in or near the vegetable garden to increase the insect diversity and to eat while waiting for the vegetables to be ready for harvest.

Henbit (*Lamium amplexicaule*) has square stems and overlapping, deeply veined leaves which are slightly furry. The tiny flowers can be white through to purple.

Medicinally henbit can be used as a blood purifier and for treating any bleeding problems. The roots of henbit are host to an array of mycorrhizal associations which would suggest that this little weed is working to increase the important biota of the soil. Given that this weed likes growing in cultivated soils which are low in organic matter, we can see that in hosting these mycorrhizae, it is helping to repair soil structure damaged by cultivation. At the same time, it is building organic matter in the soil by growing fast and dying, adding organic matter as it composts. This is a reminder to not underestimate the value of some of the smaller, less significant weeds. We may not be able to see the important work they are doing, but that does not mean that the work is not happening.

I personally am not fussed on the flavour of this weed as a salad green but am happy to toss some leaves into a cooked dish. In the garden I enjoy knowing it is beneficial so am glad to let it be there.

Henbit is usually easily managed by hand weeding, light hoeing, vinegar or boiling water. It is an annual weed so will be short lived. It will usually emerge early in spring. Mulching the soil will prevent the seeds from growing.

Henbit is a widespread invasive weed throughout the UK, Europe, North America and southern Australia and New Zealand. In warmer areas this weed is less aggressive and therefore less problematic.

Japanese Knotweed

Fallopia japonica syn Polygonum cuspidatum

Japanese knotweed is one of the world's worst weeds and much hated almost everywhere it is found. This remarkable weed is one of the few that can out do couch grass and nut grass for growing through concrete! It has deep rhizomes and an incredible will to survive. This ability to grow through concrete and asphalt has seen it cause a lot of damage to homes and infrastructure and highlights just how tenacious it can be. This is a survival mechanism in its native habitat where it is well adapted to regenerating after being buried under larval flows on the side of volcanoes. If only Nineteenth Century botanists had considered this remarkable survival strategy before taking samples home to add to botanic gardens!

Japanese knotweed has proven so troublesome that in the UK you can have trouble getting insurance or a mortgage if you have it on your property. This weed apparently increased the cost of building the 2012 Olympic stadium by 70 million pounds. The enormous cost was due to the difficulty of dealing with Japanese knotweed. It must be carefully and completely dug out of the soil, and then disposed of by burying it more than five meters deep or at a licensed site. Every piece must be bagged and transported by a licensed contractor. You can be fined 5,000 pounds or spend two years in prison if you allow contaminated soil or plant material to spread into the wild. That is serious stuff! I am not aware of any other weed having this much impact at an urban level.

Japanese knotweed (*Fallopia japonica*) has hollow stems and obvious, raised nodes. New leaves are reddish, turning to green as they unfurl.

Japanese knotweed has already spread through much of North America but is considered to still be invading Australia and New Zealand. In Australia there are currently only around 20 locations where it is established, all located in southern states. It has been recorded as naturalised in isolated pockets in Australia since 1979. I would suggest that if in that time it has not become the terror here that it has in the UK, Europe and North America, it is probably unlikely to. But I can understand why we need to proceed with caution!

While I have encouraged you to see weeds in a positive way throughout this book, the damage this weed can do certainly seems to outweigh any redeeming features. And yet there are more and more foragers saying they are finding it easy enough to control, once you understand it.
It is edible and medicinal but that is little recompense for its ability to spread, to survive and to form very dense monocultures to the detriment of all other species. There is some work on the possibilities of harvesting it to make medical supplements (it is a good source of resveratrol, the antioxidant found in red wine and berries that can be beneficial for the heart)

but at this stage this is not likely to solve the weed problem. As with Arundo reed, it shows promise as a biofuel but again, this is more an idea than a reality at this stage.

Most weed management websites suggest that the only alternative to digging up every tiny piece of this weed, is to use the strongest herbicides available, repeatedly for three years. Wow, that is hard to kill. The crown and rhizome can survive burning, which is not surprising if it evolved to withstand larva and can remain dormant for many years until disturbed. Like *all* plants, the root system will eventually become exhausted if it is harvested enough and not allowed to replenish itself - this means harvest *all* shoots before any have the chance to develop fully and photosynthesize. Reports suggest that fortnightly mowing of the shoots will exhaust the rhizomes in two years. Japanese knotweed becomes dormant in winter, so you will get a break from your war on this weed but be ready to take up the fight as spring arrives and new shoots appear. Breaking of dormancy is the most vulnerable stage for the plant, (think of animals coming out of hibernation, they have used up their fat stores and tend to be skinny and hungry) so any efforts to control it will have greater impact at that time.

The young shoots are edible and can be controlled by livestock. Cows and goats will keep these young shoots in check. As the new shoots are supposed to be a good asparagus substitute in savory dishes, perhaps if you don't have livestock, eating these young shoots yourself might do the job. It can also be added to sweet dishes where the flavour has been described more like a lemony rhubarb. I haven't eaten it, so cannot comment on how good it may be. It can only be eaten when the shoots are young and soft. As the stems develop and become woody, the leaves can cause blisters in the mouth. The best possible way of controlling this weed without poisons is continual harvesting.

I have seen tarps recommended as a means of smothering this weed. It works by watching for little *"tents"* appearing as the shoots push up. Stand on these and break off the shoot. A specially developed material made of reinforced polyethylene laminate has been used under roads and construction sites and has been effective in stopping the shoots penetrating tarmacs and concrete slabs.

Frost damages the young shoots and can limit the spread of the weed. Summer drought can also be a limiting factor. As weather patterns shift towards more extreme weather, including more extreme frosts and droughts, this may be a limiting factor, however climate change also weakens the resilience of natural vegetation which in turn will favour weeds. As with all weeds, Japanese knotweed is a successful coloniser and is found in disturbed areas, with little evidence of it invading native forests. It is much easier for humans to blame the invading plant than it is for us to recognise the damage we have done by creating the disturbed sites ripe for invasion by weeds.

It certainly seems highly unpopular to try and tackle Japanese knotweed without using herbicides. As I have said, there is a role for careful and limited use of herbicide, and this is one case where herbicide could be a part of a combined approach to dealing with a particularly pernicious weed. Herbicide alone is not necessarily the answer as it can take repeated applications to be effective. If herbicide was a straightforward answer, this weed would not be the enormous problem that it is.

Whatever means of control you choose (and I would steer you away from herbicides as much as possible), do not expect the job of tackling Japanese knotweed to be a quick or easy one, but do not despair as persistence will pay off.

This highly invasive weed is currently widely distributed throughout the UK, Europe and North America, and has limited current distribution in Southern Australia and New Zealand. It is considered to have huge potential for future invasive spread.

Please note that the *Japanese knotweed* listed on the Brisbane City Council weed site is *not* the same plant, it is a completely different plant with very different weed characteristics, but a confusion of common names. It is *Persicaria capitata*, a low growing ground cover.

Jewels of Opar / Pink Baby's Breath

Talinum paniculatum

This weed does not seem to make it into many weed guides, probably because it is a tropical weed, common in warm areas and uncommon in cooler climates. At least, not yet. Climate change is likely to change this. The presence of this weed in your garden if you do not live in tropical or subtropical areas can be an indicator of subtle changes to climate conditions.
This is a weed capable of making the most of poor soil conditions and returning valuable nutrients to other plants nearby as it dies down for winter dormancy. It has a deep fleshy root, allowing it to survive drought and allowing it to extract an enormous amount of nutrient from poor soils – which makes it highly nutritious to us, to animals and as compost. I add it to almost any meal that you might hide (or not hide) anything green in. I have seen it growing abundantly in both clay and sandy soils. Being tropical in origin, it will die down in cooler weather, which makes it susceptible to rotting in areas with cold wet winters and heavy soils. When our winters here in Brisbane are warmer, it does not die away as completely.

It is grown in hospital gardens in the Philippines where its medicinal properties are highly valued. In Vietnam it is used to treat excessive sweating and uneven menstruation. In China it is used as a ginseng substitute, reflecting one of its common names, leaf ginseng. Although they are unrelated plants, the gnarled fleshy root of pink baby's breath (NOT related at all to the common baby's breath which is Gypsophila) does resemble the ginseng root, and like ginseng it is used for restoring vitality. Other traditional uses include as a reproductive tonic, an aphrodisiac, to treat general debility, inflammation, and coughs.

The leaves have mucilaginous properties making them great for immune support.

Jewels of Opar, or Pink baby's breath (*Talinum paniculatum*) has fleshy oval leaves. The tiny pink flowers develop into bright red seed capsules held on delicate stems. The root is fleshy and gnarly, resembling ginseng somewhat, giving rise to another common name, leaf ginseng.

The seeds are high in omega 3 and although tiny, are easy to shake into a meal along with some chopped leaves. The tiny pink flowers make this plant quite ornamental, but it is knowing that this weed is one of the most nutritious and health-giving foods I can feed my family that makes this a very welcome weed in my garden.

Eradicating any weed that has a tuber can be challenging and this one is no exception. Start by dealing with the seeds – mulch the garden well so that seeds cannot germinate. The time to deal with it is when the plant starts to shoot after winter dormancy. Dig it out if you can. If you can't, you know that your soil needs further improvement. Be aware that breaking up the roots by hoeing will only encourage those root pieces to grow! It can be readily exhausted by continual harvesting. It can also be controlled by smothering. If you have managed to dig it up, don't add the roots to the compost, instead use them to make a wonderful weed tea to feed other plants.

Although this is a pantropical weed, its range is extending, and climate change is likely to accelerate this. A couple of ornamental varieties including a variegated and a lime-coloured form are available in the US although are not particularly common in Australia yet. As this plant is becoming more popular as an ornamental outside tropical and subtropical regions, together with it being a prolific seeder and a tough plant, I think the range of this weed is one to watch.

Lamb's Quarters / Fat Hen

Chenopodium album

Lamb's quarters are an indicator of moist, high nitrogen soils. It prefers loamy or even sandy soils and summer rainfall areas. It is very tolerant of poorer conditions, but the size of the plant can be an indicator of how fertile the soil is. Under good growing conditions it can reach two metres high. Lamb's quarters have been listed as one of the five most widely distributed plants in the world.

This highly nutritious weed has been widely used around the world for centuries both as a pot herb and as a fodder plant. It is rich in minerals and therefore makes great compost. In some instances, lamb's quarters can bioaccumulate potassium, phosphorus and calcium which makes it a valuable weed for the compost if we are not eating it.

Like other members of the amaranth family of which this plant is a member, it seeds prolifically with tiny seeds that can be added to meals. In common with its close relative, quinoa (*Chenopodium quinoa*), the seeds are a nutritious food. They are high in protein, vitamin A, calcium, phosphorus and potassium. It is a prolific seed setter, capable of producing between 3,000 and 20,000 seeds per plant or more. As with the green amaranth, I like to collect the stem tips, complete with small new leaves and seeds, and use them in the kitchen. They can be dried easily and stored for later use. The seeds keep their nature, but of course the leaves crumble into a green powder when dried. These dried leaves can be stored with the dried seed, as it is simply extra goodness.

lamb's quarters (*Chenopdium album*) has waxy green leaves with a whitish underside. The older leaves are more deeply toothed than younger leaves. It has a branched inflorescence with dense but tiny white flowers.

Lamb's quarters have a long and extensive history of use as food, dating back to prehistoric Europe. Lamb's quarter seeds were an ingredient in the porridge that was the last meal of the Tollund Man, Europe's most famous bog mummy, who lived 2,400 years ago. Lamb's quarter leaves were a preferred potherb in Europe before the arrival of spinach in the Fourteenth Century. Even today they are a popular wild edible because they are fast growing, nutritious, common and easy to use in any dish that calls for *greens*. Lamb's quarters are considered an underutilised food source in our modern world, but then again, aren't so many of these very nutritious *weeds*.

Traditional medicinal uses of this weed include being used as a blood purifier, diuretic, hepatoprotective (protecting the liver), preventing scurvy, and anthelmintic against hookworm and roundworm. Pharmacological studies have substantiated the anthelmintic properties and found it to have contraceptive properties for both sexes. Best not eat too much of it if you are trying to have a family. Other studies have found this plant to have significant antimicrobial and antioxidant properties. Another reference suggests that lamb's quarters is useful for dental health and bad breath simply by chewing on the raw leaves. It can be used to treat skin issues by applying crushed leaves to insect bites or soaking a face washer in a tea made from lamb's quarters and applying that to the affected area.

A scientific study analysing both lamb's quarter and cobbler's pegs done in 2011 summed up their findings as follows:

"The results of this study showed that the leaves of *B. pilosa* and *C. album* contain appreciable amounts of proteins, fat, fiber, carbohydrate and calorific value, mineral elements, polyphenols, and generally low level of toxicants. Their antioxidant and antibacterial activities further lend credence to the biological value of this plant. Thus, it can be concluded that *B. pilosa* and *C. album* leaves can contribute significantly to the nutrient requirements of man and should be used as a source of nutrients to supplement other major sources. The plants also have high biological activities hence may be of great medicinal value."

Which basically means if you have these plants eat them! The florets can be used as substitutes for broccoli. They are smaller than broccoli but can be very prolific. By cutting the flowers off and eating them, you are effectively tip pruning, and the plant will produce even more flower heads. The seeds are easily collected but you need to keep an eye on the plant and check daily when seeds are setting. Seeds can be used in the same way as amaranth seeds or sprouted and added to salads.

Lamb's quarters are another weed with almost worldwide distribution. It is most vigorous in temperate and subtemperate zones but can also be a serious weed in subtropical and tropical zones. In warmer climates *C. murale* is more common. It is very similar to *C. album* but will have red stems and possibly veins. Both are valuable food plants and behave similarly in the garden. Controlling these weeds will rely on pulling it out before it can set seed, or if it has already set seed, creating garden conditions where seeds cannot germinate. Both Chenopodium weeds are developing herbicide resistance, and both set enormous numbers of seed per plant which can be viable for decades in the soil. The good news is that seed buried deeper than 2.5cm is unlikely to germinate, so mulching is extremely effective in managing these weeds. The seeds of these summer annuals are triggered to germinate by longer day length. You can use this characteristic against them by using either mulch or growing a crowded garden. Both reduce light levels at the soil surface and reduce seed germination.

Lantana

Lantana camara

Lantana is possibly Australia's most hated weed. It certainly is a WoNS (Weed of National Significance) here but is also a significant weed in all warm climates around the world. Approximately 30 different insects have been introduced to Australia as hopeful agents of biological control of lantana. Four of these have had limited success, and some such as the lantana bug, have become pests in their own right. It's a similar story in other parts of the world where lantana is also a weed.

Lantana (*Lantana camara*) has square woody stems. Stems and leaves are course and prickly. Flower colours are highly variable but usually feature two colours: red, orange or pink with yellow in the centre. This allows the plant to attract both insect pollinators and birds for seed distribution.

Lantana is primarily pollinated by butterflies and moths but is attractive to bees and other pollinators as well. Birds love the seeds and are the major vector of spread of this plant. Studies have shown that small areas of lantana in urban areas will actually increase the populations of small birds such as fairy wrens. In these situations, where the lantana is unable to spread due to being surrounded by urban development, perhaps we do not need to be so aggressive in controlling it and we can take the time to evaluate whether or not our control methods (usually herbicides) are doing more harm than the plant itself. There are many people who think any harm done in controlling weeds, especially those as environmentally significant as lantana, is worthwhile. I hope that I am convincing you in this book that this is not the case. Harm done to the soil in particular is likely to only encourage further weed problems. In the case of lantana in restricted urban environments where habitat is scarce, aggressive removal can be very detrimental to local wildlife populations. It is a balancing act and control should be done with care and consideration.

There are numerous ornamental varieties available to gardeners. These may have reduced seed set but they are not sterile and are able to cross pollinate with wild plants. This increased genetic diversity can make a weed far more difficult to control. For this reason, ornamental varieties are also restricted plants in Australia, and as gardeners we should not be adding to the problem by deliberately planting any variety of lantana at all.

Lantana is a restricted weed therefore you do have a biosecurity obligation to control it on your property, which is not easy! Controlling lantana is time and energy intensive, even if you include herbicides in the control regime, so it is easy to see why this weed is so hated. It has allelopathic properties so can form dense thickets, taking over open habitats and agricultural land. It has a high oil content so is highly flammable and can increase the intensity of bushfires. But as with all weeds, this evil monster has another side to it. Lantana has useful properties which, while they might not make up for its domination of the environment, might help us to find small ways of using it to our benefit.

Lantana leaves are toxic to animals and there have been significant stock losses in all areas of the world where this plant is a weed. Surprisingly our little swamp wallaby is one of the few mammals that are able to eat lantana without harm. Lantana is largely toxic to humans too. The berries are edible when fully ripe. They taste sweet and almost like chocolate. Unripe berries are not edible, so make sure your berries are completely black before eating. A few unripe berries will result in tummy ache and nausea, a lot can be serious, even fatal. Some sources, including research done at the University of Texas, has found even ripe berries to be toxic. I have eaten small amounts of berries to no ill effect, as have many other wild foragers. The berries have long been used to make jams, jellies, pies and cordials in its native Central America. As the jury is out on this one, I would suggest you proceed with caution when eating lantana berries, and perhaps don't serve them to others, even if you are comfortable eating them yourself.

The berries can cause increased photosensitivity, so even if you are comfortable eating lantana berries, don't eat a lot and then spend the day in the sun or you will be at risk of increased sunburn.

Lantana is surprisingly useful. We have already mentioned its value as a habitat plant, and the fact that the ripe berries are edible with a mild chocolate flavour, but wait, there is more. The leaves are course enough to be used as sandpaper on fine grained timber. Grab a pair of gloves and use the rough canes for weaving baskets or natural fences. The timber of lantana is resistant to rot and termites, which is not great news in the environment but does mean any furniture, baskets, garden stakes or fences you make from it will be long lasting.

The leaves can be brewed into a tea which is a very effective fungicide for use in the garden. Lantana is an insecticide, so you can also use this tea on aphids and mealy bugs. This is a tea for the garden, not for us as the leaves are toxic! If you are making garden brews such as lantana tea, have a separate set up so you are not using the same teapot for your own tea.

Crushed leaves can be added to puddles and ponds to kill mosquito larvae. This one should be done thoughtfully though, as it is a good insecticide and will also kill other aquatic insect larvae such as that of dragonflies and hover flies. The main action here is that it stops the larvae developing into adults so should not be harmful to bees, wasps and butterflies drinking from the puddle. Try floating a sprig of flowers with a few leaves attached in a bird bath to keep mosquitoes out. You can burn lantana in a jar at night in place of commercial mozzie coils. You will want relatively green material for this to ensure it smoulders rather than burning quickly. As with commercial mozzie coils, try to avoid breathing the smoke, it is not good for us.

If you are *out bush* lantana might be useful in other ways. Try using a piece of cane as a natural toothbrush. Lantana is toxic so shouldn't be eaten but has many medicinal benefits, including being a natural antiseptic and for treating toothache. In its native Central America, it is commonly taken internally as a medicinal tea, so I imagine that using a stick to brush your teeth is not going to do any harm, assuming you don't then eat the stick. The crushed leaves can be applied to insect bites, cuts and wounds to relieve pain and sterilise the wound. The crushed leaves can also be applied to sprains for pain relief.

Lantana is used medicinally around the developing world for a wide variety of complaints. It is not considered edible, so it is not going to be a bush food and you should do further research before using it medicinally.

As a weed, lantana prefers degraded and open situations, having limited shade tolerance. It tolerates a wide range of soil pH and soil types but does not like wet feet. Controlling lantana will take time and require repeated efforts. It can be controlled through repeated slashing or burning – only use burning to control lantana if you have a fire permit from your local fire authority! Burning repeatedly is an effective way to control lantana but comes with risks in a fire prone country like Australia, so must be done with great care. Repeatedly taking the top off any plant, including lantana, will exhaust the root system, weaken the plant and eventually it will die. When you take the top off the plant and expose the soil below dormant seeds will germinate. This is the perfect time to grub out these seedlings before they can establish, removing this seed load from the soil. In a smaller area this seed load can also be controlled through heavy mulching. Due to the allelopathic nature of lantana you will not be able to establish new plants until the main root systems start to die. Be careful of letting stock into a paddock where you are working to control an infestation, they may eat the regrowth. Goats will eat lantana and in some instances are a great control agent. New research is finding that the toxicity of lantana can vary by strain, so in some areas it can be eaten relatively safely by goats, in other areas it is fatal. Check with other famers in the neighbourhood before letting your goats eat lantana. This variation in toxicity is not linked to flower colour or growing conditions so is very difficult to identify and is another reason why we do not need greater genetic diversity from cross breeding with ornamental varieties throwing any curve balls into the lantana control story.

Madeira Vine

Anredera cordilfolia

Madeira vine is another weed that is much hated here and yet this weed is highly sought after in Asia and the Americas where it is eaten. The leaves and tuberous roots are edible, but the aerial yams are not. Some sources do suggest that the aerial tubers are edible, based on the fact that they have medicinal properties, but as we have already established, just because a plant has medicinal properties does not mean it is safe to make a meal of.

The leaves, stems and underground tubers are mucilaginous which would suggest it can offer immune support and indeed it does have medicinal uses as an anti-inflammatory. In Chinese medicine it is used to heal liver problems, for obesity and to improve men's libido. Apparently, the leaves are delicious lightly stir fried with garlic and ginger and a dash of soy sauce. The tubers are best baked as a starch, similar to a potato.

Madeira vine is used as food and medicine in many tropical regions of the world. Scientific studies have demonstrated that the leaves do have antibacterial properties and are efficacious in wound healing even for wounds infected with *Staphylococcus aureus.* It has been shown to be effective in the treatment of burns, fungal conditions and skin issues. The medicinal uses in different countries are varied and extensive.

The chooks also like this one but I never give them vines with aerial tubers, otherwise those aerial tubers will remain in the compost the chooks create and grow as soon as I spread it on the garden – no thank you! Ridding an area of this weed involves regular checks for any bits of roots or aerial tuber that have been left behind and started to sprout. It is possible to be rid of it in one summer if the gardener is vigilant. Constant harvesting (to eat or compost) will exhaust the tuber. Beware however, if the area is not kept well-watered the aerial tubers and the underground tubers will enter a dormancy phase which could last for up to 20 years. The arial tubers can also be dormant for many years, so even if you appear to have eradicated this weed, it pays to remain vigilant.

Madeira vine (*Anredera cordifolia*) is a vigorous vine with fleshy heart shaped leaves and warty aerial nodules. It has masses of pale creamy flowers in racemes from late summer to autumn, which are highly perfumed.

As this weed is such an aggressive and problematic vine, I do *not* recommend adding it to your weed patch, but you will not have any trouble finding a gardener or bush regenerator happy for you to harvest theirs. It is a restricted plant under Queensland legislation, and nationally is a Weed of National Significance (WoNS). It is illegal to sell or give away plants. All steps must be taken to limit its spread. If you are collecting plants to eat, make sure you bag up and remove all aerial tubers, and do not leave broken pieces of stems on the ground either as they too will regrow. It originates in subtropical South America and has been spread through all warm parts of the world, probably as an edible plant. In Australia where it is a very serious environmental weed, it is thought to have been spread by people planting it over the old outdoor dunnies (toilets) as it was used as a laxative. I'm sure the sweet, perfumed flowers were also appreciated in this setting.

Perhaps if we ate it more, we would not only be healthier, but we would be part of the weed solution. If we concentrate on eating the weeds in the garden before we try to poison them to grow vegetables in their place, we will be working towards a healthier environment and the weeds will not be so problematic.

Where you find madeira vine growing, make a point to collect as many of the aerial tubers as you can from the ground, and carefully dig the underground tubers. Broken pieces of the tuber will regrow making this a very difficult weed to eradicate. It should not be added to the compost or green waste due to its incredible ability to grow from a tiny piece but is well suited to solarisation or weed tea. Efforts to eradicate this weed can at first seem to make the problem worse. Broken pieces of the root, or any pieces of plant left on the ground will regrow and the infestation will appear to be getting worse. Keep at it! By regrowing, it is showing you the bits you missed and is giving you another chance to get them.

Herbicide is useful in eradicating this vine, as with other vines that have huge underground tubers, such as cat's claw creeper. The cut and dab method should be used. Cut one stem, dab it with undiluted herbicide immediately, then move on to the next stem. Unfortunately, the cut vines in the trees will stay alive long enough to produce lots of arial tubers. Make sure you also dab the top section of the vine so that the herbicide is drawn into the arial parts of the vine to kill it. I have seen sources suggest that the cut stems should be allowed to wick a 5% solution of herbicide for two months. That is not going to be easy to achieve, so try the cut and dab method on both sides of the cut stem first.

Whilst madeira vine is a current problem weed throughout subtropical and tropical regions of the world, it is increasingly being found in warm temperate regions so there is potential for the range of this weed to extend further into these regions. It prefers moist fertile soils but is highly adaptable to soil types. It is very tolerant of both sunny and shady situations. In shady situations it can be hard to notice the thin young vines until they are well up into a tree and accessing light. The above-ground parts of the plant are killed by frost which will limit its spread in cooler areas, but it will regrow each spring from the underground tuber, so do not become complacent if you live in a frost prone area.

Mallows

Malva parviflora, M. neglecta, M. sylvestris

Small leafed mallow (*Malva parviflora*) has small five petaled, pale pink flowers at the base of the leaf stalks. Seed pods are the cheese wheel shape, distinctive to the mallow family. The leaves have 5 – 7 shallow lobes and can have varying hairiness.

As a weed, mallows tend to occur in areas disturbed by human activities. They have a deep tap root, often growing in disturbed, compacted soils with low humates and poor drainage. They are very good for breaking up clay soils. They are an indicator of soils low in organic matter and with a hard crust, low in calcium and high in magnesium, potassium, iron and selenium. While this is a great edible weed, there is a note of caution. In areas of high fertiliser use mallows can build up nitrates which is not so good for eating and can be quite toxic to livestock. High fertiliser use might make plants grow quickly but it does not make better quality food.

Mallows tend to be very pretty and are good for attracting bees and butterflies. Mallows are also a great edible weed – leaves, flowers and seeds. Young leaves can be eaten raw or added to cooked dishes, the flowers used to decorate cakes or as garnish and the seeds (harvested while still green) added to risotto or curries and the like. Mallow seeds have a high carbohydrate content. Look for the distinctive *seed cheeses*, so called because the circular layout of the seeds resembles a cheese wheel. Mallows have been used as a staple food and medicine since ancient Roman times and are still widely eaten throughout much of the Mediterranean, Middle East and China today.

M. sylvestris is by far the prettiest of the group, with large pink flowers. Sometimes considered a weed, sometimes a desired cottage garden annual. Hollyhocks, the popular and showy cottage garden flower, are closely related, as is the true marshmallow both of which are in the Althea genus. Both are edible and have similar properties to the mallows, although marshmallow is considered the most medicinal. The first marshmallow sweets were made in Ancient Egypt using the marshmallow flowers to add colour and the roots to thicken the mixture. Modern marshmallow sweets do not contain any marshmallow plant ingredients.
To quote the ancient Greek herbalist, Pliny: "He whosoever takes a spoonful of any of the Mallows, shall that day be free from all the diseases that may come unto him." If only it were that simple! They are wonderfully safe medicinal plants, however.

All the mallows have a high mucilage content so in addition to being useful for thickening soups, stews and marshmallow sweets, they are extremely beneficial in supporting the immune system. They can be made into a soothing herbal tea to treat sore throats, coughs, stomach aches and ulcers. They have very little flavour so your herbal tea can be made tastier by adding peppermint or lemon balm.

Mallows can be used externally by crushing and warming then applying to minor wounds and insect bites or by being added to homemade creams and ointments. As an ointment it can be very soothing for inflamed skin conditions. For a good skin repair ointment try also adding some chickweed and plantain, the recipe for which can be found later in this book.

The list of conditions treated by mallows is extensive. It is an extremely safe herb without risk of overdose. In essence it is very soothing and healing being highly anti-inflammatory, regardless of what the problem may be. The medicinal benefits of this weed can easily be gained by adding plenty of it to your diet if you have it growing in abundance. It is easy to eat in salads or in any dish as an edible green. In my subtropical climate mallows are only available in winter so I like to harvest as much as I can for infusing in oil to make skin creams, or to dry and add to meals later as *green powder*.

There are different mallow species found throughout the world. All are edible and have similar medicinal properties. Be careful not to confuse them with the false mallows which are not considered edible, such as *Malvastrum coromandelianum* or *Modiola caroliniana,* which can usually be distinguished by having yellow and orange flowers respectively, instead of pink or white.

I found that the best way to rid my garden of mallows was by improving my soil, which was unfortunate, as I had not intended to get rid of them! Mallows will be more tolerant of improved soils in cooler climates where they are not such a short-lived plant. Continual heavy harvesting will exhaust the plant and reduce seed set.

Mallows all prefer cool climates and as such are less common in warmer climates. They will grow and become weeds everywhere from cold through to subtropical climates. Small leafed mallow, *Malva parviflora*, is perhaps the most heat tolerant of the mallows and the most widespread mallow weed in Australia.

Morning Glory

Ipomea sp.

Morning glory (*Ipomea indica*) is a strongly climbing vine with dark heart shaped leaves. The leaves and stems are covered in tiny brown hairs. The trumpet shaped flowers have 10 overlapping petals.

Many Ipomea species are significant environmental weeds around the world, and many are known locally as morning glory. Most (not all) are aggressive vines with underground tubers, assisting them to survive unfavourable conditions. The tubers are often part of the difficulty in controlling and eradicating these weeds.

Mile-a-minute (*I. cairica*) is a common weed in this genus and has an edible tuber, which should be cooked before eating. It is considered bitter even after cooking, so it might not be worth adding to the modern diet. I haven't eaten it myself so am giving no recommendations here.

Just because something can be eaten does not mean it should be. In my opinion there are plenty of other options for better tasting edibles amongst the weeds.

If you are in the northern hemisphere, the weed vine you know as mile-a-minute is *Fallopia baldschuanica*, and completely unrelated to these Ipomeas.

Another common weed in this genus is our well-known vegetable sweet potato (*Ipomea batatas*). While the sweet potato has highly edible leaves, the leaves of mile-a-minute should not be eaten. Like many other species of Ipomea, they have a strong purgative effect meaning it brings on vomiting and diarrhoea.

The seeds of the mile-a-minute and some other Ipomeas are useful as soap. Rub them under water to get a lather. The plant is considered a good fibre plant that is suitable for weaving. The fibres from the stems have been used to make sponges, and as with many of the Ipomeas, has been used medicinally to treat skin infections and snakebites when applied externally as a poultice.

Yet another Ipomea weed, the common morning glory (*Ipomea purpurea*) has been reported as a food plant in Africa but as it also has purgative properties, I would not suggest eating this one either. Rather, stick with the close relative (and declared environmental weed) sweet potato. Yes, our beloved food crop, the sweet potato, is a declared invasive weed in many warm regions. So too is a popular Asian food crop, kang kong (*Ipomea aquatica*), although it is mainly found in tropical areas. Both have whiteish flowers.

Kang kong is another weed with unclear origins. It is a highly regarded edible which has become a pan tropical weed. First Nations people did not seem to make much use of this plant, but this is perhaps not surprising as edible leaves did not feature highly in their diet, probably due to the high number of very tough and highly aromatic leaves amongst Australian native plants. Kang kong was present in Australia before colonisation, but First Nations people in the north did trade with Asia, so this is not surprising. Kang kong is a weed as far south as northern New South Wales and is a weed of significance in the USA where its spread seems to be controlled by watercourses freezing in winter. Freezing of watercourses is not common in Australia, which suggests that this weed has further to spread here, especially when climate change is factored in.

There are around 50 native Australian species of Ipomea. Some are known as bush potato and their tubers were a food staple for First Nations people in northern desert regions. Worldwide there are a few hundred species. With so many Ipomea species looking very much alike, it is important to know which is which before you start sampling them. Think purgative and you will probably be cautious enough! One reference suggests that the flower colour is a clue.

Purple, blue and red flowers are not normally edible but white flowers usually are - usually, but not always! If you have weedy ipomeas, I strongly suggest you make sure you know exactly which one you have before you experiment with eating any part of it.

Part of the attraction of these weeds is their magnificent flowers. The dark purple flowers of morning glory (*Ipomea indica*) have seen this spread as a desired garden plant, albeit one that proved almost impossible to control. There are numerous ornamental varieties, such as *Heavenly Blue,* which are still commercially available and not considered a weed. I would still treat these with extreme caution. Plant it only where you can control it without it spreading into nearby hedges or trees and prune it to prevent seed set. The flowers of all of the Ipomeas are enjoyed by bees.

Eradicating any of the ipomea weeds can be very difficult due to the deep root systems and underground tubers. Being vines, it is important to keep them out of tree canopies where they can do a lot of damage. Pieces of stem can regrow very easily, so take care to remove all the pieces from the ground when you are clearing it. As I am pulling out the vines, I hang them on tree branches to die. This way they cannot take root on the ground but will dry out and die, then fall and compost, returning what they have taken from the soil. As for those tubers, it is not always possible to dig them out and get them all. If you have easy access, you may be able to exhaust the tuber by constantly removing the tops, otherwise the cut and dab herbicide method can be useful.

Morning glories are happy to grow in temperate, Mediterranean, subtropical, and tropical climates. Ipomea weeds are found worldwide but do tend to be less of a problem in colder climates. The related convolvulus weeds are also found all over the world and have greater cold tolerance, especially the dreaded bindweed which is the gardener's enemy number one in the UK. Like the ipomeas, the convolvulus weeds also have rhizomatous roots, spreading far and wide out of sight under the ground, and can form underground storage tubers.

Onion Weed

Nothoscordum inodorum

Onion weed tends to prefer poor soils, so soil improvement will play a huge part in successful management of this weed. It can often be found in heavily compacted clay soils which makes digging out the tiny bulbs almost impossible.

It is related to onions and garlic but lacks flavour, so while it is technically edible, there is no reason to eat it. Other related weeds such as wild garlic and three-cornered onion are far more flavourful and can be used in cooking if they are growing in your area.

Onion weed (*Nothoscordum inodorum*) is a bulbous plant with flat, strappy green leaves. The bulb is usually surrounded by numerous bublils that break away to form new plants. The flower stem is cylindrical and hollow. Flowers are star shaped, borne in clusters in an umbel arrangement at the end of the stem. Each white flower has 6 overlapping petals and prominent stamens.

Onion weed is much hated where it has become weedy but sought after elsewhere as an ornamental for its pretty perfumed flowers. Where it occurs en mass in a garden, it can be quite lovely. It makes a very good cut flower, and a bunch will fill an entire room with perfume. This is one weed that could do with a fresh perspective. We are taught that it is bad and must always be fought. If we loosen our desperate grip on neatness in the garden, this weed really is not so bad. Look at it like this – it is a pretty and perfumed bulb that will happily grow en mass to give a lovely meadow style to a lawn or garden. Massed bulbs are very hard to do in warm climates, and yet here we are fighting one which will work for us if we let it. Just like freesias and daffodils in cooler climates (where they are often declared environmental weeds), onion weed can easily be mown down throughout the year and will come up and flower in spring before the grass needs to be cut again. If we have it anyway why not appreciate it? As it is difficult to get rid of, being resistant to both poison and pulling out, eradication can be almost impossible. I know of gardeners who have tried to dig each bulb out, who have spot poisoned, poured boiling water over it and still it comes back. Boiling water works best if you scrape the soil back to reveal the top of the bulb first, so is ridiculously tedious in lawns. Its spread can be limited by removing spent flowers and preventing it from setting seed. I know of one gardener who likes it so much she gathered the seed to sprinkle in another part of the garden. They did not grow there as that section of her garden was well mulched and had significantly better soil than where the onion weed was growing.

Onion weed is hardy in warm temperate through to subtropical climates. Other allium weeds prefer cooler, less humid climates.

Paddy's Lucerne, Sida retusa

Sida rhombifolia

Sida retusa (*Sida rhombifolia*) develops woody stems. The leaves are arranged alternately. They are paler on the underside of the leaf. Flowers arise single on stalks and are yellow with five slightly overlapping asymmetrical petals.

This weed has a tap root and a half and is very difficult to pull out once it has taken hold. That means it is drawing nutrients up from deep in the soil. I have seen it growing equally well in both clay and sandy soils. It has a high magnesium content so compost it under gardenias or other plants that like a lot of magnesium. It is indicative of soils that are low in calcium, phosphate, iron and sodium but high in potassium. As with many other weeds, it prefers to grow in soils with low organic matter and lacking soil microbes.

It is edible (as is the closely related weed *S. cordifolia*) and can be used as a tea substitute, although it does not have a strong flavour. It has a high mucilage content and is good for respiratory and sinus conditions. It has a wonderful ability to soothe the digestive system and can help alleviate both constipation and diarrhoea simply by chewing a couple of leaves. The entire plant is used medicinally. The roots of the plant contain ephedrine. Ephedrine is closely related to the key ingredient in a number of hay fever drugs however it can cause heart arrythmia, so prolonged or heavy use is not advised, especially for those with heart conditions. Ephedrine levels are higher in *S. cordifolia* and herbal preparations of this weed are banned in the USA because of this, despite a long history of safe use in Ayurvedic medicine. Both *S. rhombifolia* and S. *cordifolia* are highly regarded in Ayurvedic medicine.

This is another cosmopolitan weed with a long history of use. In Australia, First Nations people used it to treat diarrhoea, the Europeans to soothe mucus membranes, the Indians to treat malaria and in Mexico it was considered calming to smoke it. It is in the mallow family, and like all mallows has very soothing healing properties. As this herb acts to soothe mucus membranes it is very useful in treating inflammatory gut conditions and digestive issues.

The whole plant can be used to make a healing herbal tea or crushed and made into an effective cough mixture. I often eat the leaves raw or add them to salads or cooked dishes. A few leaves a day is very beneficial for anyone who has chronic sinus conditions, as I did before I started nibbling this weed regularly. I had a lovely experience when a lady came up to me at a garden show and hugged me saying that I had changed her life by advising that this weed was good for reactive sinuses. She tried it and found that it freed her from the constraints of chronic reactive sinuses and in particular, a reaction to perfumed flowers. I was thrilled but not entirely surprised, it really is a very effective weed. It has done the same for me.

I have found at times when this is growing too abundantly that it is easy to harvest leaves and dry them. Once dried (placed in the sun on a couple of hot days is enough) they crumble easily into a green powder which is easy to sprinkle into any meal for added goodness.

One common name for this plant is Indian hemp. It was once used as a commercial fibre plant, so could be fun for anyone interested in fibre crafts to have a play with.

I have also heard anecdotes of it being used as a toothbrush in Fiji, simply by chewing on the highly fibrous sticks. Given that the stems are also medicinal, having anti-inflammatory and antimicrobial properties, they would probably be very effective as a toothbrush.

Sida retusa prefers a tropical or subtropical climate but is not uncommon in temperate and Mediterranean climates. Related *Sida sp* and *Mallow Sp* are found in every climate zone.

Pepper Tree

Schinus molle and *S. terebinthefolia*

Brazilian pepper tree (*Schinus terebinthefolius*) has dark green leaves which are compound, meaning each leaf is made up of from 3 to 15 leaflets arranged in pairs with a single leaflet at the tip of the leaf rachis.

Both the Peruvian (*S. molle*) and the Brazilian (*S. terebinthefolia*) pepper trees are noted as environmental weeds here in Australia, and in subtropical regions worldwide including Florida and subtropical regions of the United States. They are both small trees and both can be found in gardens. Here in Brisbane, it is not hard to find the broader leafed Brazilian pepper tree as a weed tree in older gardens. Although introduced mainly as an ornamental, both trees produce red berries which can be used and have been sold as pink peppercorns.

S. mole is by far the more ornamental of the two trees. It can reach as much as 15m with a gnarled trunk and beautiful weeping foliage. It is also far more drought tolerant than is the more tropical *S. terebinthefolia* and is common in dry inland regions and in the southern states. It was introduced as an ornamental plant and many old trees feature in heritage gardens and even have heritage protection. Heritage value is yet another area where we find conflicting motivations around weed plants. So many of the plants that have become weeds were the garden plants of our earliest gardens, and so if we are to give any heritage protection to these early gardens, we must also include the plants they contain regardless of weed status.

S. mole tends to be allelopathic, meaning little grows under its canopy. This helps to create the look of a dramatic feature tree in gardens but is problematic in the environment where the lack of soil cover can result in erosion problems. This problem is less pronounced with *S. terebinthefolia* and seems to only develop when the trees are mature.

These trees are in the cashew nut family (Anacardiaceae) – together with mangoes and poison ivy, and contain highly irritating chemicals, so handle them with care. I have never had a reaction when handling them, but neither am I allergic to mangoes. They are not at all related to true pepper (*Piper* genus).

As a problematic environmental weed, I would *not* advise you to go and plant one of these trees, but if you do happen to have one, I suggest you make use of it. If you collect the berries to make your own pink peppercorns, you will be preventing seed spread. You will however have to beat the birds to them. Birds are a major vector of seed spread of pepper trees, so try and include native food plants in your garden to give them an alternative food source. I have seen *S. terebinthefolia* hedged well and even a very large specimen kept pruned beautifully as a lollipop standard. In this case the extreme pruning means no flowers and fruit, so no weed spread.

The plants do have extensive medicinal uses in their native South America including using the leaf tea to treat coughs and colds. If you do want to use this tree for anything other than the berries as peppercorns (remove the outer skin of the berry first), do some research and it is probably best avoided if you have any allergies to mangoes or cashews. Even burning the dried branches can cause a reaction if you have sensitivities.

A related tree, *Toxicodendron succedanuem*, or Japanese Wax Tree is also a reasonably common weed. It too has edible berries, but they do need to be prepared first to remove highly irritating chemicals from the shell of the berry (as do cashew nuts).

While some of our weeds do have some very interesting properties and are able to be eaten, I tend to think that if there is a chance that we could do ourselves harm by not preparing them correctly, they are best avoided. There are plenty of weeds that make excellent eating without needing special preparation and without risk.

Pepper trees have become an invasive species in many Mediterranean, subtropical and tropical climates.

> **Other Weed Pepper Substitutes**
>
> If you are keen to find a pepper substitute, but don't have a weedy pepper tree, try dried paw paw seeds. I use them mixed 50/50 with true peppercorns. It is a great way of using the abundant seeds when the paw paws are in season, with the added benefit of being extremely good for gut health and anthelmintic. Anthelmintic means they get rid of worms. If you have young children, it will be well worth adding some dried paw paw seeds to your pepper grinder. Paw paws are generally not considered an environmental weed, but for any gardener in warm climates who has ever thrown the seeds into the compost, they can easily become one in your garden.
>
> There is another group of weeds that are used as a black pepper substitute - *Lepidium spp.*, the peppercresses. These small weeds in the brassica family are often unnoticed until they flower and seed. The leaves are edible and peppery in flavour, but it is the seed pods that are used as pepper. The seeds are distinctive, being contained in small round disc shaped seed pods. The entire peppercress plant, like all brassicas, is edible raw or cooked. The flavour can vary a little between species, but they all contain a pungent pepperiness. *L. bonariense*, with its ferny foliage, has an unusual peppery aniseed flavour.
>
> One of the most common of the peppercress weeds is Virginia peppercress, *L. virginicum*. It originated from the Americas but is found throughout most of the world. It has a long history of medical use, including for expelling intestinal worms (similarly to paw paw seeds), and for treating poison ivy rash. If you find yourself having a skin reaction to the pepper trees discussed above (which are related to poison ivy), you could try rubbing the rash with peppercress leaves.

Plantain

Plantago major and *P. lanceolata*

Plantain can be an indicator of low calcium, low organic matter and low moisture in the soil. It can also indicate that other minerals are high in the soil. Where it dominates in lawns, you are mowing too low. The name is derived from the Latin *planta*, meaning the sole of the foot. Plantain flourishes in well-trodden areas, which usually means highly disturbed places with compacted soils and low fertility.

Ribwort plantain (*Plantago lanceolata*) forms a rosette of narrow leaves with strong parallel veins. The flower stems are slightly hairy and leafless. At the top of the stem is an ovoid inflorescence of tiny flowers each with a single white bract.

Plantain has long been a popular potherb throughout Europe and has followed European migration around the world.

Seeds of the closely related *P. psyllium* are sold in health food stores as psyllium husks, a source of soluble fibre. Psyllium husks are used extensively in fibre drinks to help regulate gut health. Seeds of all the plantains are very high in mucilaginous soluble fibre and therefore are very good for gut health. Collect the seed head of any of the plantain weeds you have, chop finely and add to your breakfast or green smoothie.

The young leaves are good eating and have a subtle nutty flavour. Older leaves get a bit fibrous but can still be used when cooked. Plantain has many medicinal uses and is so good for us and so useful medicinally that I consider it amongst my absolute must have weeds.

It is a band aid plant – useful for wrapping cuts and abrasions to accelerate healing. For other skin issues, even bites and stings, chew the plantain leaf a little to release the juice first then apply to the site for good relief. This used to be common knowledge. Shakespeare mentions using plantain for broken skin in three plays - *Love's Labours Lost*, *Two Noble Kinsmen* and *Romeo and Juliet*. Not that Shakespeare is a medicinal authority, but I do urge you to try it. Plantain features in herbal history, being favoured by the Romans and Greeks, King Henry VIII and even the church. For the Greeks, Plantain was the representation of a maiden sent seeking her lost love by the Goddess Demeter. In the Middle Ages when the use of herbs was forbidden by the church, plantain was still allowed because it was thought to represent the footprints of those who followed Christ. To the Native Americans plantain was known as white man's footsteps because it seemed to grow wherever white people went. All are references to the ability of plantain to spread where humans travel, as a weed and as a valued plant which is spread deliberately. Who are we to dismiss a weed with history like that?

Plantain is well known for being a very good skin herb, as are mallows and another favourite weed, chickweed. It works very well in salves to sooth inflamed or irritated skin, or when simply softened and applied externally. As mentioned, it can stop bleeding and can help heal bruises. It has a strong drawing action, which can be good for drawing splinters or for cleaning wounds. For this purpose, mix it with some unprocessed honey to make a poultice. I have found this exceptionally effective at cleaning wounds and accelerating healing. I personally found it very soothing and stopped the throbbing pain of a messy and dirty cut almost immediately. Hours later I removed the poultice and found the wound perfectly clean. The wound healed very quickly. It is important that the honey used for this purpose is sourced from a beekeeper and is unprocessed except for being strained. Raw honey contains a full complement of natural enzymes and other potent healing properties, whether it is manuka honey or not. I have personally used plantain many times on sometimes rather serious cuts on myself and when helping others. It has never failed to stem the bleeding, draw dirt from the wound and promote fast healing without scarring.

Plantain is a very valuable herb for supporting the mucous membranes. This means respiratory and gut health. It is an excellent lung herb and is one of the best for coughs and colds or any stubborn and difficult bronchial complaints. My winter go-to tonic is a tea combining plantain, cobbler's pegs and paddy's lucerne. It is also useful in soothing and treating any of the many inflammatory gut conditions.

Plantain is easy to add to the diet. Young leaves can be added to salads, older leaves chopped and used as cooked greens. The leaves and seeds can be used in green smoothies. All varieties of plantain are worthwhile. I have grown a couple of ornamental varieties. One is a *P. major* cultivar with reddish leaves, and another is a smaller variety with green and white leaves. I also grow buckshorn plantain, *P. coronopus* which is less fibrous and great in salads. In addition, I encourage a tiny native plantain, *P. dentata*, which is easy to miss as it is so small.

Occasionally I do find people who, even after learning what a wonderful plant plantain is, want to get rid of it. It is not hard to hand weed with a forked weeding tool. Work on improving the soil, be that garden, lawn or pasture, and you will have less plantain. This is a plant that does like compaction and will thrive with foot traffic. As the soil structure improves, plantain no longer dominates and can be easily outcompeted. It is not very shade tolerant and will not cope with being crowded by taller plants.

Both *P. major* and *P. lanceolata* are very widely distributed and common all over the world, although *P. major* is less heat tolerant than is *P. lanceolata*. There are numerous other Plantago species as well, all with similar uses. Wherever you are in the world chances are you will have a plantain weed, and possibly also a native plantain.

Prickly Lettuce

Lactuca serriola

Prickly lettuce is usually found in heavily disturbed soils and is very tolerant of dry, compacted soils. It can be an indicator of soils lacking in organic matter with hard crusts and low pH (acidic), with low calcium and high magnesium, potassium, manganese and iron. This wild relative of lettuce is often overlooked or mistaken for a thistle due to the prickliness on the stem and leaves. It may be related to our delicate modern lettuces, but this is one tough plant. It can often be found growing in cracks in the footpath or even along the rough bitumen edges of highways. Like modern lettuces, it is edible. The young leaves are best eaten before the plant sends up the flowering stalk and is still in the rosette form. Leaves can be cooked or used in salads. I personally never find these young enough for salads, as the low growing rosette stage is short lived and the plant often goes unnoticed until it shoots skyward, so I always eat it cooked.

The white sap in these wild lettuces contains a substance called lactucarius which has sedative and analgesic properties. It was used in Ancient Greece to suppress sexual desire, and by the ancient Egyptians as an aphrodisiac. As it happens it is all in the dose. Small amounts act as a stimulant, larger amounts as a sedative. Too much and it is a purgative which means vomiting and diarrhoea.

It is often confused with another wild lettuce, *Lactuca virosa* and the two have been used interchangeably. *L. virosa* can be distinguished by being far less prickly and having a distinct red/purple tinge to the stems. Both have the common name of opium lettuce due to the properties of the sticky white sap. A tea can be made from the leaves and stem for pain relief and works in the same way as a very mild opiate. The medieval herbalist Hildegard von Bingen suggested that prickly lettuce was a useless plant because anyone who ate it became mindless. She also recommended wrapping cooked lettuce around a man's loins to reduce excessive lust. I have not yet found a willing volunteer to test this recommendation.

Prickly lettuce (*Lactuca serriola*) has a row of small spines on the central rib on the back of the leaf, and on the edge of the leaf. The leaf is lobed and a waxy grey green. The flowers are small (approx. 1cm) and resemble lettuce flowers, or miniature dandelions.

I do recommend caution however if you are thinking of using this medicinally. As mentioned above, the effects can vary enormously based on the dose and both sedatives and stimulants can interact with medication and alcohol. I have found a cup of tea made with dried leaves and stems to be effective in helping myself and others to sleep, especially when dealing with a painful injury such as a broken bone. It is often recommended that a tincture be made from this plant, but I find that as a tea it is strong enough to be effective and is much easier to make. There are a number of weedy Lactuca species, all are edible before they send up a flowering stalk. Like cultivated lettuce, they become far more bitter once they start to flower. None of the wild lettuce species has been bred for sweetness and form, unlike our cultivated lettuce, therefore they all have a much stronger flavour. They also all have a much higher component of phytochemicals and therefore are far more nutritious and medicinal than cultivated lettuce.

Breeding experiments have shown *L. serriola* to be the wild ancestor of all modern hearting lettuces. This is a classic example of how distantly removed our modern vegetables are from their wild origins. Lettuce as we know it is not valued particularly as having significant nutritional or medicinal values. This is not the case with its wild ancestor and is a classic case of less goodness and more sweetness being bred into our food. Hearting lettuces were not recorded until 1543 in Europe.

Prickly lettuce is depicted in 6,500-year-old Egyptian paintings. Lettuces have been cultivated as a vegetable in China for over 1,000 years. Modern Asian lettuces are not hearting and are largely used as a cooked vegetable, although they too look very different to these wild lettuce ancestors.

Prickly lettuce and its related weeds are short lived annual plants that spread by seed. They are easily removed by hand pulling (with gloves as they are prickly), cutting at ground level or hoeing. To stop the next generation of weeds, improve the soil and create a garden environment which does not allow seed to grow; you know how to do that by now - mulch and dense planting.

L. variosa is hardy in cool to warm temperate zones. *L. serriola* is hardy in warmer climates. *L. serriola* is the most widespread of all the Lactuca species and is found on all continents (except Antarctica).

Purslane

Portulaca oleracea

Abundant purslane indicates that the soil may be rich in phosphorus. Being a succulent, this hardy little plant will grow in some pretty harsh and tough places. Hot dry conditions are preferred by this low growing weed, but if drainage is good, like in the sand between pavers, it will flourish in hot wet conditions as well. It is shallow rooted and so will grow in both sandy and clay soils so long as there is an exposed dry crust for the seeds to germinate in. This weed is easily smothered by mulch, but you may not want to get rid of it. The leaves, stems and seeds are all edible. They are very high in protein, in particular ALA (alpha-linolenic acid) Omega 3 fatty acids, as well as other vitamins and minerals including Vitamins A, B, C, E and calcium, magnesium and potassium. They can be eaten as a snack while gardening or added to salads, used as a pot herb or anywhere else you may add greens. It also works well as a pickle in vinegar.

This herb is considered a longevity herb in China and was apparently appreciated by King Henry XIII to alleviate problems associated with urination. First Nations people used the seeds to make flat breads before white settlement, highlighting the very widespread nature of this so-called *weed*. Purslane only became known to European history during medieval times but has a long history of use in Ancient Egypt, Greece and Rome as well as China. In Vietnam purslane is used to expel worms (crush 50g of the plant and drink the extract for 3 nights), and it is used externally to treat eczema and pimples.

Purslane (*Portulaca oleracea*) has smooth stems which can be tinged with red. The fleshy leaves may be alternate or opposite but are clustered at the leaf joints or at the end of the stem. The tiny yellow flowers are located in the centre of the leaf cluster. They only open for a few hours in the morning.

Scientific studies have backed up modern herbal uses for purslane, including its use to support immune, heart, bronchial and digestive health, to fight inflammatory diseases and gut ulcers and to help control diabetes. Herbal preparations of purslane are available in health food stores and online.

To collect the seeds in any quantity, pull out as many plants as you can as they are setting seed, and lay them to dry on a clean sheet. After a few days as the plants dry out, a little shake and the seeds will collect in the sheet.

Purslane is a key ingredient of the Middle Eastern salad, fattoush. As with many of the weeds, opinion as to the flavour and joy of eating varies. Some authors dislike it raw, while as many others, me included, thoroughly enjoy it raw. As with all the foods we eat, personal taste will play a part.

It has a high mineral content, which not only makes it good for us, but it also makes it a good weed to use as a herbal salt substitute.

This weed has been bred to produce a group of very popular garden plants with highly ornamental flowers – the sun jewels. Yes, our very pretty sun jewels are *Portulaca oleracae*, and they too are edible, if somewhat less flavoursome.

If you are still not keen to appreciate your purslane and wish to be rid of it, it can be controlled easily by hand pulling and smothering. It does produce large quantities of tiny seeds, so you will need to consider how best to deal with these. They won't germinate through mulch. As they often grow between pavers, treating the area with boiling water or steam will kill the adult plants as well as the seeds.

Purslane will grow as an annual in all climate zones but as a perennial in warmer areas. It is very common in all temperate and subtropical regions of the world.

Scarlet Pimpernel

Anagallis arvensis

Like so many of our weeds, scarlet pimpernel indicates soils low in organic matter, microbes, calcium and phosphate. This little weed can be mistaken for chickweed when not in flower. It is toxic, causing extreme nausea and body pain, so well worth making sure you have correct identification! The little red/orange or blue flowers are very pretty. It was one of my favourite flowers as a small child. This weed has been associated with human habitation for millennia and has become naturalised around the world. The species name *arvensis* means *of cultivated land*, referring to its preference for disturbed habitats. It prefers light soils but will also grow in most soil types. It likes to grow in alkaline (or sweet) soils (pH greater than 7), so lowering the soil pH will help make it less favourable to scarlet pimpernel. Perhaps in addition to spraying with white vinegar, use a watering can to apply diluted white vinegar to the soil so that you not only kill the weed, but also adjust the soil conditions temporarily. Vinegar breaks down quickly so is not considered beneficial for permanently adjusting the soil pH. Follow this up with compost and organic mulch to give long term improvement and make the soil less attractive to this and other weeds.

Scarlet pimpernel was used as an antidepressant in ancient Greece, and to treat mental disorders according to European folklore. Given its toxicity, perhaps the idea was to scare the person out of being unwell! No modern studies have found any medicinal benefits at all, except that it is highly toxic to animals. In India there are reports of using a liquid made from this plant to expel leaches from dogs' noses, but if the dog swallows the liquid by accident, it can be toxic. I can't help being surprised that there are enough cases of needing to expel leaches from dogs' noses to find this out. It can be used externally in skin creams to fade freckles, skin pigmentations and spots. You can use the salve recipe given later in this book and substitute the other weeds for scarlet pimpernel. Make sure if doing this, you keep the infused oil well labelled as accidental ingestion might lead to regret.

Scarlet pimpernel (*Anagallis arvensis*) is a weakly sprawling plant with square stems and leaves arranged in opposite pairs. The 5 petalled flowers are radially symmetrical. Flowers only open when the sun is shining.

The name *scarlet pimpernel* is directly associated with the fictional French hero, and it is thought to be his floral emblem. His calling card featured a red flower. This seems a long bow to draw. I have been unable to find any reason why this might be *the* red flower, but this sort of detail can get lost in the retelling of the tale over time.

Another interesting feature of this plant is the misrepresentation that the flower colour is temperature dependant, being scarlet in cool climates and blue in warmer climates. I have seen both colour variants growing in close proximity. I tend to find more of the orange than the blue here in the subtropics which turns this theory on its head. There are many other much less common colour variants, but always on separate plants. Flower colour is consistent within individual plants. Spanish research has suggested that hours of sunshine is causal to the colour variations, and while this may explain why it is predominantly red in England and blue in Spain, does not explain why it is not uncommon to find the two colours, and various other colour morphs, growing in the same location. Other sources suggest that the colour difference is due to pH, similarly to hydrangeas. This makes more sense, but it has not been researched enough to be sure. If you have this weed, look at what colours you may have and see if you can see any patterns to which colour grows where.

Scarlet pimpernel is a more problematic weed in cool to warm temperate climates but is widely distributed throughout the world in all climate zones.

Scurvy Weed

Commelina spp

Commelina species like moist shady places in the garden. They can be surprisingly deep rooted which can help them survive periodic dry conditions well.

All species of Commelina have very pretty blue flowers, are hard to get rid of and are very good butterfly host plants. I do not try to eradicate this one, just pull away the excess and give it to the chooks who love eating it. Having some left for the butterflies is not so bad, and in a crowded garden it doesn't get much of a chance to get away from me. At the moment I am not pulling too much of it out of my garden, it is providing a bit of shelter from the intense sun for the plants it is scrambling over and is also working very well, together with dock, as a decoy plant for the grasshoppers. While they are eating the weeds they are leaving my Brazilian spinach alone.

Scurvy weed is so called because it was used by the early settlers to keep scurvy at bay. First Nations people however didn't eat it, but then green leaves did not feature highly in their diet. Chooks and caterpillars are happy to eat it and I am happy to let them. A popular green vegetable in some areas of Asia, *C. benghalensis* is considered an environmental weed in Queensland and northern New South Wales. There are seven native Australian Commelina species, which are very similar looking with the same blue flowers. The most widely distributed is *C cyanea*. They are important forest floor habitat, but although native can become problem weeds in a garden situation. The introduced *C. benghalensis* is often called *Hairy Commelina* and has been described as commelinas on steroids. It can have a significantly larger leaf and tends to be hairier, but these are not necessarily identifying characteristics, as the native commelinas can also sometimes develop larger leaves and can often feature leaf hairs. To be sure of correct identification it is best to look at the flower. The flowers of the native commelinas all feature three even sized petals. *C. benghalensis* has a smaller lower petal while the two upper petals are of equal size. This little difference does not matter to the chooks or butterflies, nor will it matter to you if don't want it in the garden, but it will matter for those working in bush regeneration. Check which it is before assuming it is just a weed. I have seen many council workers poisoning native commelinas growing amongst trees in parkland, thinking it is an introduced weed when actually it is native and valuable habitat and ground protection.

Scurvy weed (*Commelina diffusa*) is a native plant which becomes a weed in gardens. It has narrow leaves with an obvious leaf sheath. It roots readily at the nodes. As with all of the native commelinas, the blue flowers have three evenly sized petals.

I do not find this one a very desirable weed for eating however I know others who very much enjoy it. Although it is known as scurvy weed, the vitamin C content of the various commelinas is unknown.

All of the Commelina species have bright blue flowers. The similar looking and also weedy plant with white flowers is *Tradescantia albiflora*. This species is less commonly eaten but is still edible. Allergic reactions to Tradescantia species are not uncommon so check for a skin reaction to this one before trying to eat it. You may also have a variety of other tradescantia weeds with boldly coloured foliage. These were once popular garden plants, and new cultivars are still being released. The tradescantias will have white, or sometimes pink/purple flowers, never the blue flowers of the commelinas. Given that the two are closely related and often confused, they are often grouped together as I have done here.

The name Wandering Jew has been seen as somewhat controversial of late. As with many common names the reason for the name is largely lost in modern culture. There is a biblical story of a Jewish man who chastised Jesus for pausing to rest while carrying his cross. Apparently, Jesus replied to the man: "I shall stop and rest, but thou shalt go on till the last day." This Jew became known as the Wandering Jew and stories have circulated involving this character for many centuries. For any gardener who has tried to deal with Wandering Jew, this statement by Jesus will seem to apply particularly well to this weed. As you can see, the name refers to a character, not a religious group. However, as this has become a sensitive issue, the common name is now being changed to *wandering trad*, short for Tradescantia.

These weeds are succulent ground covers, useful as living mulch in orchards as their high water content helps to keep the soil moist. When growing thickly it can be very attractive and help to crowd out other weeds.

Commelina and Tradescantia weeds can be somewhat of a pain to eradicate. Solarisation works very well if they are growing in sunny places, which they usually aren't. Smothering also works but a deep smother layer is needed for commelinas as they have deep roots. Keep an eye on your smother layer and pull out any emerging shoots before they can spread. It is shade tolerant and will use other plants as support in order to reach light, so won't be controlled by growing taller plants or cover cropping, unless they are dense and spiky like pumpkin vines. I have seen these weeds hand pulled and then hung in trees to dry out and die before composting. For this method to be successful they need to be hung in full sun and spread out, not in dense bunches which will allow the inner stems to grow. These broken stems can remain alive and able to regenerate for a surprisingly long time. During dry weather controlling this plant seems easy, only to have it come back with a vengeance when rains return. As these weeds are succulents, they cannot be added to compost or left on the ground to die. Weed tea works is a perfect solution – for composting the weeds as well as for feeding the garden.

Some commelinas, including *C. benghalensis,* have an interesting ability to develop underground stolons which produce flowers and seeds. This can mean that future soil disturbance results in a new weed infestation, as these underground seeds can be dormant for a long time. Both the above ground and underground seeds require light to germinate, so keep the area well mulched to keep the seeds dark and dormant.

Current research shows that commelinas can be used for bioremediation, as they can absorb large amounts of heavy metals. Be aware of this potential if you are foraging for it in public spaces.

There are Commelina and tradescantia weeds which will grow in cold through to tropical climates. *C. benghaliensis* is a weed of all tropical and subtropical regions of the world but is not always considered troublesome environmentally, although it much disliked by gardeners.

Sensitive Plant

Mimosa pudica

Sensitive plant (*Mimosa pudica*) is bipinnately compound, meaning the leaves are feather like and made up of a series of oppositely arranged leaflets. The leaflets fold away when touched to reveal a thorny stem. Each flower will last for only 1 day. The older the plant the more flowers it will produce.

Sensitive weed is a deep-rooted legume, two characteristics of weeds which indicate they are excellent for soil improvement.

As the name suggests, this weed is reactive, which is great fun for kids. The ferny leaves close when touched, a defence against grazing animals. Be careful, it also has thorns! As a plant native to the plains of Africa where drought and grazing are constant pressures, this plant is well adapted to harsh conditions. It thrives in warm to hot climates, is highly drought tolerant but is also tolerant of extremely wet conditions. It has a deep tap root and thrives in heavily compacted soils. It is one of those weeds that is almost impossible to pull out.

The pretty pink flowers are edible and make a lovely cake decoration or garnish. The leaves are edible, and the entire plant has been associated medicinally with relieving nervous disorders and stress. Apparently just sitting by the plant and stroking the leaves helps to relieve stress. I have a friend who runs a family day care centre. When the children get a bit wild, they are sent to sit and *pat the plant* for a couple of minutes. Apparently, it makes a big difference.

The leaves will also close with wind, excess noise and at night. This adaptation allows the plant to conserve water in dry conditions. This is a curious characteristic and one that is energetically expensive for the plant, therefore must be an effective mechanism to avoid predation from herbivores and to conserve water. Studies have found that very high concentrations of potassium chloride and calcium cause water to be withdrawn suddenly from the leaves, resulting in drooping. The cause of these minerals suddenly being in high concentrations is not so clear. This characteristic of being able to close its leaves in response to stimuli has been used to study learned responses in plants. The plant was found to close its leaves when dropped. The plant stopped doing this after a few drops, having learnt that the dropping was not a threat to its survival. When it was dropped again the next day, and the next week, the plant still did not close its leaves, demonstrating that it had indeed learnt that it didn't need to use an energetically expensive mechanism in response to being dropped. While this is truly fascinating, for me the greatest finding of this study is that we are learning just how little we really know about plants as living beings!

Herbal tea can be made from the leaves of sensitive plant to calm and heal the central nervous system. It has been reported that drinking the tea regularly has resulted in reduced symptoms of stress, lowering of high blood pressure, restful sleep, relief from shingles, MS, Parkinson's disease and other disorders of the nervous system.

It is a deep-rooted legume, and a ground cover. It provides protection and soil improvement to disturbed and exposed ground. It can often be found as a weed in warm climates growing on roadsides and areas where grass has been cut too short and scalping has occurred. It is extremely drought tolerant and therefore is able to exploit these hot dry conditions. This weed has been found to be an effective accumulator of heavy metals, which makes it a useful plant for soil remediation but also means that if you wish to use it, avoid harvesting plants grown on roadsides or potentially polluted ground.

As with any weed that is difficult to pull out, its roots are working for you in the soil. Cut the top off and compost this leguminous weed but leave the root to keep working. It can be controlled by boiling water or by smothering. As the organic smother layer breaks down it improves the soil, changing the conditions and making the garden less well suited to sensitive plant. Herbicides are not very effective for sensitive plant as the plant will close its leaves to avoid contact. How clever! Unfortunately, this has resulted in stronger chemicals being recommended and used against it.

Where sensitive plant is a weed in lawns, it is very clearly telling you that you have a real problem with your soil and the way you are managing your lawn.

Sensitive weed is a serious weed in tropical climates where it is a perennial but is also found in subtropical, Mediterranean and warm temperate climates worldwide, growing as an annual in cooler climates.

Soursob

Oxalis debilis, (formerly *O. corymbose*), and *Oxalis pes-caprae*

Soursob (*Oxalis debilis*) has a fleshy root with tiny bulbils that easily break off to form new plants. The three lobed leaves are a similar shape to but much larger than clover. The pink flowers are tubular with 5 even petals.

Both *O. debilis* and *O. corniculata* (creeping oxalis or creeping wood sorrel) prefer soils low in calcium, good drainage and good moisture. Interestingly, creeping oxalis was used in ancient China as an indicator of soils containing copper and was used to search for copper deposits.

What a lovely pest is soursob. There is no denying the cheerful little pink flowers of *O. debilis* or the vibrant yellow flowers of *O. pes-caprae* are pretty in the garden and I know many (me included) who cannot hate it for this reason alone. For others nothing excuses its ability to spread and to withstand poison, pulling or any attempt to be rid of it. I am happy to eat the leaves as I am working in the garden and find them slightly lemony and refreshing – good in salads and as a pot herb. The chooks are quite happy to eat the bulbs, as are pigs. The bulbs are fine for us to eat as well and are sweet and tangy, much like the entire plant. Digging up the bulbs to try and eradicate this weed will only aid its growth, as all the tiny bulblets attached to the main bulb break away and spread as you dig. This is best controlled by eating. Constantly removing the tops off any bulb will eventually weaken and exhaust the bulb, leading to death. The leaves can be cooked to remove some of the tanginess and reduce the oxalic acid content a little. They are also useful for making a variant of lemonade or a lightly fermented switzel.

The creeping yellow oxalis (*Oxalis corniculata*) with its exploding seed pods is also edible. This one is a low creeping plant which often takes hold in lawns that are mown too short but are well watered. If left to grow it makes quite a pretty ground cover. This oxalis is widely used medicinally in India where it is used for preventing pregnancy. All the oxalis species have been shown to have some use in healing wounds, as anti-cancer, cardio-relaxant, antioxidant and antibacterial. They can be used topically for skin infections.

All the oxalis species are edible, and as a genus there are species growing wild as weeds in almost every climate but the polar ice caps. The flowers are a pretty addition to salads or for decorating desserts. Many of the ornamental varieties such as *O. triangularis* with its eye-catching purple leaves and pale pink flowers are becoming quite sought after for edible flower mixes.

The flowers of soursobs are very pretty and abundant, making them a great filler in cottage gardens. Like onion weed, this is a highly ornamental weed which we would love if it were called daffodil or freesia, two other highly ornamental bulbs which can also spread well beyond where they were planted. They are highly seasonal, so can put on a fantastic show when the climate suits them and then disappear altogether. If you didn't know they were weeds you would congratulate the gardener on such a great floral show. The yellow flowering *O. pes-caprae* is a common weed amongst grape vines in South Australia. Viticulturalists there are finding that the weed does not compete at all with the vines, but instead, if left alone, provides a ground cover and soil protection and the flowers are attracting beneficial insects. The soursob flowers as the vines are reshooting after winter dormancy, a time when they are vulnerable to insect attack and when the beneficial insects are most needed and appreciated. Oxalis species occur as native and weed plants all over the world and in every climate except polar. They have the greatest species diversity in subtropical and tropical regions but are problem weeds throughout warm temperate, Mediterranean, subtropical and tropical climates.

Sow Thistle

Sonchus oleraceus

Sow thistle (*Sonchus oleraceus*) has flowers similar to lettuce, or miniature dandelions. The stems are hollow. The base of the leaf wraps around the stem.

Sow thistle likes high nitrogen soils. It is indicative of soils low in calcium and phosphate but high in nitrogen, and other minerals. It will grow widely but prefers moist soils which are slightly acidic. It is sold in some markets as Asian greens, showing just how valuable this common weed is. Watch the chooks and guinea pigs go mad for it! It is very high in vitamins and minerals and can be eaten raw or cooked. I find it a little bitter raw and prefer it cooked, although the very young leaves are fine and taste like the outer green leaves of lettuce, to which it is related. The flowers can be added to salads or stir fries.

In New Zealand sow thistle is known as Puha and the leaves, stems and flower buds are used in *boil-ups*. Trials there have found that greenhouse grown puha has a lower iron content than wild grown plants, but the flavour is less bitter, so the greenhouse grown plants are more popular with chefs.

This bitter flavour is valuable for stimulating digestion and supporting the liver and kidneys. The bitterness is lost with cooking, so for these medicinal benefits eat some young leaves raw in salads or add to smoothies or pestos – places where the flavour is masked by other leaves. This plant is said to have anti-fever, antioxidant and anti-inflammatory properties and has a long history of medicinal use around the world. It can be used to make a soothing cup of tea to help get a good night's sleep, can help treat bronchial disorders and has even been suggested to be effective as an anti-cancer. The leaves are high in vitamin C (which is diminished when cooking), protein and numerous vitamins and minerals, including calcium and iron. The roots can be used to make a tea which is antibacterial and anthelmintic. The white milky sap can be applied to warts and ulcers.

Nicholas Culpepper had plenty of interesting ideas on how to use sow thistle in 1653, which included adding three spoonsful of the juice to warmed white wine to ensure labour would be speedy and easy, as a facewash for clear lustrous skin, boiled in wine to stay the dissolution of the stomach, using the sap for asthma, and the juice heated and added to a little oil of bitter almonds and peel of pomegranate, then dropped into the ear for deafness or ringing in the ears. Whilst I do not suggest you try these without doing further research, this is a plant considered to have been useful for a very long time.

In the garden sow thistle is a valuable decoy plant as it will attract aphids and white fly away from other plants. It may also harbour viruses which are problematic for lettuces so are best not grown in their vicinity. Given the nutritional value of sow thistle, I would be more inclined to grow lettuce as the decoy plant to keep the bugs away from my sow thistle!

Sow thistle is sometimes confusingly called milk thistle. It is not a true thistle at all. The milk thistle that is sold as a herbal supplement is a true thistle, *Silybum marianum*. The true thistles can be identified by their purple flowers. The sow thistles all have yellow flowers and are more closely related to lettuce and dandelions. The annual sow thistle (*Sonchus oleraceus*) is the most common, but you may also find that you have the perennial sow thistle (*Sonchus arvensis),* or the prickly sow thistle (*Sonchus asper*). All are edible, although the perennial and prickly sow thistles are pricklier to handle and therefore are more likely to be eaten cooked.

Sow thistles do like high nitrogen soils and therefore are often a pest of highly fertilised crops. They are easy to dig in or pull out when they are small. Cutting mature plants off at ground level will stop them setting seed but they will regrow. Cutting plants off below ground level will kill them and root fragments will not regrow. The small seeds are wind dispersed (similarly to dandelion) and will not take hold in heavily mulched or heavily planted gardens.

Sow thistles are found on almost every corner of the earth and will grow in almost any climate.

Spear Thistle, Bull Thistle

Cirsium vulgare

Thistles like nitrogen rich soils and are often in abundance following overgrazing, since they are too prickly to be eaten by livestock. The tap root suggests they are working to repair paddocks compacted by livestock. An abundance of highly prickly weeds is a great way of Mother Nature telling us to clear out and let the land repair itself.

Spear thistle (*Cirsium vulgare*) has sharp spines on the stems, leaves and flower buds. The plant grows from a basal rosette with smaller leaves on the upper stem. The leaf lobes are spear shaped, hence the common name.

Thistles are very valuable habitat plants. They are popular nectar sources for bees and a wide variety of butterflies, as well as other pollinators. A UK study looking at nectar content per flower in wildflower meadows found that both *C. vulgare* and *C. arvense* far outranked most other flowers tested, beaten only by the common ragwort (*Senecio jacobaea*) and closely followed by dandelion and false dandelion. It has been found that small seed-eating birds enjoy the seeds of these thistles, and the down attached to the seed is taken by birds for nesting material. I would go further and suggest that the extreme prickliness of this tall weed provides shelter for small birds, and probably also small mammals, lizards and insects. Small birds which are in decline in urban areas due to lack of dense plant cover are often seen in fields with this weed, even when no other protection seems to be around.

Spear thistle is best dealt with by tilling. Its extreme prickliness makes it one we prefer to have very limited close contact with. It does have a tap root but will not regrow from broken root pieces. Beware and be sure of your identification – some thistles, such as the creeping thistle (known as Canadian Thistle in northern America), *C. arvense* will regrow from broken root pieces. Creeping thistle should not be hoed, but instead cut the tops off the plant before it has the chance to set seed. Cutting it down will need to be done repeatedly to exhaust the root. If your thistle has seeded, ensure you are mulching the garden well and not allowing seeds to germinate.

Thistles are native to much of Europe and the UK, despite being declared as weeds there, and are a naturalised weed in Australia and northern America.

Interestingly, thistles were one of the earliest weed problems in the Australian colony. The Scotch Thistle Act (1852) was passed in South Australia in an attempt to control them. This was the first weed legislation passed in Australia and possibly even the world. Although it was called the Scotch Thistle Act, it covered all purple flowering thistles, of which the spear thistle was the most common. The true Scotch thistle, *Onopordum acanthium*, was also established as a weed in South Australia at that time. As other completely unrelated plants became weeds, they became classified as *thistles,* so that they too fell under this weed control act.

Spear thistle is widespread throughout the world and considered a serious weed in Australia, Canada and the USA.

Spurges

Euphorbia sp

There are a few different spurge weeds here in Brisbane and all are wildly different in form, as is typical of this huge genus. Further afield there are other spurge weeds which are completely different in appearance again. Euphorbias are widely spread and highly diverse. There are over 20 different Euphorbia weeds in Australia. Wherever you are, there is likely to be multiple spurge weeds. All have dangerous milky white sap, and all are poisonous.

One of the most common here is the painted spurge (*Euphorbia cyathophora*). This is a pest that spreads readily but is also much favoured by native bees. It is highly ornamental, looking somewhat like miniature poinsettias, which are also a species of euphorbia.
Along our southern coastline sea spurge, *E. paralias* is a weed of beaches.

Radium weed, or petty spurge (*E. peplus*) is becoming increasingly appreciated for the ability of its sap to burn off sunspots. There is a very expensive cream available on prescription made from radium weed. It is not hard to use the weed directly if you do a little research first – if you don't know what you are doing, you may find yourself covered in blisters unnecessarily. Radium weed often grows amongst chickweed, so be careful and check that you are not eating it by mistake as it is poisonous. You will know if you have accidently eaten a bit of radium weed. Your mouth will start to burn, and you will spit it out, thereby saving yourself from any poisoning. You will however have an uncomfortable mouth for a little while. The chickweed you were eating it with is very soothing to your upset mouth, so check more carefully that your chickweed is *not polluted* with other weeds and keep eating it, after rinsing your mouth first with milk.

Radium weed (*Euphorbia peplus*) is easy to miss due to the nondescript small, oval, green leaves up to 3cm long. It has green flowers in 3 rayed umbels, which are also very easy to miss. It is readily identified by breaking a stem to expose the milky sap.

I have used radium weed to treat sunspots. The fresh sap should be applied directly to the spot and avoid contact with the rest of the skin. Use extreme care around the eyes. It will cause blistering. If the spot turns out not to have altered cells, the blisters will heal and nothing else will happen. If the cells are altered in some way (which may or may not mean they are pre-cancerous), the radium weed sap will attack them. One drop of sap onto an external spot can cause redness to spread from the area. This is the sap travelling along the nerve pathways to connected altered cells and working to not only attack these altered cells, but to stimulate our body's own immune reaction to fight off abnormalities. Given that skin cancer is a major killer, use of radium weed cannot replace the importance of regular skin checks and medical advice, however, a major pharmaceuticals company would not have produced a patented cream from this plant if it were not highly effective!

The sap from all euphorbias, garden plant or weed, is caustic and can burn. The degree to which it burns will vary from species to species, but all can be utilised for burning off warts and even corns. All euphorbias need to be treated with care due to this highly caustic sap. Getting some sap on your fingers, forgetting, and wiping sweat from your face later can result in the tiniest amount of sap in the eyes and a trip to hospital. I know of professional gardeners and tree loppers who will not handle large euphorbias such as firesticks (*E. tirucalli*) due to the dangers posed by the sap. Asthma weed (*E. hirta,* now *Chamaesyce hirta*) is closely related and also has milky white sap. It is not regarded as edible but has a long list of medicinal uses. Given that it has potentially toxic sap, this one is interesting, but I suggest you do your research well before trying to use it medicinally.

All of the spurges are very good at extracting boron from the soil, so when composting them, do so under passionfruit vines or other fruit trees which will often fruit better with a little extra boron.

Due to the diversity of form of euphorbia weeds, there is no single method of eradication. They do all tend to have waxy leaves so if you are using vinegar, dilute it first and add a little dishwashing liquid to help it stick to the leaves. Boiling water and steam are also effective on the smaller species that tend to like growing in pathways. In the garden low growing species can be smothered effectively. Larger species will need to be removed very carefully by hand. They can be composted but take a long time to break down and be aware that they will regrow if left lying on the ground.

Petty Spurge (radium weed) grows well in temperate and subtropical climates. There are numerous spurge weeds in most climate zones. Petty spurge is common throughout Europe, the UK, the USA, Australia and New Zealand.

Stinging Nettle

Urtica sp

Stinging nettles like rich, acidic soils (pH below 7), so raising the soil's pH with an application of lime will help make it less suitable for them to grow. Nettles can also be an indicator of soils low in calcium and phosphorous but high in other minerals, soils that are compacted and periodically waterlogged. Nettles are able to extract calcium from soils which are low in this mineral, making this calcium more available to other plants in the surface layers of the soil as it composts. They will give the best growth and tastiest greens if grown in nutrient rich, moist soils. You will know you have nettles in your garden when you try and pull the plant out and find your hand is stinging or burning for no apparent reason. There will usually be something nearby to help – rub it with chickweed, dock, billy goat weed, basket plant or new unfurled fern fronds to relieve the sting.

Stinging nettle (*Urtica urens*) has round, toothed leaves covered in stinging hairs.

Nettles are a very nutritious food for people and animals. Horses will happily eat them, which is why I love using horse manure on my garden and seeing the nettles that come up (as do mallows and fat hen, which I am happy to have). Medicinally, nettles have many uses, one of which is joint and muscle pain – including rheumatoid arthritis. Apparently, the sting stimulates healing, but I think these days we would rather use pain free treatments. Anecdotal evidence suggests that nettle is still more effective in the long-term treatment of severe arthritis and pain than are modern drugs. I tried testing this on my ex-husband, using nettle in combination with aloe vera which is also extremely beneficial for pain relief and arthritis. He did not enjoy the test treatment, especially knowing that modern medicine offers pain free alternatives. He did however find it effective. While the stinging effect, known as urtication, is very beneficial, it is not the only way to use nettle. A compress (a face washer soaked in a strong nettle tea and applied to the affected area) is also very beneficial in treating arthritis, inflammation, sprains, mild burns, gout, eczema, tendonitis and sciatica.

Nettle is a popular and sought-after vegetable in much of Europe, and its many medicinal benefits can be accessed by eating it or by drinking nettle tea. It is highly beneficial not only for healing pain, but contains histamines which relieve allergic responses, serotonin which relieves stress and associated nervous disorders and is a powerful detoxifying agent – amongst many other uses. Nettles are very high in minerals including bioavailable silica, so are excellent for strengthening all body systems. This high silica (together with their ability to dynamically accumulate calcium, sulphur, magnesium and nitrogen) make nettles an ideal fertiliser and nettle tea is often recommended in permaculture or organic gardening guides.

Nettles have a very long history of human use as food, medicine and fibre. Archaeological studies of the Bronze Age have discovered shrouds made of nettle fibre; Saxons included nettle as one of their eight sacred herbs; Roman soldiers used it to rub on their bodies to keep warm (ouch!) and relieve cramps; ancient Olympians used it to relieve aching muscles after games and French folklore suggests it enhances virility, (although my ex-husband flatly refused to test this one out for me!). Native Americans believed it was one of the first herbs God gave man, believing the sting is to protect it from the greedy and to ensure it was only for the worthy. Throughout millennia nettles have been prescribed for almost every condition you can think of. It is a very safe herb to eat, once the sting has been neutralised. To gain the maximum benefit, nettle can be eaten in large amounts – the more the better.

The leaves can be added to a green smoothie, or even pesto and will lose their sting on pulverisation. Other ways to use it are: as a herbal tea, infusion or tincture; nettle beer brewed similarly to ginger beer; within herb or weed salts; or as a classic Irish dish, nettle soup. Whichever way you use nettle there is much to be gained in terms of nutrition and health. Nettle seeds can also be eaten, if you can find a large enough nettle patch to harvest a worthwhile amount. Like all seeds, they are a good energy food. They can be eaten raw or cooked, although can be a bit of a stimulant so best not eaten before bed. Nettle plants and seeds have been recommended for supporting the thyroid and endocrine glands as well as being extremely nourishing for the adrenals, making them very valuable in supporting chronic fatigue, stress and severe burnout.

Nettle weeds are usually annual plants but might be either annual or perennial in warmer climates. They can be easily controlled by cutting back using a whipper snipper and then smothering. The seeds will not grow through the mulch. As a short-lived plant which propagates by seed, your best means of keeping this weed out of the garden is to create a garden environment where seeds can't grow.

Urtica urens, the annual nettle, is the most common nettle weed in most temperate climates. There are many species of nettle found worldwide in climates ranging from subtropical to subtemperate.

Sword Fern

Nephrolepis cordifolia

Sword fern is a common spontaneous urban plant in many cities around the world. Being a fern, this plant likes moisture, at least periodically. It is happy in many soil types as it is not deep rooted, but generally will not cope with heavy compacted soils. It prefers slightly acid soils with a high humus content so is frequently found growing in trapped leaf litter, such as in crevices in walls. Concrete retaining walls on the side of major roads are a common place to find it. Water storage nodules on the roots make it surprisingly drought tolerant. Technically, these water storage nodules are swollen stolons, not tubers. The plant cannot regrow from these. These stolons allow the plant to grow as an epiphyte or lithophyte (growing on rocks) in the wild.

Sword fern (*Nephrolepis cordifolia*) has bipinnate fronds with simple to lanceolate leaflets. The petioles (leaf stems) are covered in brown scale, which can appear furry. The rhizomes develop hairy tubers which are water storage nodules.

This fern has been shown to be very effective at drawing up heavy metals, making it a useful plant for decontamination. Of course, if there is any risk of contamination the plant needs to be disposed of as contaminated material. It should never be eaten or added to compost or green waste under these circumstances.

Yes, this one is edible. The water stolons can be used as a substitute for water chestnuts or Jerusalem artichokes, although with a little less flavour. They can be eaten raw or cooked and make a great snack while weeding – just brush off the dirt and crunch away. The rhizomes and roots also have various medicinal properties, although making a paste of the rhizome to relieve headache is probably effective in that by the time it takes to prepare the reasonably fine rhizome, the headache has gone by itself.

The sword fern is often confused with the Boston fern and they are closely related. The Boston fern (*Nephrolepis exalata*) can be easily distinguished by looking at the roots. Only the sword fern (*N. cordifolia)* has stolons. It is native to Australia and to the Himalayan foothills of Nepal where it is regularly eaten. It's natural range here extends from the northeast of Queensland into northern New South Wales. Outside of this range it is considered a naturalised environmental weed. Even within this range it is considered a pest, although I have to say I think it is wonderful to see huge concrete block walls on the side of freeways covered in this native plant.

While this fern makes a great pot plant, it can be a nuisance in the garden, forming large clumps. It is very shallow rooted, so it is easy to dig out the clumps using a garden fork. It can be composted, although I find the fern stems become brittle and sharp as they die and may take a long time to break down in the compost. Put them through a garden mulcher first if you can or use them in weed tea. Where they are growing in palms or in retaining walls, they are much harder to get rid of. If you cannot reach the crown (the part where the roots and shoots join together) the plant can grow back. Regularly taking the tops off will exhaust the plant. Boiling water is unlikely to be effective here as the crown and roots are well protected amongst the rocks. Flame weeding may be more effective but whichever method you choose, you will have to repeat as any crowns which have been protected enough to survive will grow back. It might be more useful to see them as a great way to green up a space in the garden where you would otherwise be unable to grow plants.

It will tolerate temperatures as low as 0°C, but it is a tropical plant and prefers warm wet conditions. It has become a weed in warm temperate through to tropical regions of the world.

Vervain

Verbena officinalis

Vervain is not particularly fussy about soil types but does prefer a dry alkaline soil. Vervain indicates soil very low in calcium and phosphate and high in potassium. This is a pretty weed with a long history of use. It is a good ornamental plant, popular in cottage gardens and is highly attractive to bees, butterflies and other pollinators. The closely related *Verbena bonariensis* is more ornamental with larger more showy flowers and is favoured by gardeners, although it too is a declared weed in many areas. A third closely related species known as blue vervain, *V. littoralis*, is more spindly and taller than *V. officinalis* with smaller flower heads. This species prefers warmer climates, but all three species have naturalised in Australia and much of the world. All three species have at times been garden favourites and there were once many cultivars available. It is thought that *V. bonariensis* was introduced to Australia and elsewhere as a garden plant. *V. littoralis* was most likely introduced in ships ballast or packaging material. *V. officinalis* is the only one of the three to be considered a medicinal plant and as such has a much longer history of spread around the world.

Vervain, (*Verbena officinalis*) has coarse, toothed leaves. Older leaves can be lobed. Flowers have five petals, are light blue to purple and are borne in determinate inflorescences (new flowers open at the top of the stem). The relatively large seed (compared to the flower size) clings to the stem once the flower has finished.

Historically, vervain was a key ingredient in the potions that made witches brooms fly. It has also been used in strong infusions to bring on dream states in shamans, which might be how the witches actually *flew.* It features in Christian lore, as it was supposedly used to staunch Christ's crucifixion wounds. Vervain is rich in folklore and mythological references. In Ancient Egypt it was believed to have sprung from the tears of the goddess Isis upon the death of the god Osiris. Other ancient cultures also believed vervain to be sacred, including the Druids, Persians, and Norse cultures. It was considered a holy plant by both the Greeks, who called it *hierobotane* and the Romans, to whom it was known as *herba sacra*. The generic name of the plant, Verbena, means leafy bunch. This refers to an ancient practice of brushing the alters of temples with bunches of it.

During the Middle Ages, while witches were using vervain to make their brooms fly, others were using it to protect them from the evil of witches. Another name for it from this time is herba veneris, meaning herb of love, and reflecting its popular use as an aphrodisiac.

None of these folkloric uses are recommended by modern herbalists. It does have some valuable herbal uses such as easing cramps, insomnia, as a nervous tonic, for treating anxiety and depression, anti-inflammatory, analgesic and antimicrobial, however in high doses it is a painful purgative so treat it with caution! A tea made from vervain is very bitter, so the chances of over imbibing are small. It should also be avoided by pregnant women as it is an abortifactant.

There are accounts of the leaves being edible once boiled, and the flowers and seeds are considered edible. In Turkey the flowers are used to flavour salt. Apparently, a tea made from the leaves can be added to the bath for a soothing soak.

Do not confuse vervain with a related weed, blue snake weed, sometimes known as false verbena, *Stachytarpheta cayennensis*. This weed tends to be showier with clear blue flowers. It is a garden escapee and now a pantropical weed which is still often sold as vervain. If you find this one in the garden, keep it in check and enjoy its ability to attract butterflies. Like its cousin vervain, it has been attributed medicinal values, mainly for treating malaria, but is not considered to be edible. Blue snake weed seems to have a greater ability to spread and is more problematic in the environment than are the vervains, which are usually found in highly disturbed places.

All of the vervain weeds can be dealt with by hand weeding or cutting them below the base of the stem to prevent regrowth for those with a tap root. Mulching will prevent seed germination. Small plants can be dealt with by hoeing, boiling water, steam or vinegar.

Blue snake weed is a prolific weed in tropical and subtropical climates. The true vervains are found from temperate through to subtropical environments. They have limited tolerance for high humidity. Vervains are weeds in much of the world, mostly on highly disturbed sites.

Wild Brassicas

Brassica spp

Wild brassicas are happy to grow in compacted soils and will often be seen along roadsides. They are recognisable by their flowers, which range in colour from whites and creams through to yellow. They look very much like mustard or rocket in flower, to which they are related. All are edible and somewhat peppery. Young leaves are best for edible greens. The seeds of all varieties can be used in cooking similarly to mustard seeds. They all also have the many health benefits of the more familiar brassicas such as broccoli or kale, and the medicinal benefits of mustard, which are extensive.

Brown mustard (*Brassica juncea*) is a very common roadside weed in Australia, probably escaped from farmland. It resembles many other closely related *Brassica sp* which can also be weeds. It is a highly variable species which includes many cultivars grown commercially for the leaves, seeds, stems or roots.

Brassicas are used as green manures extensively worldwide, and mustard seeds are available commercially for this purpose. The role of a green manure is to produce rapid plant growth which is chopped into the soil while still green to compost and improve it. The act of digging the crop in while green seems to be highly effective in activating beneficial soil microbes. Significant research into the use of mustard green manures in potato cropping has been done at Washington State University. Australian scientists at the Commonwealth Scientific and Industrial Research Organisation (CSIRO) have been able to find similar benefits for using mustard green manures between wheat crops. Amongst the many benefits they have been able to prove, they have found brassicas to be *biofumigants*. This refers to the ability of brassicas to reduce soil pest populations through the release of phytochemicals from the plant roots and shoots.

Brassicas have been shown to have slight allelopathic properties which may inhibit the germination of other weed seeds nearby. This variety is often seen growing in dense stands of just one or two different types of wild brassica, and very few other weeds.

If you have any type of brassica weed growing, consider what benefits it may be offering your soil. Digging in brassicas as green manure can do nothing but good for your soil. Even leaving them to grow will be beneficial. They can be highly effective for soil borne fungal diseases, so if your garden is prone to fungal problems, growing some wild brassicas can be very useful. In addition to these soil benefits, all brassica flowers are highly attractive to pollinators and beneficial insects. If you have wild brassica weeds, allow them to flower and watch the amazing array of mini wildlife they bring to your garden.

There are many common weeds which are related to the wild brassicas; they are in the Brassicasea family but not the brassica genus. These include shepherd's purse (*Capsella bursa-pastoris*), lesser swine cress (*Lepidium didymum*), peppercress (*Lepidium spp.*) and flickweed (*Cardamine hirsuta*). With the exception of flickweed, which is very common in nurseries, all of the wild brassicas prefer the cooler months of the year here in the subtropics but will be found in spring and summer in cold climates. They are all edible.

With so many different weeds in this group, you will find them in a wide variety of situations. Many of the peppercresses (*Lepidium sp*) are very tolerant of dry conditions. Shepherd's purse likes cool weather and moist fertile soil. Flickweed likes free draining soils with plenty of moisture, which has allowed it to become a nuisance weed in nurseries. Watercress (*Nasturtium officinale)* loves fresh water and is a weed in creeks and wetlands.

The brassica family is a large and diverse group, so lumping them together here is an oversimplification. They do however have some shared characteristics which are useful. As they all have the peppery taste similar to rocket or cress (both also brassicas), they are quite recognisable on first bite. This flavour is due to the presence of mustard oils.

Flickweed, (*Cardamine hirsuta*) is a small rosette forming plant. Most of the leaves are within the basal rosette with a few on the stems. Leaves are pinnately divided into 8 - 15 leaflets. The terminal leaflet is larger than the other leaflets. It has tiny white flowers and upward pointing, elongated seedpods which open explosively.

Nasturtiums (*Tropaeolum majus*) also contain mustard oils, have the peppery taste and have similar health benefits based on the mustard oils. Nasturtiums, which are a weed in many areas, are the only plant outside the brassica family to contain mustard oils. The name is a little confusing, the common name *nasturtium* came about because they taste like water cress, not because they are related.

The stronger the taste, the more mustard oil is present and the greater the healing benefits will be. It will also make it much harder to eat – for culinary purposes, stick to eating young leaves fresh and older leaves cooked to reduce their pungency. Experiment a little with whichever wild brassicas you have in your garden. They may not be the stars of your next salad, but, like rocket, they can certainly add some extra excitement to a meal. Don't just stick to the leaves, the flowers are edible too and most have a delicate sweetness combined with a mild pungency. The cottage garden favourite, sweet alyssum, is also a brassica, and the flowers are delicious. Within the Bach Flower Essences, mustard flowers are used for dispelling gloom and depression. They can be a little flavour surprise so why not add some wild brassica flowers to a salad when we need cheering up.

The seed pods are also edible. You can collect the ripe seeds to use as a mustard seed alternative. They are great in curries, or for making pickles and preserves. The unripe seed pods can also be used. Harvest before the seeds are ripe and eat fresh, or lightly roast them as a peppery snack similar to wasabi peas. Eat them as a snack with beer or add them to a cheese platter. The seeds of all the wild brassicas can be used as sprouts or for sprouting microgreens. To get the healing benefits of the mustard oils, a tea or soup can be made with the older leaves. If you are not keen on drinking the tea, try using it as a foot soak. This is great for tired, inflamed feet and also a way for the body to soak up the goodness, which is beneficial even for colds and congestion. Be aware that mustard is hot and when used externally it has the potential to burn the skin. Don't soak your feet for longer than 20 minutes.

Mustard has a strong drawing action and has been used for centuries as an external poultice to draw the congestion of a cold, or to add warmth, stimulating blood flow and relieving pain, including back pain and sciatica. This works along the lines of a topical liniment or anti-inflammatory cream.

Lesser swine cress, (*Lepidium didymum*) is a sprawling ground cover with pinnate (fern like) leaves. It has tiny white flowers and seedpods that form round capsules.

To make a mustard poultice, crush some dried mustard (usually seeds but you can also use leaves, or use the leaves to make a tea and use this in place of the water component) and mix with water to make a paste. Thicken the paste with flour or beaten egg whites if need be. Spread the paste over a piece of cloth and apply it to the skin. You should start to feel the warming action very quickly. If this warming becomes uncomfortable remove the plaster. As it has the potential to cause burns and blistering if left on too long, be aware of your comfort level and never leave it on for more than half an hour.

The amount of, and therefore the therapeutic value of the mustard oil varies from species to species. The best way to find out if your weed is likely to be of value medicinally is to taste the wild brassica you have available. The more pungent (peppery) it is the more mustard oil it contains. This particularly applies to the seeds. If you have a mild brassica, it may be less value medicinally, but much easier to eat. Either way make use of it in the kitchen in any way that suits your palette.

One brassica worth singling out for special mention here is shepherd's purse (*Capsella bursa-pastoris*). This is such a small weed that we tend not to notice it until it is setting seed. The seed pods are small and heart shaped. If you believe in the school of thought that the shape of a fruit will indicate what part of the body it is good for (The Doctrine of Signatures), you won't go wrong with this one. Shepherd's purse has long been valued as a remedy for bleeding. It is effective against all forms of bleeding – bleeding noses, regulating menstrual problems, internal bleeding, high and low blood pressure and haemorrhage. It can be used by eating the leaves, although as it is a small rosette they are often missed until the distinctive seed pods appear. The leaves are still edible at this stage, as are the seeds. If you are experiencing nose bleeds, try crushing a leaf and putting it inside the nose for relief.

The seed capsules of this plant have been found to attract and kill nematodes. The purpose of this characteristic is unknown, but one theory suggests it is a means of providing fertile soil for the seeds to germinate in. Whatever the reason, it could be useful if you have problem nematodes in the garden.

Shepherd's purse (*Capsella bursa-pastoris*) is a low growing, rosette forming plant with lobed leaves. The tiny white flowers form in loose racemes followed by distinctive heart shaped seed pods.

Brassica weeds are widespread worldwide. This is a large group of weeds, and most climates will have multiple varieties. They are very tolerant of poor soil conditions and will seed abundantly. Many are short lived annuals, but the seed can have a long soil life. The seed is often spread by water runoff, which is why they are often found along creek corridors. In the garden brassica weeds should be dug into the soil to get the benefit they offer as a green manure. They are easily hand pulled and added to compost. To reduce future generations of this weed, keep your garden densely planted and well mulched.

Wild Carrot / Slender Celery

Cyclospermum leptophyllum

Wild carrots are an indicator of worn out or low fertility soils. They have quite a tap root so are very good for aerating and improving the soil. Use this one as compost. It can be eaten and tastes a little like carrot crossed with parsley. It is related to both, but possibly most closely related to celery. It makes a good edible garnish. If you have an abundance of it, it can be used as a mildly flavoured parsley substitute. Try it wilted in garlic butter and served with pasta.

Slender celery (*Cyclospermum leptophyllum*) is a small branching plant with threadlike green leaves. The tiny white flowers are round and form in umbels. The seeds are relatively large in comparison to the flower size.

The seeds can also be eaten. Celery seed is becoming a fad super food, often sold in health food stores. It is indeed very good for you, as is the seed of the wild carrot, but unlike celery seed, wild carrot seeds are free. By eating the seeds (or sprouting first then eating the sprouts), you are not just getting free health-giving food, you are controlling a weed from becoming a problem. The seeds are used in Ayurvedic medicine as a sedative, antifungal, antibacterial, anthelmintic, for rheumatism, and chronic skin conditions.

The tap root is very thin, so does not make much of a meal but tastes similar to carrots. The tap root can be significantly longer than the plant is high, a feature we rarely see given that it is so hard to pull the root out of the ground intact as it prefers compact soils.

To control this weed, soil improvement will be essential, as will creating a garden environment which makes it difficult for seeds to germinate.

It is in the Apiaceae family together with carrots, fennel, parsley and celery. All of these plants have clusters of small flowers, usually white, borne in umbels (meaning umbrella shaped) which are highly attractive to pollinating insects. The flowers of the wild carrot are especially tiny but are still appreciated by pollinators.

Slender celery can be found worldwide in temperate through to tropical climates.

Kate Wall

Weed Recipes

Now that you have discovered the amazing world of edible weeds you may be wondering how to eat them. As a general rule, think of weed leaves (the edible ones that is!) as a spinach substitute. Use them in the same way you would other greens – young leaves raw in salads and on sandwiches, older leaves cooked. I use weed leaves in almost every meal. They get added into my smoothies, chopped finely into pasta dishes and curries, or added to pizzas.

Weed seeds are also wonderful additions to our diets. I like adding the seeds of green amaranth - the most abundant seed in my weed garden, to risottos, brownies, or my morning porridge. Another way of utilising the seeds is to use them to grow your own sprouts or microgreens.

If you would like some more inspiration on how to eat your weeds, read on! The following recipes have all been written by my dear friend and fellow weed eater, Sharr Ellson, of Sharr Herbs, and I am delighted to share her fabulous recipes with you here. Sharr and I have collaborated on creating weed feasts. Sharr cooked and I (and our guests) feasted. I can absolutely vouch for the deliciousness of her recipes!

The only exception is the recipe for weed teas and tinctures. This is based on traditional herbal lore.

These recipes are not just a way of using edible weeds to create delicious meals, they are nutritionally dense and are supporting your health and wellbeing.

"Let food be thy medicine, and medicine be thy food" Hippocrates.

Weed and Cheese Cobb Loaf Dip

Ingredients

1 large cob bread loaf (450g)
Dip:
200g weeds, washed and finely chopped (a mix of weeds work well here)
3 green spring onions thinly sliced
2 cloves garlic, crushed
250g block cream cheese, chopped, at room temperature
200g Greek feta, crumbled
300ml sour cream
1 tbsp lemon juice

Instructions

Using a serrated knife, cut the top quarter off the cob loaf to form a lid. Pull away the soft bread from inside the loaf, leaving a 2cm-thick shell. Tear the soft bread and the bread in the lid into large pieces. Place loaf, lid and bread pieces on an oven tray lined with baking paper.

To make dip, heat an oiled frying pan over a medium heat. Add onions, weeds, and garlic. Stir for about 1 minute, or until the weeds are wilted. Drain off excess liquid. Cool.

Process cream cheeses, feta, sour cream and juice in a food processor until smooth. Stir into weed mixture. Season to taste.

Spoon mixture into loaf. Cook in a moderate oven (180C) for 15 minutes, or until golden and crisp. Remove.

Serve with the torn bread.

Some weeds that work well in this recipe are amaranth, chickweed, dandelion, fat hen, mustards, mallows, nasturtium leaves, purslane, sorrel, stinging nettle and dock.

Raw Weed Cheese

Ingredients

1 cup cashews (walnuts work well too), soaked in clean water overnight (8 hrs)
1 tablespoon lemon or lime juice
1 teaspoon garlic powder or 1 small clove of fresh garlic smashed
2 teaspoons nutritional yeast
2 teaspoons miso or make it 2 tablespoons of nutritional yeast in total
Pinch of salt (not if you are using miso)
Pinch of pepper

¼ cups clean water, although you may not need all of the water

1 handful of weeds, finely chopped

Instructions

Soak nuts overnight, drain and rinse.

Place in a food processor/ninja, along with weeds, lemon or lime juice, salt if using it and pepper.

If you can, start slowly. Add only a little water as you really don't want to add much water at all. Process until completely smooth.

Remove from the food processor/ninja and place the mix into a bowl, add the nutritional yeast or miso.

Mix everything together, cover and place in the fridge for a few hours to allow the flavours to marry before serving.

Some weeds that work well include dandelion, fat hen, mustards, mallow, nasturtium leaves, purslane, sorrel, pink baby's breath and stinging nettle.

Raw Weed Crackers

Ingredients

1 cup raw flaxseeds

½ cup raw sunflower seeds

½ cup raw pumpkin seeds

1 cup chia seeds

Water for soaking

1 medium onion, chopped

1 medium capsicum, chopped

½ cup veggie pulp left over from juicing (if you do not have pulp from juicing, you can add an additional half cup of weeds)

½ cup fresh weeds

1 teaspoon sea salt

1 teaspoon garlic powder

2 tablespoons of any dried or fresh herb such as rosemary, chives, all-herb or a pinch of chilli

Instructions

Place the flax, chia, sunflower seeds, and pumpkin seeds in separate bowls. Cover each seed with water and allow to soak for about 6 hours. Cover the flax and chia with just enough water to make them into a gel. It's about 1 to 1½ cup for each bowl. Rinse and drain the sunflower seeds and pumpkin seeds.

Throw the onion and capsicum into your food processor, and process until it's almost a liquid consistency. Add the drained sunflower and pumpkin seeds, weeds, the juice pulp, herbs, garlic powder and salt then process until well combined. Add the chia and flax gels and blitz again until all combined.

Scoop the mixture out and spread evenly and thinly (2mm) onto non-stick sheets in your dehydrator.

Score the crackers into the shape and size you'd like, using a sharp object like a pizza cutter or knife being careful not to cut your non-stick mat.

Set your dehydrator for 57°C and dehydrate for about 6 hours. Peel the non-stick sheets off and turn the cracker sheets over directly onto the mesh screens and dehydrate for a further 6 hours, or until completely dry and crispy.

Store in a sealed container.

You can use any weed greens for this but the ones high in minerals will be tastier. You can also add seeds from weeds, such as green amaranth and fat hen. Add these seeds to soak with the sunflower seeds, they will not form a gel like the chia and flaxseeds do.

Stinging Nettle Hummus

Ingredients
1 can chickpeas (drained and rinsed)
½ cup fresh stinging nettle leaves
1 large lemon juiced
2 tablespoons well-stirred tahini
¼ cups olive oil
½ teaspoons smoked paprika
1-2 cloves of garlic, chopped
sea salt to taste

Instructions
Combine tahini and lemon juice in a food processor and blend for 1 minute. Scrape sides and bottom of processor bowl then process another 30 seconds.

Add olive oil and smoked paprika. Process for 30 seconds; scrape sides and bottom of processing bowl to ensure even blending then process another 30 seconds.

Add half of the chickpeas to the food processor, process for 1 minute. Scrape sides and bottom of bowl.

Add in the stinging nettle and process 20 seconds, then add remaining chickpeas and process for 3 to 4 minutes or until thick and smooth.

If the hummus is too thick slowly add 2 to 3 tablespoons of water until the consistency is perfect.

Store your humus in an airtight container and refrigerate for up to one week.

Weed Chips

Ingredients

500g weeds (large leaves are the best, try dandelion, mallows, plantain, dock or sorrel)
6 tablespoons olive oil or coconut oil
Here are three seasoning flavour combinations to try:
½ fresh tomato chopped up, 4tbs Parmesan cheese, 2 x garlic cloves smashed
½ tbs fresh black pepper, 1 whole lime juiced
½ tbs sesame oil, ½ tbs hoisin sauce, 1tbs sesame seeds, 1tbs honey, ½ chilli fresh or dried

Instructions

Wash weeds and dry.

In a large bowl mix olive oil and your chosen flavour combination. Massage this mixture into the weeds firmly with both hands, like kneading bread. Place prepared weeds on a dehydrator tray or you can even use your oven. Dehydrate on 52°C for about 8 hours.

The oven can be faster, it can be done at 150°C for 8 to 10 minutes but keep an eye on the edges as they can burn quickly.

Take them out while they are crunchy. Eat-em up, as they don't last long or keep well.

Note: - do not add salt, they will be salty enough; greens are quite salty when dried.

Wild Burger Patty

Ingredients

2 tbsp extra-virgin olive oil, divided
1 small onion, diced
2 cloves garlic, minced
1 cup cooked brown/white rice
1 can cannellini beans, drained and rinsed (you can use other beans, I like these ones because they are white and creamy)
½ cup fine breadcrumbs or almond meal, oats, corn meal
2 tbsp chia seeds (optional)
½ tsp chilli powder (if you like chilli)
2 tbsp fresh parsley
1 pinch good quality salt
1 pinch ground black pepper, or dried paw-paw seeds, pepper tree berries, pepper cress

2 cups weeds, all the yummy ones

Instructions
Place a large pan over medium heat. Add 1 tbsp of olive oil and onion and garlic. Cook, stirring frequently, until the onion is translucent and soft. Wipe the pan clean as we are going to use it later.

Place rice, beans, breadcrumbs, chia seeds (if using), weeds, chili powder, parsley, salt, and pepper in a food processor and process until mixture is smooth-ish, being careful not to overmix as you will lose texture. Form into 4 equal patties.

Place the pan back on medium heat and add remaining 1 tbsp of oil. Add patties to the pan and cook until golden brown.

Wild Weed Pesto

Ingredients
2 cloves of garlic, minced
½ cup of extra virgin olive oil
2 cups freshly picked young mixed weeds
1 cup fresh picked basil leaves
¼ cup freshly grated parmesan cheese (for a vegan alternative you can leave out the cheese)
Teaspoon of sea salt
½ cup of cashews (or any nuts you have available)
4 tablespoon of lemon juice
1 whole lemon zest

Instructions
Place all the ingredients in a food processor with the nuts at the bottom. Slowly add the olive oil when the food processor is running. Blend well until you get a paste consistency. Adjust seasoning according to your taste. Enjoy.

You can use any mix of edible weeds (both leaves and seeds) for pesto but do be careful if you are using bitter tasting weeds. Too much will give you a bitter tasting pesto, use weeds such as dandelion or sow thistle as part of a mix of weeds, not on their own. Try a mix of cobbler's pegs, chickweed, dandelion, dock, fat hen, scurvy weed, purslane, young thistle leaves, nettle, and pink baby's breath.

Wild Mustard Mayonnaise

Ingredients

2 whole eggs
1 tb dried wild mustard seeds: - wild brassicas, shepherd's purse, flickweed, wild rocket.
2 tbs lemon juice
2 cups of mild olive oil
Pinch of salt

Instructions

Combine the whole egg, lemon juice, salt and mustard in the blender cup. Pulse with the blender a few times to break up the yolks.

Add 1 cup of the oil a little at a time. With the blender running, add the first 1 cup of oil a few tablespoons at a time. Make sure each addition of oil is completely blended before adding the next. The mixture should start to thicken and lighten. Once you've made this a few times and have a feel for it, you can try going more quickly.

Add the remaining oil in a steady stream. Once the first half cup of oil has been added, you can add the rest more quickly. Add as much of the oil as needed to reach the consistency you prefer; the more oil you add, the thicker the mayonnaise will become. You may not need to use all the oil. If the mayonnaise becomes too thick and you'd like to thin it out, blend water, 1 teaspoon at a time, into the mayonnaise until you reach your desired thickness.

Transfer any mayonnaise not being used immediately to a storage container. Homemade mayonnaise will keep for about 1 week in the refrigerator.

Green Goddess Dressing

This is such a great dressing that you will be using it not only on your salad but with cheese platters, sandwich spread and chippy dip. And what a smart way to get more weeds and herbs in your diet with little effort.

Ingredients

1 cup plain Greek yogurt or a 50\50 mix of Milk Kefir and yogurt, or sour cream, or cashew cheese
1 cup packed fresh weeds (dandelion, wild carrot, chickweed, baby cobber's pegs, soursob, wild brassicas, stinging nettle)
2 tablespoons fresh herbs leaves
1 medium clove garlic, roughly chopped
Pinch of sea salt
Black pepper to taste (or substitute the black pepper for crushed dried paw-paw seeds, pepper tree berries, or pepper cress)

Decorate with wild garlic or wild brassica flowers

Instructions
Combine all of the ingredients to a food processor. Process until smooth and green.
Taste, and add more salt or one of the peppers you chose if needed. Use it now or cover and refrigerate for later (it's even yummier later). This dressing will keep well in the fridge for 7 days.

Weed Oil

Apicius wrote "We eat first with our eyes" over 2,000 years ago. He would be happy with this recipe for weed oil. It delivers vibrant green splashes on the plate and is full of wonderful phytonutrients. This oil is largely used as a garnish due to its bright green colour. You can enhance the flavour by adding garlic flavoured weeds (in the allium family), mustard flavoured weeds (nasturtiums or wild brassicas) or lemon flavoured weeds (Oxalis and Rumex species). The flavour addition from these weeds can be subtle if they are added to a mix of other green weeds, or stronger if you use mainly these weeds.

Ingredients
4 cups loosely packed fresh soft, clean leaves of weeds (no stems)
1 cup good quality olive oil

Instructions
Create an ice bath by adding some ice to a large mixing bowl and then adding a few cups of water to create a cold wet bath. Put aside.
Set a medium size pot of water over high heat. When the water is boiling, add the fresh weeds. Let the weeds cook for about 20 seconds MAX, until they wilt and darken slightly in colour. Quickly transfer the weeds from the boiling water to the ice bath.
Remove the weeds from the ice bath and squeeze out as much excess water from the weeds as possible. Take your time with this step, really try to get as much water out of the weeds as possible.
Transfer the squeezed weeds to a blender. Add the oil and blend on the highest speed for 2-3 minutes.
Line a fine strainer with cheesecloth and put a large mixing bowl underneath. Pour the oil from the blender through the cheesecloth-lined strainer. Don't force the oil through the strainer, just let the oil drain naturally through. This may take about 1 hour.
When the oil has fully drained through the strainer, you can store it in a small container in the refrigerator for up to a few months. Use this oil to garnish anything savory. Pizza, eggs, avocado on toast, pasta.

Weed Salt

When making a weed salt, you have the option to create either a flavoured salt, or a salt substitute.

Choose weeds which are high in minerals and flavour. Purslane, chickweed, stinging nettle, dandelions, comfrey, plantain and wild carrots are all good. Try adding some of the wild brassicas, or wild garlic for extra flavour. The weeds need to be dried thoroughly to make a weed salt. Use a dehydrator, in the oven on a low heat or even just leave them out in the sun for a few days in hot dry weather. The front seat of the car with the windows up makes a good herb dehydrator in hot climates. Lay the herbs on a tea towel and then park the car in the sun for a day.

The dried leaves can be crushed to a fine powder with a food processor or mortar and pestle and then stored for use in seasoning food. For people on low salt diets this can be a great way to add extra flavour and minerals. Even if you are not on a low salt diet, this green powder is an excellent way of boosting flavour and nutrition in meals.

The dried herbs can be blended with a good quality rock salt in a salt grinder to produce a flavoured salt. You can add any strongly flavoured herb such as rosemary, all-herb or oregano and dried garlic for additional flavour. I like adding the dried leaves from celery tops to my herb salts.

For a lemon salt try using soursob or dock.

Chocolate Bark

Ingredients

300g quality chocolate buttons or chopped chocolate block (milk, dark that's up to you)

¼ cup raw nuts (almonds, pecans, macadamia, pistachios, coconut shaved)

¼ cup weed seeds such as green amaranth, plantain, wild carrot seed, fat hen, pink baby's breath, roasted wattle seeds (*Acacia fimbriata* is an Australian native that has become a weed outside its native range)

¼ cup dried cranberries or dried cherries, barberries, apricots, or candied ginger, chopped if large

2 tablespoons dried weed flowers or flower petals (dandelion, soursob, wild brassicas, madeira vine, cobbler's pegs) collect and dry on paper towel weeks before, store in a paper towel lined container

About ½ teaspoon flaky sea salt

Instructions

Heat frypan over medium/low heat and add the nuts, spread nuts evenly over the pan surface and keep stirring for about 3-4 minutes. Don't take your eyes off them and use your nose; when they start to smell fragrant, they are done. Burnt nuts taste awful.

Remove from heat and let cool on a tea towel or baking paper.

Transfer the nuts to a cutting board and roughly chop them.

Place a saucepan on the stove, medium heat, and add 3-4 cms of water to the saucepan.

Place a dry, heat-safe mixing bowl over the saucepan. Don't let this bowl touch the water in the saucepan.

Add chocolate to the mixing bowl. Don't let any water get into the chocolate.

Stir until all of the chocolate has melted.

Cover a medium, rimmed baking tray with baking paper. Use a silicone spatula to spread chocolate evenly over the baking paper — aim for about 2-3 cm thickness.

Sprinkle the nuts evenly over the chocolate, followed by the dried fruit. Add the flaky salt, then sprinkle petals and weed seeds over the chocolate between the nuts and fruit.

If you're in a hurry, place the tray on a flat surface in the fridge to harden for about 15 minutes. If you're not, let the chocolate cool on the bench for 2 to 4 hours, until completely hardened.

Once the chocolate is completely hardened, use your hands to break it into pieces. Serve immediately or wrap up for gifts.

Iced Dandelion Mocha

Ingredients

2 cups water

2 tablespoons roasted dandelion root, ground

1 tablespoon cacao nibs

1 cinnamon bark or quill

2 tablespoons honey

½ - ¾ cup milk or milk of your choice (rice, almond, oat, goat)

Instructions

Place water, dandelion roots, cinnamon and cacao in a saucepan. Bring to a boil, then reduce the heat to allow it to simmer for 5 minutes to infuse. This step can also be done in a teapot.

Pour root, bark/quill and nibs through a fine mesh strainer into a pitcher.

Add honey to taste, stir in well, now let it sit to cool down.

Pour the mocha mix over ice in a glass until it is two thirds full. Add milk to each glass and serve.

Soursob Lemonade

A very refreshing lemonade-like drink can be made using the leaves and flowers of any of the oxalis species.

Gather a cup full of leaves and blend in one litre of water. Add a spoonful of raw honey for added sweetness. Blend in a food processor until the leaves are fully chopped and you have a green liquid. Let the mix sit in the fridge for a few hours or overnight. The drink will be a light green colour but very tasty and refreshing. As there is no heating the vitamin C content of the oxalis remains high. When combined with the healing powers of raw honey this drink is not only yummy but also a great immune boost.

Sun Kissed Weed Tea

I love the saying "work smarter not harder" and this sun kissed tea is just that. Let the sun infuse your beautiful weeds, flowers and herbs to make a delish, refreshing and invigorating drink.

Ingredients
8 cups water
Petals from 3-4 fresh hibiscus flowers
1 lemon, quartered
Handful of mix tasty weeds such as soursob, cobbler's pegs, purslane, plantain, mallow, Wandering trad, blackberry nightshade berries, clover flowers, chickweed and fat hen
Handful of fresh mint or basil leaves
3cm piece of ginger, peeled, sliced
2 tablespoons of raw honey
Ice cubes and additional fruit and herbs for serving

Instructions
Pour all ingredients into the glass jar and making sure all the ingredients are submerged. Don't stress if not ALL are submerged it is not a long brew.
Stir, cover and place in the direct sun too steep for 2–4 hours, depending on how strong you prefer it.
Once finished, transfer to a pitcher filled with ice cubes and additional garnishes of fruit, mint, or weeds. Alternatively, refrigerate it in an airtight container to keep it fresh and chilled.
Drink within 2 days.

Recipe – weed tea, infusions and tinctures for coughs and colds

My go to formula for cold and flu season is a mix of plantain, cobbler's pegs, paddy's lucerne and ground ivy, in roughly equal parts or as you have it available. It is fine to include stalks, leaves and flowers of the cobbler's pegs and paddy's lucerne. Add some other highly medicinal weeds such as chickweed, nettles, mallows, soursob, wild brassicas, pink baby's breath, sow thistle, dandelions and false dandelions, mullein, elderberries, violets or red clover, depending on what you have available. All of these weeds are medicinal and beneficial when the immune system is low. The simplest way to prepare and consume these herbs is as a herbal tea.

To make a simple herbal tea, add a handful of herbs, roughly chopped, to a teapot and cover with hot water. Steep for five minutes and drink warm. This is a soothing tea with a mild green flavour, similar to green tea. If you are coughing, an added dash of honey can be soothing to the throat.

To make a stronger brew, steep a little longer or make an herbal infusion. The darker the colour of your brew, the stronger the brew will be and the greater healing benefit you will receive.

Herbal infusions are best made with dried herbs, so chop and leave the weeds on a tray to dry for a day or two before making this one. Add 30g of dried herb to the bottom of a 1L glass jar and cover with 1L of boiling water. Cap tightly and leave on the kitchen bench overnight (or for four hours). In the morning strain the mix and refrigerate. Drink it over the next 36 hours. It will end up with a somewhat dark and muddy appearance.

To get an even stronger and more long-lasting formula, you can make an herbal tincture. Tinctures are prepared with alcohol. They can be made with fresh or dry herbs. There is something of a science to making and prescribing tinctures, especially as they can provide a strong therapeutic dose, best supervised by a qualified naturopath.

A common at-home version of a tincture is to infuse herbs in a bottle of vodka. Chop the fresh herbs and add to a bottle of vodka. Store in a dark cool place, inverting every day for two to four weeks. The mixture can then be strained and will keep for six months or longer if refrigerated. Make sure it is well labelled! When taking, it is best to have only a small amount at a time – one small shot per day is plenty. <u>Any use of herbal tinctures should be supervised by a qualified naturopath.</u>

Weed Oxymel

An oxymel is an ancient herbal remedy which is primarily used for immune support and to treat respiratory and breathing disorders. It is basically herbs infused in vinegar and honey to make a medicinal drink. To gain the enormous medicinal properties that this drink offers, you will need to ensure you use unprocessed (raw) honey and unfiltered apple cider vinegar which still has some of the mother. These are both extremely medicinal products on their own, and when unprocessed and unrefined. By combining them in an oxymel with healing herbs you can make a fantastic and easy to take medicine for when you are unwell or for when you are rundown and trying to prevent getting sick.

Ingredients
1 garlic bulb smashed

½ cup fresh weed leaves roughly chopped (any of the medicinal weeds are good here, including chickweed, plantain, sida retusa, dandelion, cobbler's pegs, mallows, fat hen, sow thistle, gotu kola)

1 cup raw honey

1 cup raw apple cider vinegar

Instructions

Put the smashed garlic and chopped weeds into a jar. The jar should be about one third full of herbs.

Fill the jar about halfway with raw apple cider vinegar.

Add raw honey to the vinegar and weeds to fill the jar. Don't worry if the honey is thick, the vinegar will help it to dissolve and combine.

Put the lid on and give it a few shakes to combine. In winter this may take a bit longer to combine, don't be too fussy it will come together.

Put the oxymel in a cool place out of direct sunlight to infuse for at least a week and up to 30 days in winter. Shake jar at least 3 times a week to keep the weeds under the honey and vinegar, then strain out the weeds and garlic with a fine mesh strainer before using.

Store the oxymel in a cool place out of direct sunlight. It will keep for 6 months on the bench. It can be refrigerated for a longer shelf life.

Dose: Adults take 1-2 tablespoons 2-3 times per day when you feel a sickness coming on. Children can be given half this amount. **Oxymels should not be given to children under the age of one due to the raw honey.**

Skin Repair Ointment

Ingredients for herbal infusion

6 medium mallow leaves, small handful of chickweed, 6 medium plantain leaves chopped finely.

½ cup carrier oil such as olive oil, grape seed, jojoba, apricot kernel, avocado oil

Instructions

Pick the mallows and other weeds at mid-morning, when the dew has dried on the leaves and the flowers are open. Don't wash the leaves but pick them over and discard any dirty ones. It's important to use only dry plant material – any trace of moisture will cause the oil infusion to go off. Fill a smallish jar with finely chopped leaves. Pour oil into the jar and make sure all leaves are coved. Close the jar tightly, shake and place in a bright sunny spot inside. Shake the jar daily every day for the next 4 to 6 weeks.

After 6 weeks strain the weeds from the oil, I do this with a colander lined with cheese cloth held above a jar to catch all that liquid gold oil. Take your time and don't be tempted to squeeze out any last oil from the plant material as this can also squeeze out any water contained in the plant material and cause your infused oil to spoil. Label the jar and store in a cool dark space. If you have a larger jar, you can increase the herbs and oil proportionally.

Skin Repair Salve – Step 2
Ingredients for salve
30 mls of your infused oil
10 g beeswax
30 g shea butter or coconut oil

Instructions
Heat the beeswax and shea butter or coconut oil in a double boiler over a very gentle heat. Stir until all is fully melted, which should only take one or two minutes. Once they are melted turn off the heat and add your infused oil. Stir to combine and take away from heat as quickly and safely as you can, as you want to keep the properties of the infused oil in a stable condition, which means not overheating. Pour the warm salve into a clean jar. (This quantity will make 4 lip balm size pots). Cover and let it cool until it becomes solid. Label your pot.
If you wish to make a lip balm, increase the quantity of beeswax so the resulting salve is thicker, or use the balm recipe below.

I use this recipe to make an amazing skin cream every year using mallows, chickweed and plantain. You could add cleavers to this if you have it (it does not grow here in the subtropics). It is a little oily to rub on but is absorbed by the skin beautifully and is incredibly soothing, nourishing and healing. It can be used as an everyday full body moisturiser.

Weed Balm

A balm is a thicker ointment made without adding the shea butter / coconut oil. You could use weeds and herbs to make healing salves or balms for other external purposes such as sore muscles, insect bites, irritated skin, or minor wound healing. Suggestions of weeds to use for healing balms include:

<u>External antiseptic cream or insect bites:</u> billy goat weed, plantain, tea-tree (*Melaleuca quinquenervia*), fleabane, lantana, bittersweet nightshade or blackberry nightshade (*Solanum dulcamara* and *S. nigrum*).
<u>Minor wound healing:</u> plantain, tea-tree, chickweed, wild carrots, fleabane, lantana, blackberry nightshade.

Irritated skin including dermatitis and eczema: chickweed, bittersweet nightshade, blackberry nightshade, wild carrots, plantain, mallows.

Aching muscles and sprains: basket plant, comfrey, sow thistle, stinging nettle.

Ingredients
1 cup weed infused oil
30g beeswax
1 small jar to hold 170mls of product

Weed Infused Oil - The alcohol intermediary method.
Finely chop 1 cup of dry weeds (I use a blender) and put into a jar with 1 shot glass of vodka (30mls). Let everything sit for between 6 and 12 hours.

Remove the lid, add enough oil (200mls) to cover the herbs and put this jar into a yogurt maker at 38°C, stirring at least once a day for three days.

When this time is up strain out the weed matter using a nut milk bag or clean fabric over a strainer over a bowl.

Put your infusion in a clean labelled jar (the label should include the weeds used, the carrier oil and the date it was made) and store in a cool dark place.

This method is not only faster than the traditional infused oil method used in the skin cream, but also far more intense, extracting more goodness from the weeds, and resulting in a darker coloured infused oil. You can use either method to create infused oils or your skin creams and balms.

Instructions for the balm
Use the double boiler method to melt your beeswax, as you did for the salve. Take it slow and easy – don't get the wax any hotter than it needs to be.

Add one cup of infused oil once the beeswax is melted, stir gently until all is blended. Turn off heat.

Pour into desired container and allow to cool and set. Label your container.

I use an old grater to grate the beeswax before adding it to the pot. This helps it to melt faster and more evenly at a low heat. It will be a good idea to set aside old kitchen tools which will be dedicated to your salve making, as beeswax is very difficult to clean off kitchen utensils.

Kate Wall

References

1. Eat The Weeds, and other things too. Greene Deane 2018 http://www.eattheweeds.com
2. Weeds In Australia. Australian Government 2018 http://environment.gov.au/biodiversity/invasive/weeds/index.html
3. Oxalates In Spinach and Other Leafy Greens: Can Oxalic Acid In Green Smoothies Devastate Your Health? June 5, 2012, http://greenreset.com/oxalates/
4. Some notes on oxalic acid for foragers. Adam Grubb and Annie Raser-Rowland http://www.eatthatweed.com/oxalic-acid/
5. Oxalic Acid Information 2018 http://oxalicacidinfo.com/
6. Oxalic acid concentrations in Purslane (Portulaca oleraceae L.) is altered by the stage of harvest and the nitrate to ammonium ratios in hydroponics. Scientia Horticulturae Volume 102, Issue 2, 1 November 2004 Usha R. Palaniswamy, Bernanrd B. Bible, Richard J. McAvoy
7. The Weed Forager's Handbook: A Guide to Edible and Medicinal Weeds in Australia by Adam Grubb and Annie Raser-Rowland Hyland House, 2012
8. CABI, 2018. Invasive Species Compendium. Wallingford, UK: CAB International. www.cabi.org/isc.
9. City of Gold Coast. Kang Kong, Ipomea aquatica http://www.goldcoast.qld.gov.au/mobile/environment/kang-kong-ipomoea-aquatica-16949.html
10. Weeds Australia, An Australian Weeds Committee National Initiative 2018 http://weeds.ala.org.au/
11. Useful Tropical Plants, Ken Fern 2018 http://tropical.theferns.info
12. The Poison Garden, John Robertson 2018 http://www.thepoisongarden.co.uk
13. Entheology; Preserving Shamanism's Ancient Sacred Knowledge, Keith Cleversley 2018 http://entheology.com/plants
14. Corangamite Region "Brown Book" - How to optimise your soils to enhance productivity. Corangamite Catchment Management Authority, AS Miner Geotechnical 2103 http://www.ccmaknowledgebase.vic.gov.au/brown_book/29_Weeds.htm
15. The Old Farmer's Almanac, Weeds as Indicator Plants, What Weeds Can Tell You About Your Soil. Mar 28, 2018, https://www.almanac.com
16. Monsanto to Pay $289.2 Million in Landmark Roundup Lawsuit Verdict Baum, Hedlund, Aristei, Goldman. 2018 https://www.baumhedlundlaw.com
17. Common Weed Killer Linked to Bee Deaths Sept 24, 2018, University of Texas. https://news.utexas.edu/2018/09/24/common-weed-killer-linked-to-bee-deaths
18. Glyphosate perturbs the gut microbiota of honeybees. Erick V. S. Motta, Kasie Raymann, Nancy A. Moran. Proceedings of the National Academy of Sciences Sep 2018, 201803880; DOI: 10.1073/pnas.1803880115
19. Open-Source Food: Nutrition, Toxicology, and Availability of Wild Edible Greens in the East Bay. Philip B. Stark, Daphne Miller, Thomas J. Carlson, Kristen Rasmussen de Vasquez

20. The Weed Book. Identifying and removing weeds and introduced species from your garden. Mark A. Wolff. 2011 New Holland
21. Weed. The Ultimate Gardener's Guide to Organic Weed Control. Tim Marshall. 2010 ABC Books
22. Edible Wild Plants of Vietnam, The Bountiful Garden. Yoshitaka Tanaka and Nguyen Van Ke, 2007, Orchid Press.
23. How Can I use Herbs In my Daily Life. Isabell Shipard. 5th edition 2011 Published by David Stewart. Nambour
24. The Wondrous World of Weeds, Understanding Nature's Little Wonders. Pat Collins 2017 New Holland
25. Wetland Weeds Causes, Cures and Compromises. Nick Romanowski 2011 CSIRO Publishing
26. Organic Control of Common Weeds. Jackie French 1989 Arid Books
27. Medicinal Plants in Australia Vol 3 – Plants, Potions and Poisons. Cheryll Williams 2012 Rosenberg Publishing Pty Ltd.
28. How to Plant and Grow Wild Asparagus, January 24, 2018. Penelope Hart. https://dengarden.com
29. How healthy is urban horticulture in high traffic areas? Trace metal concentrations in vegetable crops from plantings within inner city neighbourhoods in Berlin, Germany. Säumel I1, Kotsyuk I, Hölscher M, Lenkereit C, Weber F, Kowarik I.
30. Can Urban Soil Offer Edible Weeds Fit for Foraging? Eden Stiffman, 21 Sept 2018 https://civileats.com
31. Innovators look to "accidental crops" as a nutritious, environmentally friendly and free source of food. Natalie Parletta, Sept 28, 2018, https://ensia.com
32. Chipurura, Batsirai & Muchuweti, M & Bhebhe, M. (2013). An assessment of the phenolic content, composition and antioxidant capacity of selected indigenous vegetables of Zimbabwe. Acta Horticulturae. 979. 611-620. 10.17660/ActaHortic.2013.979.66.
33. Chipurura, Batsirai & Muchuweti, Maud & Kasiyamhuru, Abisha. (2013). Wild Leafy Vegetables Consumed in Buhera District of Zimbabwe and Their Phenolic Compounds Content. Ecology of food and nutrition. 52. 178-89. 10.1080/03670244.2012.706094.
34. Arlene P. Bartolome, Irene M. Villaseñor, and Wen-Chin Yang, "Bidens pilosa L. (Asteraceae): Botanical Properties, Traditional Uses, Phytochemistry, and Pharmacology," Evidence-Based Complementary and Alternative Medicine, vol. 2013, Article ID 340215, 51 pages, 2013. https://doi.org/10.1155/2013/340215.
35. This Nasty Weed Could Save your Life: Bidens. Joybilee Farm 2018 https://joybileefarm.com
36. The Growth of Clovers at Different Levels of Soil Acidity by A. J. McNeur, Ecologist, Grasslands Division, D.S.I.R., Palmerston North. 2018 https://www.grassland.org.nz
37. A Dock a Day May keep the Doc Away – Harvesting Wild Docks, Dan de Lion. June 20, 2012, http://returntonature.us
38. Philippine Medicinal Plants 2018 Godofredo U. Stuart Jr., M.D. http://www.stuartxchange.org/Talinum.html
39. Culpeper's Complete Herbal, Nicholas Culpeper. Originally published in 1653, Wordsworth Editions Limited, 1995
40. Beyond Organics, Gardening for the Future. Helen Cushing. ABC Books, 2005
41. Garden Talk, Colin Campbell. Hyland House Publishing 2009

42. The Organic Garden Doctor, Jackie French. Angus and Robertson Publishers, 1988
43. The Permaculture Garden, Graham Bell. Thorsons, an Imprint of Harper Collins Publishers, 1994
44. Magic and Medicine of Plants, Reader's Digest 2010
45. Modern Ailments Ancient Remedies, a healing manual. Gillian Kerr and Dr Yvonne Bloomfield. Lansdowne
46. Gather Victoria, Ancestral food. Magical Cookery. Seasonal Celebration. 2018 https://gathervictoria.com/
47. Wild Food Girl. Foraging the wild for plants and stuff to eat. Dina Falconi, 2014 https://wildfoodgirl.com/
48. Plantain, First Aid in your Backyard. Corinne Wood. July 2005 Weed Wanderings Herbal Ezine with Susan Weed. Vol 5 No 7
49. Healing Wise. Energise and Enjoy with Nettle. Susan Weed. October 2008. Wise Woman Herbal Ezine with Susan Weed. Vol 8 No 10
50. Nourishing Herbal Infusions. Sandra Nanka. Sage, Queensland Herb Society Inc Newsletter Vol 41 Issue 2
51. Herbal Tinctures. Bettina Schmoll. Sage, Queensland Herb Society Inc Newsletter Vol 41 Issue 3
52. Wild Herbs of Australia and New Zealand, Tim Low. Angus and Robertson Publishers, Australia 1991
53. A New Book of Herbs. Jekka McVicar Dorling Kindersley Limited London 2004
54. Quinn, L.D., Endres, A.B. & Voigt, T.B. Biol Invasions (2014) 16: 1559. https://doi.org/10.1007/s10530-013-0591-z
55. Not Ready for Prime Time: Making Fuel Out of Invasive Plants. Michael Todd Nov 20, 2013, Pacific Standard Magazine
56. A New Leaf: Making Paper from Weeds Lisa Conti Oct 7, 2008 Pacific Standard Magazine
57. Weeds: control without poisons. Charles Walters 2nd Ed. 1999 Acres USA Inc
58. Commonsensehome.com Prickly Wild Lettuce – Garden Lettuce's Wild Cousin – Weekly Weeder #24 March 13, 2017, by Laurie Neverman
59. Weeds, Guardians of the Soil. Joseph A Cocannouer the Devin-Adair Company Old Greenwich • Connecticut 1950, reprinted 1980
60. Weeds as Indicators Of Soil Conditions by Stuart B. Hill and Jennifer Ramsay Ecological Agriculture Projects, McGill University (Macdonald Campus) 1977
61. Deadly Nightshade vs Black Nightshade. Mr Homegrown. Www.rootsimple.com 4 November 2011
62. "Natural products derived from plants as a source of drugs" Journal of advanced pharmaceutical technology & research vol. 3,4 (2012): 200-1.
63. Making Natural Dyes from Plants. June 19, 2012, Pioneerthinking.com
64. Soil Restoration: 5 Core Principles. October 17, 2017, Dr Christine Jones EcoFarmingDaily.com
65. Options for Reducing Glyphosate. Integrity Soils, The Biological Education Specialist. Don Campbell. 2018
66. Penn State. "Recruiting ants to fight weeds on the farm." ScienceDaily. ScienceDaily, 18 December 2018. www.sciencedaily.com/releases/2018/12/181218115142.htm
67. Marina Semchenko *et al*. Fungal diversity regulates plant-soil feedbacks in temperate grassland. *Sci. Adv.* **4**, eaau4578(2018). DOI:**10.1126/sciadv.aau4578**
68. The Sad Story of Nitrogen (but there Can be a Happy Ending) Part 1. Graeme Sait. 5 December 2018http://www.nutri-tech.com.au
69. Willows poisoning at Daylesford Lake 'a disaster' for heat: activists. Hayley Elg. Bendigo Advertiser January 18, 2019

70. Yarmolinsky, Ludmila et al. "Anti-Herpetic Activity of Callissia fragrans and Simmondsia chinensis Leaf Extracts In Vitro" open virology journal vol. 4 57-62. 11 May. 2010, doi:10.2174/1874357901004010057
71. Callisia Fragrans' plant has medicinal value. By Trung Hieu - Translated by Uyen Phuong. Saigon Online. Thursday, January 31,
72. The Biology of Australian Weeds vol 2 and 3. FD Panetta, RH Groves and RCH Sheperd. 1998 RG and FJ Richardson, Melbourne Winning the War on Weeds. Mark A Wolff. 1999 Kangaroo Press
73. Don't Judge Species on Their Origins, Mark A Davis NATURE | VOL 474 | 9 JUNE 2011, Macmillan Publishers Inc.
74. Goats and Weed Control. By Jim Johnson, Soils and Crops Consultant and Robert Wells, Ph.D., Livestock Consultant. Noble Research Institute Posted Oct. 1, 2007
75. Vegetation management expert turns to goats for effective weed control. Jennifer Nichols. ABC News. 23 September 2016
76. Green Manuring with Mustard. Improving an Old Technology. Andy McGuire, Agricultural Systems Educator, WSU. Agricultural and Environmental News. Washington State University. June 2003, Issue 206
77. Mobile goats prove to be a natural weed killer. Joshua Becker. ABC News 22 October 2015
78. The palatability, and potential toxicity of Australian weeds to goats. Helen Simmonds, Peter Holst, Chris Bourke 2000 Rural Industries Research and Development Corporation
79. Clean soils the brassica way the biofumigation project. GroundCover™ Issue: 25 | 01 Jan 1999 Australian Government Grains Research and Development Corporation.
80. Managing Herbicide Resistance in Northern NSW. Andrew Storrie, Tony Cook, Paul Moylan, Alan Maguire, Steve Walker and Michael Widderick Australian Government Grains Research and Development Corporation
81. Glyphosate Worse than We Could Imagine. "It's Everywhere" F. William Engdahl. Global Research, April 27, 2019
82. Glyphosate from Monsanto's Roundup Decimates Microbes in Soils and the Human Gut – New Science. Isabelle Z. Global Research, February 16, 2018
83. The biology and non-chemical control of Japanese knotweed (Fallopia japonica (Houtt)) W Bond, G Davies, RTurner HDRA, Ryton Organic Gardens, Coventry, CV8, 3LG, UK November 2007
84. Aggressive Japanese Knotweed is Making Its Way Across U.S., Pushing Out Native Species in its Path by Jan Wesner Childs. The Weather Channel, Environmental News 9 May 2019
85. Hicks DM, Ouvrard P, Baldock KC, et al. Food for Pollinators: Quantifying the Nectar and Pollen Resources of Urban Flower Meadows. PLoS One. 2016;11(6): e0158117. Published 2016 Jun 24. doi: 10.1371/journal.pone.0158117
86. Ground Ivy Herb Use. Deb Jackson and Karen Bergeron. Alternative Nature Online Herbal 2019
87. Weeds that Indicate Soil Conditions, Four Season Garden: How Weeds Can Help Identify and Correct Soil Problems. by BC Farms & Food – Permalink. May 16, 2017
88. University of California Agriculture and Natural Resources. Statewide Integrated Pest Management Program. http://ipm.ucanr.edu/index.html 2019
89. University of Illinois Weed Science. http://weeds.cropsci.illinois.edu/index.htm 2019
90. Great Britain Non-Native Species Secretariat. 2019 http://www.nonnativespecies.org/home/index.cfm

91. Global Invasive Species Database 2019. http://www.iucngisd.org/gisd/
92. Shenefelt PD. Herbal Treatment for Dermatologic Disorders. In: Benzie IFF, Wachtel-Galor S, editors. Herbal Medicine: Biomolecular and Clinical Aspects. 2nd edition. Boca Raton (FL): CRC Press/Taylor & Francis; 2011. Chapter 18. Available from: https://www.ncbi.nlm.nih.gov/books/NBK92761/
93. The Biodynamic Education Centre Library. Section Six. Weeds Pests and Disease. May 2013 http://www.biodynamiceducation.com
94. Bala (Sida Cordifolia) Medicinal Use and Health Benefits. Bimbima Daily life experience of ayurvedic medicines, complementary therapies. Anupama July 15, 2014, https://www.bimbima.com/ayurveda/herb-information-balasida-cordifolia/614/
95. When Weeds Talk. Jay L McCaman. Copyright 2013
96. Weeds. How Vagabond Plants Gatecrashed Civilisation and Changed the Way We Think About Nature. Richard Mabey. Profile Books 2010
97. QUT Grand Challenge Lecture Series. Rapid Evolutuion in Introduced Species: Will Weeds Become Our Future Natives? Professor Angela Moles, UNSW
98. Organic Soil Fertility and Weed Management. Steve Gilman. NOFA Chelsea Green 2011
99. The Value of Weeds. Ann Cliff The Crowood Press 2017
100. Weeds and What They Tell Us Ehrenfried E Pfeiffer Floris Books. Translated from the original Germany written in 1950.
101. Shreemantra Herbs. Lantana camara, The Unusual Wild Herb. 2020. Shreemantra.com/the-unusual-wild-sage
102. Health benefits of common lantana. 2020. healthbenefitstimes.com/common-lantana
103. Cavalier - S&W Seed Company (swseedco.com.au)
104. Dai H, Wei S, Twardowska I, Han R, Xu L. Hyperaccumulating potential of Bidens pilosa L. for Cd and elucidation of its translocation behavior based on cell membrane permeability. Environ Sci Pollut Res Int. 2017 Oct;24(29):23161-23167. doi: 10.1007/s11356-017-9962-9. Epub 2017 Aug 21. PMID: 28828736.
105. Xuan TD, Khanh TD. Chemistry and pharmacology of *Bidens pilosa*: an overview. J Pharm Investig. 2016;46(2):91-132. doi: 10.1007/s40005-016-0231-6. Epub 2016 Mar 30. PMID: 32226639; PMCID: PMC7099298.
106. Purslane (Portulaca Oleracea): The Weed with Extraordinary Benefits (Science Based). Jenny Hills, 2019. Healthyandnaturalworld.com
107. Uses and benefits of Virginian Peppercress Lepidium virginicum 2020 healthbenefitstimes.com/virginian-peppercress.
108. Grounds for testing: Delprat Phytoremediation Garden | Landscape Australia Andrew Toland, May 2022
109. Puha - the unsung hero of superfoods | Te Ao Māori News (teaonews.co.nz) Peata Melbourne, 2016
110. Plentiful Puha. Julia Sich (juliasedibleweeds.com) 2016
111. Qualifying Dynamic Accumulators: a Sub-Group of the Hyperaccumulators. - The Permaculture Research Institute (permaculturenews.org) Dean Brown 2015
112. Which Dynamic Accumulator Plants are Actually Helpful for your Garden, According to Science? – Earth Undaunted. Erin Alladin, 2022 earthundaunted.com

113. Achira (Canna edulis) - The Cultivariable Growing Guide, William Whitson. cultivariable.com
114. Glechoma hederacea - Southern Cross University (scu.edu.au) SCU Medicinal Plant Monographs. Glechoma hederacea. Jessica Gatti 2008
115. Roberts, H.R., Warren, J.M. & Provan, J. Evidence for facultative protocarnivory in *Capsella bursa-pastoris* seeds. *Sci Rep* **8**, 10120 (2018). https://doi.org/10.1038/s41598-018-28564-x
116. Study shows glyphosate impairs learning in bumblebees (2023, July 25) retrieved 1 April 2024 from https://phys.org/news/2023-07-glyphosate-impairs-bumblebees.html From University of Knostanz
117. Oxalate (Oxalic Acid): Good or Bad? Franziska Spritzler 2023 (healthline.com) https://www.healthline.com/nutrition/oxalate-good-or-bad
118. Foods High in Oxalates. Medically Reviewed by Minesh Khatri, MD on December 11, 2022, Written by WebMD Editorial Contributors (webmd.com)
119. A Modern Herbal | Nightshade, Black (botanical.com) Based on A Modern Herbal by Mrs M Grieve, 1931.
120. Solanum nigrum: Current Perspectives on Therapeutic Properties Ramya Jain (Grad. stud.); Anjali Sharma (Grad. stu.); Sanjay Gupta, PhD; Indira P. Sarethy, PhD; and Reema Gabrani, PhD. July 5th, 2016. Alternative Medicine Review, Vol 16, No 1.
121. Contaminant Berries in Frozen Vegetables, Leo J Schep, Robin J Slaughter, Wayne A Temple. The New Zealand Medical Journal, 3 April 2009, Vol 122 No 1292; ISSN 1175 8716
122. The Lost book of Herbal Remedies, The healing power of plant medicine. Nicole Apelian, Ph.D & Claude Davis, 2021.
123. Smithsonian Magazine. What Did Tollund Man, One of Europe's Famed Bog Bodies, Eat Before He Died? Nora McGreevy July 22, 2021
124. Acta Poloniae Pharmaceutica ñ Drug Research, Vol. 68 No. 1 pp. 83ñ92, 2011. Comparison of the nutritive value and biological activities of the acetone, methanol and water extracts of the leaves of Bidens pilosa and Chenopodium album. Adeolu Adedapo (Center for Cardiovascular Diseases, College of Pharmacy and Health Sciences, Texas Southern University, Houston TX, USA), Florence Jimoh and Anthony Afolayan (Department of Botany, University of Fort Hare, Alice 5700, South Africa)
125. Kalita, Sanjeeb & Kumar, Gaurav & Loganathan, Karthik & Venkata, Kokati & Rao, Bhaskar. (2012). A Review on Medicinal Properties of Lantana camara Linn. Research Journal of Pharmacy and Technology. 5. 711-715.
126. The palatability, and potential toxicity of Australian weeds to goats. Helen Simmonds, Peter Holst, Chris Bourke. Rural Industries Research and Development Corporation. 2000
127. Alba, Thainara & Pelegrin, Carla & Sobottka, Andréa. (2020). Ethnobotany, ecology, pharmacology, and chemistry of Anredera cordifolia (Basellaceae): a review. Rodriguésia. 71. 10.1590/2175-7860202071060.
128. Yuniarti WM, Lukiswanto BS. Effects of herbal ointment containing the leaf extracts of Madeira vine (*Anredera cordifolia* (Ten.) Steenis) for burn wound healing process on albino rats. Vet World. 2017 Jul;10(7):808-813. doi: 10.14202/vetworld.2017.808-813. Epub 2017 Jul 22. PMID: 28831227; PMCID: PMC5553152.

129. Singh, Ajeet &, Navneet. (2018). TRADITIONAL USES, ANTIMICROBIAL POTENTIAL, PHARMACOLOGICAL PROPERTIES AND PHYTOCHEMISTRY OF SIDA RHOMBIFOLIA LINN.: A REVIEW. 6. 10.21276/IJIPSR.2018.06.02.263.
130. Weeding Between the Lines; An anthology of essays about our relationship with nature. John Dwyer. Australian Garden History Society. 2023

Index

agapanthus, 44, 45
aloes, 46
amaranths, 40, 49, 55, 110, 149, 150, 158
arum lilies, 49, 67, 69
asparagus, 16, 75, 80, 86, 117, 118, 119, 155
balloon vine, 112
bamboo, 35, 67, 68, 69, 80
billy goat weed, 74, 109, 122, 123, 226
bindii, 35, 46, 124
bindweed, 35, 40, 49, 65, 67, 68, 69, 80, 100, 171
black wattle, 61
blackberry, 35, 61, 67, 69, 74, 127, 128, 226, 227
blackberry nightshade, 128, 226, 227
blue snake weed, 204
Bracken, 45
brassicas, 74, 93, 100, 205, 206, 207, 208, 209, 219, 221, 223
Brazilian cherry, 129
broom, 48
brunsfelsia, 80
bulrushes, 118
burr medic, 70, 100, 130, 132
buttercups, 35, 43, 46, 49, 59
cactus, 46
cadaghi, 29
callisia, 42, 43, 57, 59, 64, 84, 121
caltrop, 42, 125
camphor laurels, 67, 113
canna, 49, 69, 109, 110, 132, 134
capeweed, 46
cat's claw creeper, 63, 108, 112
cat's claw creeper, 67, 68, 69, 75, 80, 83, 84, 108, 113
cestrum, 108
chickweed, 34, 42, 43, 46, 48, 49, 52, 87, 91, 134, 135, 136, 139, 168, 179, 184, 197, 199, 214, 218, 221, 223, 225, 226, 227
chicory, 48
Chinese elms, 53, 66, 84, 108, 113

Cissus, 112
cleavers, 43, 48, 56, 110
clover, 42, 46, 69, 70, 109, 113, 124, 130, 137, 138, 224
cobblers pegs, 15, 16, 34, 35, 43, 54, 56, 82, 87, 91, 106, 138, 179, 218, 223
coconuts, 28
Cocos palm, 84
comfrey, 48, 69, 221
commelina, 59, 83, 112, 186, 187, 188, 189, 218
coral berry, 110
couch, 35, 63, 67, 69, 71, 79, 80, 83, 153
creeping charlie, 43, 59, 65
creeping indigo, 42, 70, 131
crepe myrtle, 66, 80, 108
crocosmias, 44, 45
dandelion, 17, 35, 40, 46, 48, 49, 55, 70, 91, 109, 113, 124, 141, 142, 144, 195, 214, 215, 217, 218, 221, 222, 224
dock, 40, 48, 49, 91, 110, 144, 199, 214, 217, 218, 221
duckweed, 48
Dutchman's Pipe vine, 27
Easter cassia, 42, 66, 84, 86, 87
elderberry, 46, 110, 224
emelia, 94
Eupborbia, 39
false dandelion, 40, 49, 141, 142, 195
false mallow, 40, 87, 103
fat hen, 34, 48, 55, 158, 199, 214, 215, 216, 218
fennel, 46, 48
fireweed, 47, 74, 101
fleabane, 17, 73, 146, 147, 148, 226
flickweed, 93, 206, 219
freesias, 17, 45, 172
galant soldiers, 43
garlic mustard, 27, 40
giant hogweed, 28
giant reed, 31
glossy nightshade, 128
glycine, 42

goldenrod, 110
gorse, 60
grass weeds, 47, 60, 64
ground elder, 35
hawkweed, 144
heliotrope, 47
henbit, 43, 152
Holly leaved senecio, 61
ivy, 35, 112, 113, 176
jewels of Opar, 44
khaki weed, 125
kikuyu, 71, 73
knotweed, 67, 68, 69, 80, 81, 119, 153, 154, 155, 156
lantana, 17, 27, 60, 105, 108, 110, 112, 162
lesser swine cress, 42, 206
leucaena, 60
liquid amber, 66
love lies bleeding, 68
madeira vine, 57, 67, 69, 166
mallows, 40, 48, 52, 60, 91, 110, 167, 168, 174, 179, 185, 199, 215, 217, 223, 225
mare's tail, 18
mare's tail, 35
Mexican poppy, 87
Mexican sunflower, 74
Mickey Mouse bush, 16, 60, 66, 86, 108
Mile-a-minute, 169
mints, 65, 151
morning glory, 35, 67, 68, 69, 80, 84, 108, 110, 169, 170
Morning glory, 29, 69
mother-of-millions, 59, 64
mugwort, 49
mullein, 46, 49, 110, 224
mustards, 27, 205, 206, 207, 208, 219
nasturtium, 91, 214, 215
nasturtiums, 207
nettle, 35, 43, 48, 49, 52, 56, 100, 103, 110, 146, 199, 200, 201, 216, 217, 218, 221, 223
Noogoora burr, 74
nutgrass, 34, 43, 44, 45, 60, 63, 67, 69, 73, 74, 75, 80, 88, 89
onion grass, 45
onion weed, 34, 43, 44, 45, 57, 59, 60, 73, 80, 172, 173, 192
oxalis, 16, 34, 35, 57, 59, 74, 80, 91, 191, 192, 222, 223

paddy's lucerne, 39, 40, 94, 139, 179, 223
Patterson's curse, 46, 47
pepper tree, 175, 177
peppercress, 93, 206
pink baby's breath, 91, 157, 215, 218
plantain, 34, 46, 48, 49, 70, 109, 110, 124, 139, 168, 178, 179, 180, 217, 221, 223, 225, 226, 227
plumbago, 80
poke weed, 110
Prickly lettuce, 180, 182
privet, 60
purple loosestrife, 49
purslane, 28, 34, 46, 48, 49, 87, 91, 182, 183, 184, 214, 215, 218, 221
quack grass, 49
Radiata pines, 115
radium weed, 136, 197, 198
ragweed, 43, 49, 74, 99, 100
ragwort, 48, 195
red natal grass, 45
Ruellia, 112
scarlet pimpernel, 136, 184, 185
sensitive weed, 40, 189, 191
sheep sorrel, 46, 49
shepherd's purse, 48, 206, 219
sida retusa, 28, 60
silver leafed desmondium, 56, 70
Singapore daisy, 63, 64, 67, 68, 69, 73, 80, 81, 84
snake plant, 30, 84, 87, 88, 110, 111
sorrel, 46, 48, 110, 144, 146, 191, 214, 215, 217
soursob, 60, 88, 113, 221, 223
sow thistle, 15, 16, 48, 52, 73, 83, 193, 194, 224
sow thistles, 15
speedwell, 49
spiny emex, 125
Spiny emex, 125
spurge, 196, 197, 198
spurges, 39, 46, 48, 198
St John's wort, 47
swine cress, 93
Sword fern, 201
thickhead, 43
thistles, 34, 40, 48, 49, 70, 100, 194, 195, 196
Thunbergia, 113

tick trefoil, 37
ti-tree, 67, 226
tradescantias, 57, 59, 112
tree lucerne, 42, 100
trefoils, 40, 42
velvet leaf, 60
vervain, 46, 204
vetch, 40, 42, 49, 70
vinca, 98

violets, 65, 224
wandering Jew, 35, 42, 64, 65, 188
watsonias, 45
wild carrot, 39, 40, 46, 49, 93, 210, 221, 226, 227
wild marigold, 46
willow, 27, 48, 98, 108, 114
yarrow, 49, 110

ABOUT THE AUTHOR – KATE WALL

Kate Wall is an in-demand gardening coach based in Brisbane. Her career changed from environmental science (with scientific qualifications in biology) to professional gardening after the 2011 floods when her local community was badly affected. Kate's volunteer efforts to restore flooded gardens saw her become Australia's most experienced horticulturalist in the field of garden recovery after flooding. This culture of caring has set the theme for Kate's approach to gardening as she works towards improving people's lives through making gardening a pleasure and a success. It is her mission to teach gardeners how to really understand and master their own patch so that they can easily create their own dream garden.

Kate specialises in teaching people to garden in harmony with nature, ensuring beautiful and highly successful gardens for gardeners of all levels of experience. By working with nature Kate focuses on a very sustainable approach to gardening which is not only better environmentally but also makes the job at hand so much easier. As a resident of a subtropical city, Kate is a keen proponent of subtropical gardening. She encourages gardeners to understand and appreciate our unique climate and to use it to our advantage, regardless of the style of garden. Kate has her own highly successful subtropical cottage garden, producing food, herbal medicine and an incredible abundance of flowers and joy. Kate often has as many as 100 different types of plants in flower at one time in her small 600sqm suburban garden – including the many weeds she appreciates in her garden!

Kate is a popular garden speaker and workshop facilitator and the creator of online gardening courses which can be accessed via her website www.katewall.com.au

Books by Kate

Working With Weeds; a practical guide to understanding, managing and using weeds

Earth Repair Gardening: the lazy gardener's guide to saving the Earth

Gardening After A Flood

Awards

2011 Ray Phippard Fellow Award, Lions International (Qld and Nth NSW)

2021 Merit Award from the Australian Institute of Horticulture for Working With Weeds

2022 Anita Boucher Award for Outstanding Achievement in Horticulture from the Horticultural Media Association of Australia (HMAA)

2024 Finalist in the HMAA Laurel Awards for Gardening After a Flood.

RECIPE AUTHOR – SHARR ELLSON

For the last 20 years Sharr Ellson has operated as the head chef of a Steiner childcare program in Brisbane, providing children with unique, diverse and nourishing meals daily, with many of the ingredients sourced from her own garden. The love to provide nourishment and enrichment to people is embodied in the way Sharr lives and her guiding moto of "food is a gift to yourself 3 times a day, make it worthwhile" can be seen on every plate, in every product and with every recipe.

Sharr's experience, passion and love for the community has led her to cook for any and everyone, from the sickly, mumma bears post-partum, families in need and school fetes to club fairs such the annual fair of the Queensland Herb Society. Sharr's cooking has nourished, supported and enriched the tummies of so many people.

She runs private workshops where she can disseminate her learnings with likeminded individuals to develop a collaborative understanding of how we can better love our ingredients and get the most out of them. Sharr regularly contributes to magazines, newsletters and blogs with her unique and creative recipes.

Sharr has embedded these values into her family life where she has employed a "from scratch diet" – if we want to eat it, we have to make it. Sharr has spent a lifetime cultivating her understanding of how to bring the best out of the bountiful produce the world affords us, be that produce from her own kitchen garden, wild foraged herbs and weeds or connecting with other organic growers. For those willing to engage, Sharr brings a culinary and personal care adventure.

The Herbal Estate (Sharr's Etsy store) stocks many different organic weed and herbal balms, salves, powders and creams all produced in small seasonal batches. Her tallow chickweed balm is one of her most in demand products and sells out quickly.

To purchase products from the Herbal Estate visit https://www.etsy.com/shop/TheHerbalEstate

You can follow Sharr's creative adventures at https://www.instagram.com/sharrherbs/

www.ingramcontent.com/pod-product-compliance
Lightning Source LLC
Chambersburg PA
CBHW080357030426
42334CB00024B/2910